THE REAL HIPHOP

THE REAL HIPHOP

Battling for Knowledge, Power, and Respect
in the LA Underground

Marcyliena Morgan

DUKE UNIVERSITY PRESS *Durham and London 2009*

© 2009 Duke University Press
All rights reserved.

Printed in the
United States of America
on acid-free paper ∞

Designed by Jennifer Hill
Typeset in Scala by
Keystone Typesetting, Inc.

*Library of Congress
Cataloging-in-Publication Data
appear on the last
printed page of this book.*

For Julie,
Maurie,
and the
Good Life

CONTENTS

ACKNOWLEDGMENTS

Art is a discovery in itself. Seen in
detail it is a series of discoveries,
perhaps intended in the first
instance to stave off boredom.
In a long range view, art is the
setting up of monuments to the
ordinary things about us, in a
moment and in time.

ZORA NEALE HURSTON,
*Folklore, Memoirs, and
Other Writings*

HIPHOP IS A MONUMENT to the youth, both black and brown, who
resided in low-income communities in the New York area in the 1970s. In
the act of living their lives and doing ordinary things, they created an art
form that now resonates for the masses throughout the world. When
hiphop began to move stealthily into the mindset of youth in the United
States and elsewhere in the world, some of its fans were sitting in class-
rooms at colleges and universities. These students considered hiphop to
be as serious as traditional academic study about the importance of knowledge, and as a result they presented new challenges to the establishment
and to hiphop itself. Students and fans of hiphop began to agitate for
classes, radio stations, artistic representations, research projects, and general inclusion in institutions at every level. I began developing the Hiphop
Archive around 1995 when I was teaching at University of California, Los
Angeles, in the department of anthropology and the Center for African
American Studies. In 2002 I formally established the Hiphop Archive at

the W. E. B. Du Bois Institute at Harvard University. I wanted hiphop to have the same level of respect as any area of study in the academic world. What's more, I wanted the issues, ideologies, and love of knowledge and sense of fairness that is fundamental to hiphop culture to become part of academic culture. I thought hiphop could level the academic playing field for students of color and for working-class students, as well as bring skill and merit back into the academic game the way skill and knowledge have become the foundation of hiphop culture. My research on hiphop, and on Project Blowed in particular, has been possible because of the support of many people.

Early on I received a UCLA Senate Grant to study hiphop language. I also received a Dean's Award from the Graduate School of Education and the Faculty of Arts and Sciences at Harvard University. Encouragement and feedback on this project has been provided to me by many people, including Nicole Hodges Persley, Dionne Bennett, Lidet Tilahun, Josef Sorett, Brooke C. Minters, Sumeeya Mujahid, Jenigh Garrett, Jessica Norwood, Chhay Chhun, Erin Ransom, Monique Matthews, Michael Jeffries, Dawn Elissa Fischer, Brian Cross, Valerie Smith, Bakari Kitwana, Glenda Carpio, Evelyn Hammonds, Evelyn Higginbotham, Jamaica Kincaid, Werner Sollars, John Jackson, Dorinne Kondo, Michael Dawson, Tommie Shelby, Lawrence Bobo, Stephen De Berry, Tarek Captan, Tasha Wiggins, Lori Caldwell, Dara Caldwell, Elizabeth Caldwell, and Ben Caldwell. I owe special gratitude to Henry Louis Gates Jr. and the faculty of African American Studies at Harvard University who encouraged me throughout this project. Stephen De Berry worked as my research assistant in the early stages of this study, and Dionne Bennett and Dawn Elissa Fischer have provided feedback and assistance throughout the project.

I am forever grateful to all of those at Project Blowed who allowed me to be there as they worked their magic and lived their dreams. I especially want to thank Ben Caldwell, Charletta Johnson, Lori Caldwell, Badru, Eddie Hayes, Mone Smith, Tasha Wiggins, and Paul Cheatham for their time and insight.

Finally, I want to thank my husband, Lawrence Bobo, for his insight and unfaltering support during this long project. Many Thursdays I left our home in the early evening only to return well after midnight. He was a constant source of inspiration, friendship, and encouragement. He has both my love and my respect.

I Am Hiphop

LOS ANGELES IS A CITY perched on the edge—and everyone who lives there knows it, especially when they are young. It has its borders, but the Pacific Ocean is the only true demarcation line between LA and the rest of the world, since to look east and toward the other coast— and everything in-between—is to miss the point. Gazing onto the Pacific Ocean from Los Angeles can mean for some that they have arrived at the last chance to make this country work for them. It is the end of the city, the country, and the American dream. And to drive on Sunset Boulevard east to west throughout the city is to witness the immigrant dream and nightmare all lacquered in a shimmering glaze that makes you question whether your mind can thoroughly register what your eyes do see. Mexico as well as Central America and all of South America exist in Los Angeles, whether in cruising La Cienega, searching within the rising streets of Silver Lake for Micheltorena, or looking for Aztlan in Eastlos (East LA). Africa and the diaspora exist in LA too. They can be found at the annual African Marketplace, the Pan African Film Festival, the area known as Little Ethiopia, and in memories of 5th Street Dicks, where black men—young and old—sat outside and played chess while jazz sounds streamed onto Leimert Park, as strong coffee and equally strong opinions were dispensed with conviction. And Asia and the Pacific Islands rise prominently in all their hues, dimensions, neighborhoods, and celebrations. It is in the debates over the best shiatsu—Koreatown or Little Tokyo?—in the churches and business organizations and the parades and restaurants, clubs, swap meets, temples, and in the times when Samoans dance the mele mele as they lead their schools to victory.

To chant Westsiiiiiide!—bobbing heads and hands (with fingers formed in the letter W) to a real and imagined beat—is not simply a claim to a coast, but a claim to a city that myopically refers to the West Side as the rich and the white. Beverly Hills, Brentwood, Bel Air, Santa Monica, Pacific Palisades, and Malibu are some of the places that the shortsighted call home. It is also where the parents of many urban youths work—cooking, cleaning homes, caring for other people's children, and satisfying the pleasures and needs of the wealthy. It is no surprise that LA's diverse communities scoff at interlopers who do not understand "the real LA."

One does not drive through LA but rather rides within it—with the sun beating down on the car's exterior creating a reflection that balances the color, speed, and contradictions of everything around. On a Saturday night, streets and freeways seem to stretch from one end of LA to the other as cars glide through neighborhoods and past nationalities—all while the radio blasts the latest beats. When heading back to the hood after a long day at Venice Beach, there are always many answers to the questions "Where you goin'?" "Where you from?" and "Where you at?" The answers include streets and neighborhood landmarks like Crenshaw, Degnan, Florence, Leimert, Slauson, Pico Union, Little Tokyo, Koreatown, Culver City, Baldwin Hills, Silver Lake, Inglewood, LBC (Long Beach), Carson, Compton, Venice, Watts. It is a place where being in high school means negotiating with Samoans, Filipinos, Koreans, Japanese, Chinese, Vietnamese, Chicanos, Ethiopians, Belizeans, Fijians, African Americans, Salvadorans, Hondurans, Caucasians, and wannabes. And one cannot ignore the car clubs that come out to cruise and low-ride on a Sunday evening down Crenshaw and into Thursday nights at Project Blowed as they all cry out to their collective community—Westsiiiiiide!

When I arrived in LA in the mid-1990s its underground hiphop scene,[1] at a venue known as the Good Life, was the main gathering spot for practitioners and guardians of hiphop culture.[2] If you were a young person who loved hiphop and could rhyme, dance, write, and draw, and you searched for *real* knowledge and wanted to be recognized and respected—and had respect for others—then the Good Life was a lyrical heaven on earth. In many ways it was the only glimmer of hope for young people of color in LA, and its followers understood that they had to stand tall in order to "represent" for the love of hiphop. This was no easy matter, however.

In the mid-1990s the low- and middle-income communities of color in Los Angeles had to cope with escalating gang organization and activity, police harassment and corruption, the demonization and criminalization of the black male as superpredator, the rise in teenage pregnancy, the rise of HIV/AIDS, the spread of crack cocaine, the abandonment of public schools, and more. It is no surprise that this period also marked the rise of gangsta' rap in Los Angeles. The group N.W.A (Niggaz With Attitude), with its founding members Eazy-E, Ice Cube, Dr. Dre, MC Ren, and Yella, provided a thorough and unforgiving description of the LA landscape in terms of police corruption, the deterioration of families and communities, gang activity, and much more.[3] In their popular release "Fuck tha Police" (1988), N.W.A situated their rhymes in a courtroom to expose what they consider to be police corruption and racism, and they defend their own aggressive response to it. Their courtroom drama includes a judge (Dr. Dre), a court clerk (MC Ren), and the defendant (Ice Cube). This song also includes one of the most repeated lyrics in hiphop: "So police think they have the authority to kill a minority."

MC REN: Right about now, N.W.A court is in full effect, Judge Dre presiding in the case of N.W.A vs. the Police Department. Prosecuting attorneys are MC Ren, Ice Cube, and Eazy-Motherfuckin-E

DR. DRE: Order, order, order Ice Cube, take the motherfuckin' stand. Do you swear to tell the truth, the whole truth and nothin' but the truth so help your black ass?

ICE CUBE: You goddamn right!

DR. DRE: Well won't you tell everybody what the fuck you gotta say?

ICE CUBE: Fuck the police comin' straight from the underground
A young nigga got it bad 'cause I'm brown
And not the other color
So police think they have the authority
To kill a minority
Fuck that shit, cause I ain't the one
For a punk motherfucker with a badge and a gun
To be beatin' on, and throw in jail
We can go toe to toe in the middle of a cell
Fuckin' with me cause I'm a teenager
With a little bit of gold and a pager
Searchin my car, lookin' for the product
Thinkin' every nigga is sellin' narcotics
You'd rather see, me in the pen
Than me and Lorenzo rollin' in a Benz-o

There is little question that gangsta' rap expressed hopelessness and nihilism. Still, N.W.A emerged as an insistent force determined to tell what was happening and what was destroying its communities—even if its members sometimes ended up being a destructive element themselves. In spite of its potential, rather than creatively focusing on the tension between real events and a dynamic critique of society, N.W.A's story only served as a mirror of life in South Central LA because it seemed to glorify the destruction at hand. While society's reaction to N.W.A's story of the real world was seen as a harsh, cruel, and overly negative reality, some of LA's youths wanted to do more than yell "fire" about their predicament. In the midst of the destruction around them, a group of young people in LA looked to the Good Life and Project Blowed for leadership. They relied on it. Word spread among them about the skill and performances of MCS, b-boys and b-girls, and legendary lyrical battles! It was always amazing to me when teenagers would recall details about Project Blowed—even if they had never been to a performance. They knew and would recite its history, rules of operation, the names of artists, style of rapping, etc. They used expressions like "verbal prowess" and "lyrical genius" to describe the MCS who reigned there and they talked about how Project Blowed was organizing and building the underground. It was the underground this and the underground that, repeated again and again with pride and respect. Project Blowed was something to believe in, something that believed in itself,

4

something that could not be destroyed or taken away. It was something that they could look forward to and be proud of—no matter what happened. It did not simply fan the flames of urban decay and societal attacks. Project Blowed was putting out the fire.

I began this study in the mid-1990s in order to understand what happened at Project Blowed that made young people gravitate to it and consider it a monument to their existence. I was interested in how a performance venue organized around hiphop's language ideology of the Word and developed by young people with few resources could become a social, cultural, and artistic symbol for Los Angeles and hiphop nationwide. As one young man excitedly explained to me, "The Blowed's style is like a virus. Once you hear it you want to do it and it's uncontrollable and spreads and spreads and spreads. If you're not careful, you'll catch it!" I wanted to learn about Project Blowed, about them, about how they created and maintained it and how they evaluated and understood the development of lyrical MCS. I was also concerned with the urgency that many Project Blowed supporters felt and their argument that their cultural and social lives—their reality—was misrepresented in the mass media, that their everyday activities were criminalized, and that they were under constant surveillance.

In the midst of my quest to understand why so many youths gravitated to Project Blowed, I too began to rely on the project. I developed a respect for hiphop culture because in spite of all its excesses and some of its deserved criticism from society, it remains a rare place where young black people and brown people are valued and awarded by their peers. They are treated as gods and goddesses and put on pedestals for searching for and "representing" truth and knowledge and recognizing and being proud of who they are and where they come from. It is a space of hard work, skill, approval, and dreams. These youths strive in an uncensored yet scrutinized space where their discourse is meticulously monitored, judged, and applauded or ridiculed based on their skill and ability to express their lives. Through this constant quest for better skills and control of the microphone (mic), hiphop redraws the urban grid and transforms ideal spaces into problematic ones and decaying spaces into fertile, creative landscapes. Hiphop creates a "real" LA where communities of poverty and people of color are suddenly visible and the source of future dreams. It is also the discourse space where "the juke joint has gone public" (Perry 2004, 6). Participants do not deny the variety and contradictions of opinions and styles in the hiphop and African American community. Instead, hiphop encourages a critique and discussion about itself, but only from those who care about it. It is accustomed to those who hate young people of color and haters in general. In their argument for the "real" hiphop, youths have lifted the veil and curtain into the African American community and America in general, and behind it for all to see is sexism, misogyny, and nihilism as well as the organic and formally educated intellectual, the family, church, black nationalism, schools, mosques, the altar, and the aesthetic. Because they choose to represent their real world as complex, in spite of what a particular MC may perform or say, hiphop youths stand for something and are willing to fight for what they believe in through hard work, loyalty, commitment and their search for the good life. Eventually, this commitment may also extend to academia where hiphop's presence is mainly the result of student agitation and loyalty to hiphop.

The Birth of the Hiphop Scholar

Hiphop's incursion into higher education took place within the same tradition as black studies, Chicano studies, Asian American studies, women studies, etc. In the 1960s and 1970s, students used nonviolent protest as well as arguments of standards and inclusion to achieve the representation of the significance of all minorities and their contribution to the academic curriculum. Hiphop's appearance in academia began in the 1990s, around the time of Project Blowed's beginnings. College students, many of whom were beneficiaries of affirmative action and desegregation efforts, challenged the academic and scholarly representations of the lives of lower-income youths of color. They argued that urban youths could be best represented and understood by analyzing hiphop culture since they had created it for themselves. Though the students were seldom from the communities described by hiphop artists, they experienced and witnessed the same racism described in hiphop lyrics and had extended family members who remained in low-income neighborhoods. These students were not content to be complacent as a result of their inclusion in elite institutions. Moreover, as they listened to and participated in hiphop culture, they recognized the emergence of theories, ideas, and critiques that reinvigorated intellectual debates and challenged societies and nations to address issues of justice, freedom, and equality. Students protested the established way of studying hiphop by bum rushing their campuses, and they coun-

6

tered by introducing hiphop radiobroadcasts and offering hiphop classes on their own while lobbying faculty to teach the new curriculum. Their critique of academic institutions' analysis of larger social and political arguments is exemplified by Dionne Bennett, who as a student had argued for the inclusion of hiphop courses by stating: "The reason that we should all be intrigued with Tupac's 'Dear Mama' is that it is a direct critique of the Moynihan Report. I think sociologists should be made aware of that critique!"

The support of hiphop by college students was a way to reach out to peers in poor communities while acknowledging and problematizing their advantages. As college students in the 1990s struggled to claim a voice and introduce growing ideological, gender, and social class struggles developing in communities of color, public intellectuals and academic writings on hiphop also emerged. The publication of Tricia Rose's book *Black Noise: Rap Music and Black Culture in Contemporary America* in 1994 and Russell Potter's *Spectacular Vernaculars: Hip-Hop and the Politics of Postmodernism* in 1995 introduced critical analyses of hiphop as an artistic, social, and cultural phenomenon. Hiphop had finally arrived as a medium of study as well as a very public spectacle. Though there was general focus on the Word, much of the scholarly work was concerned with the effect of hiphop on dominant cultural values rather than on how it operated as a system of language and discourse. For example, there was the First Amendment free speech issue associated with the group 2 Live Crew that drew the public comments of Henry Louis Gates Jr. and Houston Baker Jr.[4] In the 1990s both bell hooks (1993, 1994) and Angela Davis (1993) had conversations with Ice Cube about politics and feminism. The significance of hiphop in African American culture was also addressed by the philosopher Cornel West (1993), the historian Robin D. G. Kelley (1996, 1997), the political scientist Michael Dawson (1997, 2001), and the sociologist Paul Gilroy (1994), who celebrated and critiqued the impact of the relentless and often problematic images, philosophies, and personas materializing in hiphop culture.

The analysis of hiphop by some of the leading scholars of the time eventually opened the floodgates for public intellectuals who either critiqued hiphop within its artistic, cultural, and social form (e.g., Cornel West, Michael Eric Dyson) or vilified it as an irreverent, self-loathing, and destructive force for youth (e.g., John McWhorter, Stanley Crouch, Adolph Reed). Irrespective of the focus of the analysis, hiphop has established itself as one of the most influential academic forces of the last two decades. While it is no longer necessary to argue that hiphop should be the subject of scholarly attention, it is still important to identify the contradictions inherent in including it as a subject of study.

I wasn't "there" in the Bronx when DJ Kool Herc began his reign as a master DJ who rocked the party over the mic or when Grand Wizard Theodore first scratched on vinyl. I wasn't there when party MCs ceded their supremacy and passed the mic to lyrical MCs who moved hiphop to the next phase. I wasn't there when Afrika Bambaataa turned his DJ leadership skills into building the Zulu Nation and when Grandmaster Flash cut and scratched his way into hiphop history. Narratives about these moments are rich, expansive, and prophetic, and they represent significant moments that signal the founding of hiphop culture.[5] I didn't participate in these regional firsts or any others—I didn't even witness the beginnings of LA underground hiphop. My commitment to hiphop began like many who claim they grew up in hiphop culture. It was simply something I had to do.

My graduate school life was composed of classes, study, working in adult literacy programs, watching martial arts movies on kung fu Saturdays, being aware of all the latest music, dancing at clubs, and in the summer working with urban youths. In the 1980s, these young people lived and breathed hiphop until it affected virtually every aspect of their lives. There were b-boys and b-girls dancing at the clubs I went to, and whenever I saw my family in Chicago or ended up in cars with younger cousins we recited our favorite lyrics. Between working with young people in the summer and other social activities, I appreciated virtually all aspects of hiphop. I was living the hiphop litany: recognize, represent, come correct, build, maintain, respect. However, nothing prepared me for how it appeared in the academy.

In the late 1980s I attended a conference in Philadelphia where educational researchers who had been working in "the community" invited local "rappers" to perform for the gathered scholars. It was a conference of about five hundred academics who studied (and I think cared about) mainly poor students and making the education system more effective. There were only a few people at the conference who came from working-class backgrounds, and I counted only seven people of color (including myself) in attendance. The local rappers invited to perform were two young black men in their early teens, full of stage presence and self-importance. As they began, one acted as a human beat box by making percussive sounds from deep in his chest, with his lips at times protruding and at other times drawn back in. The other was a b-boy who could pop lock and do spins and head stands and freezes as well as rap. I watched them with intensity and delight until I noticed that many of those present were looking at the performance—and me—with sheepish expressions. It was as if we shared a guilty little secret at the pleasure involved in watching black bodies as entertainment that made us satisfied and very, very comfortable in our positions of power (cf. Lott 1993). My feelings about the experience were similar to those described by the journalist Nelson George (1998). He compared the audiences and spectators of hiphop performances to the battle royal, a boxing match that existed in the rural South in the 1930s where young black men gathered in a boxing ring, blindfolded for a slugfest as entertainment for white onlookers.[6] As George describes it, "For the young black men who pummeled each other in the quest for a bit of spare change, it was a chance to prove their toughness to friends, rivals, and themselves. For the biggest and most brutal participants, it was a way to get paid and, in a weird way, flaunt the physical power that the white viewers otherwise feared in everyday life. For white audiences, the heated bout allowed them to see the blacks as comical figures whose most aggressive urges were neutered for their amusement" (George 1998: vii). True, my colleagues were not taking bets on the bodies of those young black men. In fact, they would be horrified to think I would even suggest it. Yet somehow our careers were tied to the rapping and spinning youths before us, and my colleagues seemed extremely uncomfortable with themselves as they watched nascent performances by rappers who would go on to become famous—DJ Jazzy Jeff and the Fresh Prince.[7] Indeed, the bulk of scholarship at the time not only bordered on cultural voyeurism but also treated young black men, and hiphop culture in particular, as simultaneously "socially pathological," an "endangered species," and "at risk" (Males 1996, 1999). The need for more scholarship on hiphop culture becomes clear exactly at moments like those described above when scholars recognize hiphop's existence but treat it as coming from the Other and thus as a curiosity or a problem and not as intellectually, politically, and artistically important.

I was there when hiphop appeared in the academy. I also cosponsored the first academic hiphop conference in 1999 at University of California, Los Angeles, in order to demonstrate faculty support and respect of hiphop to students, scholarly institutions, and those involved in hiphop culture and industry. With the collaboration of the students La'Tonya Rease Miles and Tarek Captan (DJ Dusk),[8] the Power Moves Hiphop Conference brought together MCs, radio, club, and studio DJs, b-boys and b-girls, journalists, scholars, artists, filmmakers, graffiti artists, international artists, and community organizers. I described it as "a two-day conference on hiphop culture dedicated to promoting meaningful dialogue between critical theorists, ethnomusicologists, executives in the music industry, performers, students and academics, among others." Many conferences sponsored by the academy followed, including the Feminism and Hiphop Conference at the University of Chicago in 2005, which was sponsored by Cathy Cohen. These conferences and others were designed to engage the elements of artistry, conflicts, contradictions, research, social organization, and so on that have developed through hiphop culture. They treated hiphop in the same serious way that they would address any important area of academic study. These forums were also often complemented by student-organized conferences on college and university campuses.[9]

I was there for hiphop's first moments in the academy, and unlike hiphop's beginnings in its everyday locations the challenges associated with its future were in academia immediately clear. And although many embrace hiphop now, at the beginning they came to it kicking and screaming with their students pushing them from behind.

The Real Hiphop

When hiphop's party DJs on the East Coast mixed tunes and moved the crowd in the 1970s, they also verbally directed the crowd to keep the beat moving and the mood flowing. They eventually ceded the speaking role to the MC, who raised it to an art form beyond party yells. Soon graffiti art, which had already spread throughout East Coast cities became the artistic backdrop for hiphop events. This was accompanied by groups of dancers who worked on routines that not only played to the break beats used by DJs but also visually represented them. The elements of hiphop—DJ, MC, b-boy, graffiti—came together and hiphop was born. What distinguished hiphop's introduction was that it coalesced around these elements with artists and audiences as members and partners. Instead of the call and response and "amen" and "you go now" audience mode of African American music and preaching style (cf. Smitherman 2000), the call and response became an echo chamber that reverberated back on itself until the artist became the audience and vice versa. This was especially true for whoever was on the mic. People were not there just to enjoy and to listen; they also came to evaluate and to play a part in building their culture.

While hiphop is a combination of playful entertainment and serious art and ritual (West 2004), it also exists as a form of representation for those living in social crisis. Despite the fact that the four "elements" of hiphop are fundamental to its existence, it is hiphop's culture of critique and its verbal and linguistic representation that has galvanized many around its strengths, weaknesses, and contradictions as it works to capture the social world. Hiphop language ideology and wordsmithing skill is a test and showcase for virtually every aspect of the study of language and culture, identity and society. What is meant by language? What is a speech community? What are standards? How is language socially constructed? What is language ideology? How does the grammar work? What is a meaningful unit of sound? How do we know what someone really means? What is the meaning of meaning? What is intentionality? What is sense and reference? What is social face? What is knowledge? Who controls discourse? How does power work?

Hiphop does not simply answer questions about language, discourse, and society on a regular basis but rather it tests, teases, manhandles, and critiques those questions in order to display and analyze the social, cultural, and political reality of the local and social world as seen by the MC. The outcome can range from a narrative of epic proportions encompassing the rise and fall of empires and peoples to the fight between good and evil. It can also include the energy, desire, and values of the dance club. Irrespective of the message and style of hiphop, all MCs are tested, evaluated, and judged according to their lyrical skills, their ability to represent their community and audience, and their skill at analyzing their reality and power. Though popular music has often been included as a strategy in addressing injustices and the power of the state, this does not necessarily mean that music is used to promote progressive politics, since "popular culture creates its own micro-politics of organization, location, identity, and affiliation" (Lipsitz 1994: 152). This is particularly true of hiphop music since it insists on its right to artistically represent reality about anything and everything, and it is also relentlessly commodified and commercialized and imitated and despised. Nevertheless, hiphop practitioners eventually and consistently raise the skills bar and agitate for content and language ideology. Hiphop social practice and culture includes policing itself, criticizing itself, hating itself, imploding on itself, and loving itself once again. This is evidenced by Nas's complaints on the title song of his album "Hip Hop Is Dead" (2006):

> Everybody sound the same commercialize the game
> Reminiscin' when it wasn't all business
> It forgot where it started
> So we all gather here for the dearly departed . . . Went from
>   turntables to MP3s
> From *Beat Street* to commercials on Mickey D's
> From gold cables to Jacobs
> From plain facials to Botox and face lifts
> I'm lookin' over my shoulder
> It's about eighty people from my 'hood that showed up
> And they came to show love
> Sold out concert and the doors are closed shut

Though hiphop may be obsessed with criticism and self-criticism in an effort to both maintain and raise standards, this point is often missed by many of its most ardent detractors. Critics of hiphop seldom engage the culture's own critiques and assessments of itself. Instead, many critics impose a tired, stereotypical binary of good versus evil, urban versus suburban, black versus white, considerate versus self-destructive, and a "you said it and you get what you deserve" analysis of hiphop. Part of the reason is that, as Nas demonstrates, hiphop skill and creativity are constantly critiqued as part of the cultural practice within the genre. Detractors like Adolph Reed, Stanley Crouch, and John McWhorter either don't understand this critique or they simply do not respect it. Their unwillingness to engage existing evaluation within hiphop culture, a critique that is fundamental to hiphop's notion of inclusion and freedom of speech, suggests an inability and refusal to navigate hiphop's unrelenting system of evaluation and reevaluation. Another reason that some academics dismiss the study of hiphop is that it relentlessly questions and is often irreverent regarding traditional theories of feminism, cultural nationalism, politics, and religion (see chapters 3 and 5). Theories, ideas, methodologies, and practices can be exploited, exaggerated, and reenvisioned in order to represent a world ruled by black people, the oppressed. It is particularly irritating for those in ivory towers to deal with theorizing from young people of color who claim hiphop to be their knowledge base and for whom no theory is sacred and thus is open to critique, satire, and amusement.

Some outside of academic institutions also criticize hiphop's presence on college campuses.[10] I have participated on panels with journalists and hiphop artists who argue that it is the beats that define hiphop, and any attempt to refer to its political, educational, and social importance is not "true" hiphop. Some have actually argued that one can't be a true fan of hiphop culture and also be a college student. In contrast, there are others who insist that hiphop's existence is in fact a political statement irrespective of what its founders and followers believe.

This book does not focus on the contradictions, crises, and destructive aspects of hiphop. Instead it explores in depth how an underground hiphop venue worked; how it wrestled with all of the contradictions in hiphop, in the surrounding community, and in LA in general by focusing on what it means to be an MC and to control the mic. Hiphop lyrics and activities are concerned with the major questions of philosophy, identity, ideology, art, and existence. Thus this work also concerns how oppressed people and voices that are marked and perceived as marginal can move into dominant culture and often create a space for themselves. Whether we call this space the counterpublic or the underground, it threatens the dominant discourse about black and urban youth and forces recognition from society and its educational system. Moreover, it intentionally attacks and redesigns how urban spaces and spaces occupied by youth are conceived, lived, and perceived (Lefebvre 1991; McCann 1999). This system regularly ridicules serious questions and ideas that emerge from popular culture— especially when they originate from youth, people of color, and poor people. Students of hiphop are well aware of society's unwillingness to hear the analysis, critique, and story within hiphop, and they agitate for its inclusion.

Scholarship on hiphop now exists in education, psychology, anthropology, sociology, political science, philosophy, theater, art, business, physics, religion, English, linguistics, American studies, history, communications, music, and more.[11] While introducing hiphop to the academy has not been easy, it is also true that those involved in hiphop have been slow to support its inclusion. There are cries that hiphop will be talked about and studied to death and thus lose its vitality in the hands of academics, whose heads are in books rather than engaged with the rest of the world. It is only fitting that while this book is about how the underground hiphop scene in Los Angeles developed and sustains itself, it is also much more. It is a celebration of the level of support for hiphop and the commitment to it throughout the world for it to be incorporated into higher education without losing and compromising what it is and what it means to those who introduced it and to those who continue to develop and sustain it. By using a language ideology and system that has been stigmatized in American society, hiphop has identified with lower social classes and minority and marginalized groups throughout the world. Hiphop creates an alternative space where norms are questioned, what is stigmatized is valorized, and where the inability to control and manipulate dialects and language styles and varieties is seen as a lack of MC skill and the inability to critically analyze society in order to represent one's interests. As Ice Cube noted: "So back off genius / I don't need you to correct my broken English" (1991).

This book is concerned with three intersecting areas of hiphop culture. The first and most comprehensive area focuses on language, symbolism, identity, and the Word, and it is concerned with the work of the MC. It considers the relationship between the language ideology of the African American speech community, hiphop language and hiphop culture, and how lyrical battles are waged and shaped in discourse and in the linguistic, symbolic, and ideological principles that bring hiphop into being. The second area concerns the cultural and social aspects of hiphop. This work considers hiphop part of and a product of African American cultural, political, social, and artistic expression. It is that aspect of the American experience on which hiphop has shaped its understanding and representation of race, social class, gender, sexuality, and political power. It considers how women become active in hiphop, how they are apprenticed, and the nature of socialization and participation in the underground. Finally, it focuses on how hiphop discourse styles affect spiritual, political, and international thinking and movements, especially as these styles are employed in building political and social movements. While these areas do not represent every aspect of the hiphop underground or of Project Blowed, they do provide a way into the underground as a physical, imagined, symbolic, and powerful space.

This volume is the result of the twenty years I spent observing and supporting hiphop culture and the seven years I spent working with KAOS Network and Project Blowed. I have observed hiphop activities in schools, at work, at play, in underground venues, at open-mic sessions, and at concerts and rap contests throughout the United States. Conducting this ethnography was no simple matter; I was constantly tested and challenged by many of the individuals included in this study. I consider these challenges to be a sign of respect for my work and for hiphop culture itself. I continue to be grateful to have the opportunity to learn from the hiphop community. I was eventually able to accomplish this study because I came of age during hiphop's prehistory and followed it from its inception. Before and during this research I worked on and supported various community and arts projects developed by Ben Caldwell, creator of KAOS Network (the home of Project Blowed; see chapter 1). I continue to work on and support these projects.

I was assisted in this research by young people ranging in age from twelve to sixteen years who were involved in educational and community-sponsored hiphop activities. Another group of individuals in their late teens to mid-twenties also helped with my research. Though the focus of my research is the city of Los Angeles, I also conducted studies in Philadelphia, New York, Chicago, Atlanta, Boston, and parts of Alabama and Mississippi. While I talked to several performers and include their work here, this study is equally informed by numerous personal observations and includes videotaped performances and ethnographic and formal interviews, as well as analyses of conversations and letters and interviews from hiphop magazines, rap sheets, radio and video programs, call-in shows, and playlists. All of the events included here have been transcribed, checked, and rechecked for accuracy.[12]

It is my intention that while this book is an ethnography of the language and culture of hiphop and of Project Blowed in particular, it also contains a message from the underground. This book questions, challenges, and in some cases tests academic theories about community, social class, culture, language, performance, and power. It argues against theories that only define urban youth as "at risk," violent, emotional, predatory, and pathological since within these theoretical biases it is impossible to witness the complexity and contribution of hiphop culture. The underground conceived and birthed hiphop in defiance of and without any major support from the millions of dollars given to academics for research and study of behavior, language, testing, attitudes, etc. Hiphop activists reel off the old-school mantras—*represent, recognize, come correct,* and *build, maintain, respect*—because those philosophies enhanced their lives. Because of these experiences, they honestly believe that they have the power and are destined to change the world.

The Rise of the Underground

In 1992 while most of the country was transfixed and alarmed by the influence of N.W.A and the rise of violent West Coast hiphop with its glorification of gang culture and revenge, a small group of young people who were simply socializing and hanging out with each other renewed their commitment to hiphop culture. Their move from the Good Life to Project Blowed helped to confirm the resilience of the hiphop underground. While "underground" had been bandied about as a name during the Good Life days, its significance in hiphop and in African American culture in general should not be overlooked.

In hiphop the term "underground" is in reference to many symbols, all of which coalesce around flight, fight, and freedom. The underground simultaneously recalls the era of slavery, when a people summoned incredible desire and courage for a chance to exercise control over their own language and communication, creativity, body, culture, spiritual practice, and life itself. In African American youth communities the use of the term underground also implies that it is possible to operate clandestinely while controlling information and incessant talk about what is being planned. It is a place where truths can be told, and where people can remove their veil to expose their spirits and thoughts without fear for their life. It is the ultimate space and place of humanity.

The most recognized underground movement in the United States, especially for the African American community, is the Underground Railroad. The stories that come from this movement are compelling not only because it was an escape out of slavery but also because it simultaneously symbolized hope, horror, risk, and the unknown. If as a slave you never knew freedom or anyone who had it, then how could you predict and imagine what life could and would be like when you were free from the formal slave system? Those who successfully escaped did not return to describe what freedom was like and where it was located. Those who were caught were brought back and punished or killed as examples of why freedom was too great a risk. An essay in National Geographic Online attempts to re-create the seriousness and peril inherent in the journey on the Underground Railroad from Maryland, and in so doing it captures the urgency as well as the controlled terror that slaves must have felt:

You are a slave.

Your body, your time, your very breath belong to a farmer in 1850s Maryland.

Six long days a week you tend his fields and make him rich.

You have never tasted freedom.

You never expect to.

And yet . . . your soul lights up when you hear whispers of attempted escape. Freedom means a hard, dangerous trek.

Do you try it?[13]

What is the urgency and peril of a hiphop underground? Those who choose to participate can experience and learn the freedom and creativity of hiphop culture. Instead of being angry about society, they "get busy." Rather than only complain about bad schools, they become responsible for their own education. Rather than destroy their own community, they learn that they must rebuild new ones. But in hiphop culture, freedom requires that one have knowledge about hiphop artistic skills and the social reality of the community, region, nation, and world—since all of these things combine to form hiphop culture and define the right to membership in it. The underground embodies hiphop's persistent focus on skills, competition, and evaluation from artists and fans. This level of scrutiny was typical during hiphop's early stages: to do nothing is not being in the mix—it means that you are not hiphop.

Aceyalone, one of the founders of Project Blowed, explains how the urge for the underground develops as a need and desire for expression.

The group of people we were in . . . was like a hiphop circle. At one time I was the only one that rapped. We danced; we did graffiti. The whole hiphop culture was like a *storm* of my whole life. In-between just living regular life—maybe get in a little trouble here and there—gang banging and stuff like that, I found hiphop to be just a little more fun, a little more active, a little more fun. It wasn't like I chose to get out of trouble, it just happened that way. And I don't know . . . but it was more like, naturally, hanging out with these guys, doing hiphop, was a little more fun than hanging out with gang bangers. At that moment hiphop carved its way into my life.

Once LA's hiphop underground scene began, it was immediately clear that young black and Latino men and women were not only ready but also desperate to work together in the name of hiphop and with the support of adults and community groups. As Project Blowed's underground popularity grew, news of its philosophy and organizational structure began to spread. It represented a model of how to directly and indirectly respond to the aggressive attacks from the government, police, business, drug dealers, gangs, and alienation experienced by youth. As stated on the project's website: "Project Blowed by design is a workshop designed to challenge & sharpen the skills of all Hip Hop heads from emcees, to dancers, graffiti artist, DeeJays and, of course, listeners. So it was only right that Project Blowed be born inside of an Arts Center. The organization chosen by one of Project Blowed's founders, 'Aceyalone,' was the KAOS Network."[14] It is also evident in the 2003 posting of Abstract Rude, another of Project Blowed's founding members:

In the late 80's, early 90's a small food store began to open up its doors every Thursday night to talented emcees, the Good Life. Progress in the minds of these hard workin' musicians was inevitable. Wantin' more and thriving for success; the Good Life was growing. Later, the Good Life would migrate to Leimert Park as a "no censorship" open mic sparked off Project Blowed. Here rappers and back-packers would unite and test the skills of one another, the L.A. battlegrounds. Not too many would last, as "please pass the mic" would render any weak body to never return. Only so many made it to "hold court," The Heavy Weights. The greats of L.A., Riddlore, J Smoov, Trendsetta, Rifleman Ellay Khule, Medusa, Neb Luv, 2Mex, Pigeon John, B-Twice, Freestyle Fellowship: Aceyalone, Self Jupiter, P.E.A.C.E., Mikah 9, Rhetteric, Busdriver, Volume 10, and Abstract Rude. The saga continues, it's now 2003 and these names are what keep opening the doors for the rookies. A journey only some will understand and others will choose not to take part in.[15]

In the 1990s, the future of hiphop was being tested. Those in the underground had escaped to LA. But was N.W.A right? Do the police think "they have the authority to kill a minority"? How does one answer underground questions such as, "Do you really believe in hiphop?" "Do you live it?" "Freedom [Hiphop] means a hard, dangerous trek. *Do you try it?*" Hiphop youths face these questions everyday and it is this reality that makes hiphop more than artistic practice and play. Hiphop youths are under constant surveillance and are considered a threat, and they want to escape to freedom in hiphop culture. Hiphop youths in Los Angeles have responded to the challenge as posed by *National Geographic*: "Freedom means a hard, dangerous trek. *Do you try it?*" The answer is yes. They have worked to create art, space, and social relationships designed to build and maintain hiphop culture. They absolutely wanted hiphop, and they reclaimed it by going through the underground. They had practiced and planned for hiphop throughout their youth. They were ready to claim their turn to develop and represent their culture. Project Blowed created an alternative space that claimed Leimert Park Village and KAOS Network as "the hippest corner in LA." That is the underground's evaluation. Los Angeles, with its Hollywood glamour and excess, is not simply a city of extremes in terms of wealth and poverty. It is a deeply textual realization and display of these extremes. In order for the underground to thrive, KAOS Network and Project Blowed had to address the problems of postindustrial LA and the changes occurring in all cities throughout America.

In the following chapters I provide a glimpse into the socialization process, art, culture, and politics of underground hiphop in Los Angeles in the 1990s and beyond to the present day. Chapter 1 provides specific detail on the cultural, social, and historical development of Project Blowed. Rather than focus exclusively on the artists involved in the project, this chapter identifies the adults that support underground hiphop. I focus on the adults because they are the single most important influence, outside of family, for many of the youths involved in underground hiphop. Chapter 2 provides a discussion and analysis of the social and cultural development of the hiphop community. It explores how young people learn and develop skills and their influences. Chapter 3 is an ethnographic account of Thursday Night at Project Blowed. This chapter is among the first ethnographies that take a close look at how the artist and audience corroborate through lyrical battles, the operation of crews, and the activities and social networks that make up underground hiphop. It reveals that the lyrical battle is about representing and defending identities, ideologies, rights, and the human spirit. Chapter 4 continues with Project Blowed and is concerned with young women's involvement in underground hiphop. It provides insight into the socialization of black girls around race and feminism. Chapter 5 is concerned with how hiphop discourse shapes spiritual life and political opinions and attitudes. Finally, chapter 6 summarizes the values and attributes of hiphop culture and the discourse strategies used in underground hiphop, and it draws out the theoretical and policy implications of the study.

Hiphop's notion of the Word incorporates a system that focuses on power. Hiphop is obsessed with meaning, intention, language ideology, place, space, social context, and other symbols that can be interpreted and manipulated. The Word in hiphop developed from young people who are often the targets of dominant culture and are manipulated by it. Those who participate in hiphop may be young, but they are not neophytes in the study of discourses of power and how language manipulation works. They have served their apprenticeships as the targets and victims of the system. The artists who founded LA's hiphop community are not students of political and cultural art. Rather, they are practitioners who represent the outpouring of young people who seek a positive outlet and a resource away from a dire situation that seems relentless. The youths at Project Blowed represent and perfect their craft because that is who they are. They have no choice but to be there. Instead of lamenting their lives they erect monuments to it and celebrate their victory in maintaining and building a better future and world. Ask and each one will tell you, "I am hiphop."

The Hippest Corner in LA

What's the code?
Yo! I'd like to send a special
    shout-out to Ben Caldwell
Much respect.
Thank you for everything you've
    done.
Richard—5th Street Dick, World
    Stage—Billy Higgins.
Much respect due to the Watts
    Prophets
The Last Poets and all the other
    poets out there
Much love
What's up, A. K. Tony?

ACEYALONE, "Project Blowed"

Reality Check I

IN THE LATE 1990s, Ben Caldwell's deep mellifluous voice on the answering machine of KAOS Network greeted the caller with the following message: "This is Video 3333, KAOS Network, Digital Underground, and Project Blowed at 3333 Leimert Park, the hippest corner in LA!" The thousands of young people who eventually made their way to the underground hiphop workshop at Project Blowed on Thursday nights also delivered a message. Theirs was one of the most profound commentaries of the last quarter of the twenty-first century. First and foremost, those involved in building underground hiphop were completely aware that their commitment went far beyond artistic perfor-

CHAPTER ONE

The building at 3333 Leimert, home of Video 3333, KAOS Network, Digital Underground, and Project Blowed. Photo by Tony B, courtesy of Project Blowed.

Project Blowed on Thursday night. Photo by Tony B, courtesy of Project Blowed.

mance/ An entire generation of young blacks and Latinas and Latinos had fought the Horatio Alger fight and won by redefining the terms of inclusion. They believed that their participation, presence, and enthusiasm were proof that they would be one of most powerful voices at the end of the century. They had reclaimed art and popular and political culture by bombing cities and urban landscapes with their unique images and sounds. They were determined to challenge how youth and people of color in general are represented and treated. They claimed it their duty to expose and confront the poverty, injustice, prejudice, and other ills that affect their communities and the world./Moreover, they considered it their responsibility to hold those in power responsible for what they considered the negative state in which they lived.

Reality Check II

On January 4, 1996, around 11 PM, I was in my kitchen putting away the dishes left from the dinner party I had just hosted at my home in Leimert Park. I was feeling rather satisfied about the success of the gathering. We had achieved the dream of living in a predominantly black community that had socioeconomic diversity. My dinner party included students, bankers, actors, professors, musicians, artists—good people, good music, and good food. In fact, it was "all good" until I looked out the window and saw against the night sky a moving beam of light directed at my block, searching my adopted community. Soon I heard the sound of ghetto birds (helicopters) circling around my home and neighborhood. Then the phone rang and a friend, who had been one of the last people to leave my party, yelled, "The riot squad is getting in formation at the end of your block! There are about a hundred of them in helmets, with batons and guns drawn! What's going on?!!" In unison we both cried, "They're at Ben's!" As we spoke, the police were rushing into Project Blowed. Wearing riot gear, with guns drawn and barking orders, they swarmed over the room and the main stage area. The fire department pulled up in front. The police ordered those in attendance to lie down on the floor and spread their legs. Project Blowed was under siege.

Los Angeles is wonderful. Nowhere in the United States is the Negro so well and beautifully housed, nor the average efficiency and intelligence in the colored population so high. . . . Out here in this matchless Southern California there would seem to be no limit to your opportunities, your possibilities.

W. E. B. DU BOIS, *The Crisis*

The existence of contrasting and competing views of Los Angeles is not a new phenomenon. To many, LA's diverse population and shifting boundaries and borderlands suggests a transient metropolis unable to sustain a viable identity. However, this misunderstanding results from focusing on the wrong side of town and ignoring LA's diverse population. The historian Mike Davis argues that Los Angeles has always had its share of detractors and admirers, and that "the city of angels" is not as much planned as it is envisioned. As he summarizes: "It is hard to avoid the conclusion that the paramount axis of cultural conflict in Los Angeles has always been about the construction/interpretation of the *city myth,* which enters the material landscape as a design for speculation and domination" (1992, 21).

Davis's critique is ironic if we consider that Los Angeles, the city of angels, began as a settlement of diverse people. In 1781 the Spanish government ordered eleven families (a total of forty-four people, with equal numbers of adults and children) to leave Alamos, Mexico, and establish a settlement. This group included native Mexicans (eight), blacks (fifteen), and people of mixed blood (twenty-one). Though Los Angeles began as a diverse settlement, this diversity did not ensure a city unbiased regarding race and ethnicity. In fact, Los Angeles has not only treated many of its citizens of color unfairly, it has criminalized many of their normal activities. Thus it is not surprising that for many followers of hiphop worldwide, Los Angeles means many things. It is both home and a facade community, much like a Hollywood film lot where buildings and faces look familiar and authentic until one gets a closer look. The city myth relies on cultural, economic, social, political, and artistic reference points that are real, imagined, and Hollywood (Hollyweird) created. Intense scrutiny reveals that much of Los Angeles is literally a front—life as we imagine it without substance and depth. It is thus not surprising that there are two perspectives of LA's black community, one of which is the spectral gaze in relation to the rest of the city.

When people drive *down* Crenshaw toward their destination or home on the other side of town, with their car doors locked and windows closed, they see the poverty, the variety of religious institutions, and the endless liquor and specialty stores. *Rolling through* Crenshaw means that a person is home. Home is a familiar place that conjures memories of people, places, events, and daily life. On Crenshaw, home includes stores selling synthetic and human hair and hair supplies, music, fried chicken, pork, Jamaican food, African cloth, and Afrocentric books. One seeks Black Muslims and their bean pies, and "real" Louisiana hot links, shrimp, and gumbo, and "real" Mississippi ribs and fried catfish. Those residing in multi-ethnic LA worship in mosques, hotels, outdoors, strip malls, churches, and mega-churches that tie up traffic on Sundays and during prayer meetings. The community residents of Crenshaw in the late 1990s knew about the bowling alley and restaurant frequented by older Japanese Americans who were interned in camps during World War II. African Americans along with Chicanos and Mexicans from Ciudad Mexico and Vera Cruz, who look black and act black but speak Mexican Spanish and Chicano English, also met there. The mix of people and cultures is not overwhelming to those who see themselves as part of the landscape. Everything is familiar—not because they are in the same place, but in LA they realize they are at times (but not always) people dealing with the same things.

The current ethnic population of LA began to take shape in the 1960s with increases in the Asian American and Latin American populations after the amendment of the National Origins Act in 1965.[1] In 1990 Los Angeles County had a population of 8,863,164 people spread out among numerous cities, incorporated and unincorporated, connected by a complex system of freeways and encompassing a heterogeneous mixture of ethnic groups, social and economic classes, and community identities. By 2000 the population had increased to 13,214,158. According to the City of Los Angeles Consolidated Plan (2003–2008),[2] the communities of the City of Los Angeles that had populations of African Americans exceeding 25 percent included Adams–La Brea (47.7 percent), Crenshaw (72.5 percent), Exposition Park (28.5 percent), and Green Meadows (42.3 percent). Leimert Park reported that 55 percent of its residents were African Americans and South Vermont reported that 50 percent of its residents were African Americans.

In 1990 African Americans accounted for over one million, or 11.2 percent, of the population of LA County. Although the overall county population increased in 2000, the African American population had decreased to 9.8 percent to around 931,000 people. Within a decade, not only had LA's black population shifted, but also large swaths of the city had become associated with black and Latino gangs, poverty, crime, and overall social deterioration. The media reveled in depicting the diverse areas of the region as a monolithic pool of bad news and bad people. It was during this period that South Central was born.

Although "South Central" is a regional reference, to those living outside of its boundaries it remains synonymous with the African American population. This is true even though in 2003 the city of Los Angeles, in an attempt to contest the depiction of South Central in hiphop lyrics, videos, and movies, changed the area's official name to South Los Angeles. It is also true in spite of the fact that South Central is now mainly Latino and includes other ethnic populations, such as Asians and Pacific Islanders. Further, within its boundaries are Koreatown and Chinatown as well as parts of West Hollywood. However, because Central Avenue represented the heart of the African American cultural, artistic, and residential community in the early 1900s, South Central remains a signifier of race. The name at times includes the city of Compton as well as several other towns or neighborhoods such as Inglewood, Watts, the Crenshaw district, Lennox, Hawthorne, Lawndale, and Ladera Heights to name a few. In fact, after the public reaction to the Rodney King verdict, the curfew imposed by LA County on April 30, 1992, defined South Central as virtually any area where people of color live and regularly travel: "The area bounded by the Long Beach Freeway (710) on the East, the Santa Ana (5) and Santa Monica Freeways (10) on the North, the San Diego Freeway (405/5) to Crenshaw Boulevard and then Crenshaw Boulevard South to Lomita Boulevard on the West, and Lomita Boulevard on the South" (Gold and Braxton 2003).

Though most of the participants in this study live within the "riot" boundaries of South Central, they refer to their area as Leimert or Crenshaw. Since the 1950s, the demographic history of the Crenshaw/Baldwin Hills area has been an important part of the history of black LA. The area is a part of the eighth council district, which includes such large and distinct communities as Culver City and Inglewood. In the years before the Second World War African Americans began moving into parts of the area, and it developed through the 1950s and 1960s. Today, the combined number of merchants and professional residents of the area make Baldwin Hills, Ladera, and View Park/Windsor Hills (hereafter Baldwin Hills) the most affluent black community both in Los Angeles and in the United States overall. The area boasts of stunning views of the Pacific Ocean and downtown, and it is near the beach, Los Angeles International Airport, and Leimert Park. In response to the area's high concentration of wealth, this block of communities is also called "Pill Hill," the "Golden Ghetto," or the "Black Beverly Hills" by the black residents of LA.

With its six-figure median family income and a very low poverty rate, Baldwin Hills stands in stark contrast to most of the historically black areas of South Los Angeles. Residents who reside below the affluent hills or in what some black communities refer to as "the bottom" in places such as Hyde Park, with barred windows, chain-link fences and rows of bungalows. They also reside in the stucco two-story apartments of Baldwin Village, locally known as "the Jungle." These buildings are crammed together and are relentlessly indistinguishable, and as such they suggest that "the absentee developers ran out of imagination—and paint" (Easton 1992, 1). In the 1990s, the median family income in the neighborhoods surrounding Baldwin Hills ranged between $16,000 and $17,000 and had an unemployment rate of 30–40 percent. After the Rodney King verdict in 1992, the commercial district of the Crenshaw area saw some of the worst of the violence and looting of that event. It was many more years before the streets recovered from the burned-out remains of gas stations, markets, swap meets, and fast-food stands—some of them former landmarks of the community.

Chaos Theory Gone Wild
Betrayed in LA

The urban community of Los Angeles does not resemble the urban northeastern communities where hiphop began. However, in spite of the differences in architecture and climate and vegetation, the problems and issues are the same. Moreover, the city is characterized by a long history of both discriminating against the black community and promising changes that never occur. Though the African American population of Los Angeles is in decline today, it experienced tremendous growth decades earlier. Between 1940 and 1965 the black population of Los Angeles County increased eightfold, from 75,000 to 600,000 (U.S. Census 1979). During this period there were numerous complaints that social planning agencies were not addressing the needs of the black community in adjusting to urban living and the problems of segregation, and aggressive policing practices and hiring discrimination persisted. In the early 1960s the desperation and frustration with the situation began to surface in sporadic outbreaks of rage. For example, Mike Davis (2001) reports that black teenagers and young adults rioted in Compton, near Watts, in 1961 and on Memorial Day of that year. Another group of youngsters battled police in Griffith Park, taking over the merry-go-round with the cry that they were "freedom fighters" and "this is not Alabama" (Davis 2001, 3). At the time of the Watts disturbance in 1965, unemployment in the area was more than double the national average.[3] While the Watts "riots" may have been a shock to those outside of the African American areas, it was not surprising to those within LA's black and brown enclaves. The Watts rebellion was a collective articulation of the sense of futility experienced by those who had been consistently denied any other form of expression or control over their social destiny. The six "days of rage" that exploded on August 14, 1965, left over 30 dead, 1,000 wounded, and an estimated $200 million in damages (Horne 1995, 3).

In 1973 Tom Bradley was elected the first black mayor of Los Angeles on a wave of optimism as well as the campaign funds of a handful of powerful downtown businessmen who felt it was time for a change in leadership. There were many in South Central who campaigned vigorously for Bradley's election with the expectation that he would continue the commitment to the development of the African American community. But Bradley's own commissioned report, "McCone Revisited," noted that "critical problems" in employment and social services had not improved since Watts, while other "critical problems" of education and housing had become worse (1994, 14).[4]

The recurring sense of betrayal and abandonment by City Hall increased dramatically in 1991 when Latasha Harlins, a fifteen-year-old African American, was shot and killed by a Korean grocer. The grocer suspected Latasha of attempting to steal food from her store. Local news played and replayed the video recording of their quarreling, shoving, and the subsequent shooting of Latasha at the checkout counter. When the judge handling the trial sentenced the grocer to a period of community service, the black community considered the verdict a cruel pronouncement on the value of an African American life in white America's judicial system. The Rodney King beating also occurred in 1991, and by the time the first verdict in the case sparked the April 1992 uprising, the level of

28

frustration and futility in the community had once again swelled to the point of violent eruption. Of course, the irony of the results of the uprising is that the communities most in need were those that were most damaged. During the three days of uprising there were 18,807 arrests, and by the time it was officially over there were 58 deaths and 2,383 injuries. A reported $735 million in damages left many black-owned businesses destroyed along with those owned by Korean immigrants (Cannon 1999).

Though there were the usual commissions and promises after the riots, in the end the only thing that had changed was that fewer people could deny that Los Angeles was lacking a commitment to rebuilding a vibrant and diverse community. As Mike Davis noted at the time, although Anglo-Americans made up "only 37% of the current city population and just 12% of the public school enrollment, Anglos still comprise 70% of the active electorate and 80% of the federal jury pool for the King civil-rights trial. Needless to say, they also control 90% of the metropolis's fixed wealth and capital gains" (1992).

The call *Westsiiiiide!* yelled by urban youths from the windows of their cars and in underground venues recognizes the history of LA's African American communities and communities of color. It is a critique of LA as an ideal space. It confronts the LA establishment by laying claim to a version of "California love" that critiques the rich as well as the nation's impression that LA's urban youths have nothing to contribute. Whether in the name of Hollywood celluloid or to exploit and control the latest trend, LA (and many other major cities in America) miseducates, betrays, stereotypes, imitates, markets to, antagonizes, hunts down, and incarcerates its youth (Males 1996; Cross 1993; Davis 1992; Kelley 1996, 1997). Moreover, since LA is a city that in general aggressively feeds off of and devours the conception of youth, it must contend with its youth's discontents.

Many young people feel that there are direct and intentional attacks on them, and that these attacks seem relentless. In addition to the 1991 killing of Latasha Harlins and the events in 1991 and 1992 concerning Rodney King, numerous seemingly direct and organized attacks on youth have occurred. These attacks include Proposition 187 (also the LA police code for murder), a 1994 law to deny undocumented immigrants public education, jobs, and health services; Proposition 209, a 1995 referendum to end affirmative action; and the 1998 "3-strikes law" that turned mischievous youth offenses into hard time as it lumped violent crimes with other offenses. The 1998 law was followed in 2000 with Proposition 21, an ordinance funded by several corporations to treat youthful offenders as adults for serious crimes, irrespective of their criminal histories (Beiser and Solheim 2000), and the LAPD Rampart police corruption case. Schools in inner-city neighborhoods like South Central have become "drop-out factories" where the majority of black and Latina and Latino students attend high schools within low-income communities and where high school graduation is not the norm (Losen and Wald 2005, 6–7). As LA's urban youths prepared to begin their long march into the revitalized, newly prepped and eagerly touted corrections industry, members of California's hiphop community began to demonstrate their frustration and anger and they began to foretell what was to come.

As people began to reel from the escalating criminalization of urban youth, one response from LA's black community was an increase in organizations and enterprises that offered a space for young people to display, perform, and practice their creative talents. An example of such an effort was in the Leimert Park arts community in the Crenshaw area of Los Angeles. It was there in 1994 that the filmmaker Ben Caldwell—founder of the arts center Video 3333 and KAOS Network—offered space to a group of young people. The youths previously had been performing in a neighborhood health food store (the Good Life) and wanted to continue freestyle hiphop. This effort developed into Project Blowed—LA's most influential hiphop freestyle competition. As Project Blowed's underground popularity grew, its philosophy and organizational structure became a model and progressive response to the alienation experienced by the young people in the community. It did so in the form of a counterdiscourse, a powerful alternative medium to represent their truth.

Slipping Away on the Streets of LA
KAOS

Leimert Park Village is located in the Crenshaw district of Los Angeles. Unlike the big-city bustle of adjacent Crenshaw Boulevard, Leimert Park Village is a series of small shops and buildings on the quiet streets of Degnan and 43rd. It boasts one of the highest concentrations of businesses owned or operated by African Americans in the United States. It is the site of various Afrocentric and black cultural events and celebrations including Kwanzaa, the Martin Luther King Jr. Day Parade, blues and jazz festivals, and the African Film Festival, and it is adjacent to the annual fall

African Marketplace. Most of the businesses in Leimert Park are small shops and stores that contain hard-to-find gems of African American history, culture, and art. During the 1990s, the selection of businesses included, among others, African-themed clothing stores, the Museum in Black (a comprehensive yet eclectic collection of black memorabilia), eateries including soul food, barbeque, and Mexican food, a dry cleaner, an Afrocentric theater, performance spaces, dance and fine arts studios, the jazz and poetry performance space named the World Stage, the jazz coffee house named the 5th Street Dicks, a beauty supply store, and card and gift shops.[5]

Even though Leimert Park has enjoyed its status as the center of African American culture and arts in Los Angeles, young people throughout LA also considered it the center of their cultural movement. The KAOS Network is an arts center located on the southeast corner of Leimert Park Village at 43rd Place and Leimert. It is the venue for the Thursday night hiphop workshop known as Project Blowed. Unlike many of the businesses in the Leimert Park Village area, KAOS is well known for collaborating with community artists and young people in developing their own projects.[6] It has invited neighborhood young people onto its premises through classes, activities, and workshops that introduce them to technology and art. As the prominence of Project Blowed grew throughout the hiphop world, Leimert Park grew as proof that LA was not only "gangsta," Hollywood, and rich, but the focus of hiphop. Leimert Park was serious about "keeping it real" as well as ready to prove that there was complexity to the notion of *Westsiiiiiide.*

At first glance Leimert Park may seem to be the ideal place for an underground hiphop venue because of its history and prominence as an African American arts destination. This is not the case. The journalist A. Asadullah Samad, of the *LA Watts Times,* describes Leimert Park Village as "a pocket of community merchants, cultural artists and ethnic pride, reinforced in perpetual activity, day and night, long ignored by bureaucrats and politicians, except for some public posturing from time to time" (1997, 1). In general, the merchants are suspicious of the motives of those who try to modify their community by introducing new art forms and traditions.[7] Many of the local proprietors practice traditional southern and middle-class African American values of respect of elders and of property. Some see it as their duty to protect and represent their culture, which they view as constantly under siege. They also share a black nationalist belief that those who do not show respect for their elders have been deprived of African American culture—and good home training.

When merchants reminisce about the power and strength of African American music, art, and culture, they often mention jazz and jazz musicians. For them it is the jazzmen in particular who set the standard for how to represent African Americans throughout the world with dignity, coolness, and self-respect. In contrast to their enthusiastic support of jazz, few of the business people in the community embrace hiphop given its brashness, adolescent male posturing, and recurring critiques of refined social persona. In fact hiphop is barely tolerated, and business owners often rail against hiphop youth who, they argue, disrespect the African American family as well as political and cultural traditions and legacies. In sum, it is not unusual to find proprietors who love their culture and are courteous, determinedly independent, and ill tempered—especially when it comes to hiphop. In spite of, or perhaps in response to the proprietors' critical attitude toward hiphop, in the 1990s Leimert Park became the center for underground hiphop in Los Angeles.

Though there surely were tensions between hiphop youth and business owners, the recorded message from "the hippest corner in LA" was a significant declaration for another reason. It is ironic that such optimism existed during what may be one of the bleakest periods in the history of LA's youth. The cruelest forms of LA gang wars were in full effect in the mid- to late 1990s, controlling many once-proud black neighborhoods and producing a noxious cloud over the entire area. What's more, teenage black and Latino men and women were left to negotiate through the madness on their own. True chaos resulted from the most organized and menacing street gangs—namely the Crips who symbolized membership by donning the color blue and the Bloods who displayed their loyalty by wearing red—as well as from corruption in the ranks of the LAPD and the deterioration of the public schools. Together these factors spelled disaster for many youths of color—often irrespective of social class.

The gangs' use of basic primary and patriotic colors—red and blue— meant that anyone venturing into the wrong neighborhood or territory wearing what might be grandma's gift of a sweater in red or blue could be shot dead for it. Some were. In March 1996 a young woman who had just turned eighteen was fatally shot for wearing the wrong color in a neighborhood.[8] To make matters worse, the intricate "secret" hand signals of the gangs introduced a new era when the deaf could not use sign language in certain neighborhoods for fear that innocent communication be mistaken for rival gang signals. In fact, two deaf couples were shot in 1991 and 1994 while using sign language, which the police believed were mistaken for gang signals.[9]

This era was also that of the hard "stone cold face"—a term used in reference to the social stance of meanness, fearlessness, and coldness that young men wore on their faces and bodies. While this stance strongly suggested the view of "I'd rather kill you than see you," it helped keep away aggressors and thus see the young men through another day. It also challenged their humanity and robbed them of normal, relaxed day-to-day social interaction. As one young man asked me: "Do you know what it does to you when you have to remember not to smile outside of your house?"

Young women did not fare much better than the men. Some became gang members themselves, while others claimed unflagging loyalty to boyfriends who were gang members. These young women often assisted their partners in concealing drugs, and many received jail sentences for protecting them.[10] Others were coerced into having sex with young gang bangers and many became pregnant. Robbed of their innocence, the only thing the young girls had to negotiate was motherhood itself, and the linguistic evidence of the deterioration of familial and social ties is expressed through the rise of expressions like "baby mamma" and "baby daddy." In the terms of classic sociological literature, as reflected in St. Clair Drake's and Horace Cayton's *Black Metropolis* (1945), the "shadies" and "illegals" had obtained a tight hold on the metropolis. In a place where the car ruled, neighborhoods like Compton and areas of Crenshaw and South Central saw residents hiding behind their iron-gated doors and windows and carefully plotting their journeys between work, school, and home to avoid the crossfire of "gang-torn" LA.

But within the caustic rhetoric, community organizers and youth workers also discovered that hiphop's mandate—that MCs tell the truth—also led to something that youthful America had been without for years: the development of a critical analysis of society and a tradition where ideas and events are debated and analyzed. Some of those who were living and working with Los Angeles' black and Latina and Latino youth began to think that hiphop, and underground hiphop in particular, could save Los Angeles and its youth from itself. As one teacher told me, "I hate it! But there's something there."

The adult community activists and artists in Los Angeles who facilitated the underground movement did not do so because they were fans of hiphop. In fact they, like many people, were dismayed with the nihilism of gangsta' rap and regretted its popularity among youth. They expressed frustration that young people did not focus on politics, community, and exposing social ills. In particular, the adults did not support the widespread use of profanity, especially the use of the words "nigger" and "nigga" and the frequently misogynistic representations of women and girls. They report that they became supporters and advocates because the young people had convinced them that hiphop was not only the reason they survive but also it made them think about changing their lives.

In fact those adults who consistently supported underground hiphop include several artists, actors and filmmakers, educators, business people, physicians, musicians, lawyers, and Hollywood "industry" people who were also Vietnam veterans, former Black Panther members, former civil rights workers, and so on.[11] In many respects rather than being the clichéd "children of the 60s" they were the ones who never ceased connecting art and politics. I talked to over thirty adults who helped sustain underground hiphop between 1994 and 2000. I focus here on the interviews and observations of Ben Caldwell and Charletta Johnson, who together represent the important attributes of the adult advocates, elders, and OGs[12] of hiphop who cleared a path through the urban madness so that young people might find their way through it.[13] Ben Caldwell and Charletta Johnson also provide insight into this group's backgrounds, conflicts, and tenacity in their support of the hiphop movement.[14]

First and foremost, adults and organizations that have supported underground hiphop in Los Angeles provide a physical space for practice and performance, reasonable protection from both law enforcement and gangs, and artistic creative support. They have often done so at great risk to their own livelihoods and professional reputations, since support could be costly and often attracted harassment from law enforcement and schools. In addition to these basic yet fundamental forms of support, the adults become significant figures on how to live life with dignity and according to principles. Young people closely watch these adults as they mediate and confront power and represent youths who may be emotionally unpredictable, strong willed, creative, intelligent, and vulnerable to authority. While underground hiphop could not exist without the first form of support, it is the second that determines whether young people consider the adults supportive of hiphop.

In the pages that follow, the quotations from the ethnographic interviews are transcribed verbatim except for the use of fictitious names and the omission of most of the verbal pauses (e.g., ah, uhm, etc.).[15] The interviews reveal four fundamental qualities and beliefs found among hiphop's adult supporters. First, reliable adult supporters consistently favor a form of activism and organizing outside of typical institutions and organizations. That is, though they may use and collaborate with a variety of institutions and traditional organizations such as churches, low-income service providers, established civil rights organizations (e.g., the Urban League), after-school programs, and the like, they generally do not make an effort to do so on a long-term basis. This characteristic is true whether or not the adults are members of the organizations themselves. Second, they engage youths in projects and activities rather than directing them. They seldom refer to as "work" their activities with young people, and they do not think that age and wisdom necessarily go hand in hand. Instead, they tend to provide models for how to do things for youth by doing and often describing their experiences and conflicts in detail and with honesty, and always cloaked in wit and irony. Third, they believe that the members of their generation are alienated from young people, as well as afraid of them, and have abandoned them to "the system." For them, the system is routinely described as groups, individuals, and institutions that consistently refer to and promote stereotypes of African American and Latina and Latino youth, and whose economic livelihoods depend on society's fear and loathing of these youths and thus the need to control them. They are neither black nationalists nor committed to particular religious practices. This avoidance of particular groups and ideologies means that their work with youth is occasionally seen as in conflict with traditional community organizations and institutions and the status quo in general. Finally, they believe that youth have the power, insight, opportunity, and intelligence to change their world.

The Good Life
House of the First Sighting

The Good Life began under the direction of B. Hall and her business partner Janie Goodkin (Ifasade). Their main business and personal goal was to bring a quality health food restaurant to the Crenshaw area. Health food restaurants in the African American community are much like any health food store in the rest of the country. There are materials associated with a holistic approach to eating and life, homeopathic and natural remedies, and the diagnosis of health problems. These businesses also tend to celebrate African and African American cultural traditions. In African American neighborhoods health stores usually play jazz music, and Afrocentric materials may be available. These stores not only provide a space of respect for physical health but also one where spiritual health is an important focus—and this spiritual health is described as African. Here the term African is loosely interpreted as respectful of and dutiful to elders and ancestors, respect for oneself, and an overall belief in spirituality.

The Good Life began with the name Underground Railroad around the time that the first hiphop radio station, KDAY (1580 AM), was abruptly canceled. It became the first location of underground open-mic hiphop in LA when B. Hall's son, Blaze, who was deeply involved in underground hiphop and was practicing to be an MC, persuaded his mother and Ifasade to let him and his friends use their space after regular restaurant hours. Both women supported and worked with youth on a regular basis, although they did not employ them in their regular business practices. As Ifasade explained, their business represented them and they were concerned that their image as a healthful environment be respected.

In 1989 the Good Life became the heartbeat and pulse of underground hiphop when it opened its doors on Thursday nights. A small stage was set up and the restaurant tables were piled along the walls when performing began. Around this time Aceyalone, one of the main organizers and top MCs, got together with neighborhood kids—Mikah 9 and Self-Jupiter. Within a month, the Thursday night venue was an institution for underground and freestyle hiphop. In 1990 Acey met Peace—and they all formed the group Freestyle Fellowship. While the rest of the country viewed LA as the center of decadence, and as a-historical, reactionary, low life, and gangsta' hiphop, the underground revolution was on. Moreover, it was the hottest thing for hiphop culture in LA, though gangster hiphop and gang activity were always in competition.[16]

Acey's description of the circumstances that led to the development of the Good Life, one of the most influential underground hiphop venues in America, is unassuming: "The idea for the Good Life . . . was started by a lady—B. Hall and her son R. K. Blaze. The Good Life was, of course, an establishment, and at night it was called Underground Radio. They were just going to have an open mic, and you know, I know what it was planned to be. And I know when we got there—we made it what it was."[17] DJ Kiilu described the scene in an early interview: "There definitely was a vibe there, so thick you could feel it in the air . . . It was strictly for rappers in the beginning. No fans. It was a very hard MC vibe, a real ghetto MC underground rap vibe. If you were no good it was not for you. It was next-level shit. There are a lot of rappers with records who came to the Good Life and got booed" (Crisafulli 1996, 46).

Busdriver, another artist who performed at the Good Life, refers to it as "the ground zero for underground hiphop": "The Good Life was like the archetype of the open mic in the U.S. Before the Good Life, which started in '89, there weren't things like that. That pushed the boundaries of what hip-hop was. It really was an amazing place, mind-blowing. People from around the country would come there to check it out—Biz Markie and countless others. To me it's ground zero for underground hip-hop and any branch of music that you want to call comes from it" (Payne 2003, 1).

When a House Is Not a Home

As the Good Life venue became more popular, more problems developed between its hiphop base and the store's owners. When I spoke with Ifasade in 1997, she explained that the health food store promoted respect of others and self-respect, and thus she and Hall attempted to impose rules prohibiting misogynistic lyrics and the use of profanity while promoting tier notions of supportive styles of mentoring. "Young people needed a place to go to develop their own art," says B. Hall. "The no-cussing policy wasn't about us being uptight church people, it was about wanting the atmosphere of a serious arts workshop. Most of the crowd respected the rule; some said it made rapping more challenging, that it created more respect and brotherhood. And maybe once or twice a month somebody would blow it, but the crowd usually ended it" (Mullen 2000, 1). The no-cursing policy, though inhibiting, was not an unbearable restriction. In fact, it became a challenge for MCs to both freestyle and control their language. As Brendan Mullen reports, "The young audience, somewhat tickled by this, took to booing out anybody who did" (2000, 1).

According to many involved, the Good Life ended because of an artistic disagreement between the project's crew and the store owners. According to Ifasade, the main conflict was over the method used to designate an MC as good or bad. When an artist was not performing at the highest level of lyrical skill, the audience, comprised mainly of MCs, would chant "Please pass the mic." This chant meant that the audience no longer respected the person on the mic because that MC had not respected the audience by coming prepared. The chant included waving hands with fingers formed in the letter W, yelling, whistling, laughing, and so on. Though the chant was phrased as a polite and formal request, it was actually a clear form of rejection. Indeed, if the MC did not relinquish immediately, the chant would become insistent and loud and would continue until the MC walked off the stage—presumably in shame. The owners felt that this method was humiliating and brutal and that another strategy was required. The Good Life crew disagreed by arguing that "please pass the mic" was at the heart of the training to being an MC. Although they were willing to work within the store owners' other restrictions and censorship, the passing of the mic was the essence of what they were doing. If they couldn't evaluate according to their own standards, they would leave. The Good Life was over.

When the hiphop artists left the Good Life they began, with the help of a jazz drummer known as Daryl, a project called the Afterlife, which met at various venues throughout South Central. In the meantime, Ifasade Goodkin and Daryl (D) both independently lobbied Ben Caldwell to let the group move into KAOS Network on a permanent basis. They spoke highly of Aceyalone's leadership and enthusiasm for hiphop. Similarly, Charletta Johnson, a high school teacher, shared her experiences with students who were not interested in regularly structured English classes but were enthusiastic to share their rhymes and battle for MC skills. Ben Caldwell agreed to host Project Blowed on Thursday nights, albeit with certain restrictions. Although the MCs renegotiated the restrictions regarding what might happen on the mic regarding censorship, they all supported the restrictions regarding drug and alcohol use and respect for property. Project Blowed was now in the house.

Ben Caldwell
The Whisperer

Ben Caldwell describes himself as a Vietnam veteran and a filmmaker who began working on film projects in the black community in the early 1980s. In response to the question of what he cares about in his life and work, he

Ben Caldwell, late 1990s. Photo by
Badru, courtesy of Project Blowed.

describes his first attempts to share his love of film with the Los Angeles
black community. In 1983, he hoped to set up a program to provide screenings of art films and documentaries, and thus he sponsored a preview of
the filmmaker and MacArthur Award recipient Charles Burnett's award-
winning film *Killer of Sheep*. The turnout for the screenings was low, much
to his disappointment and surprise. As he explained, his intention was to
share what he loved with those around him, but then he began to understand that the type of entertainment offered in art films did not fit the need
for release sought on Friday nights in the neighborhood. "People think of
films as being entertaining, purely—and nothing to go to where you have
to think and figure out artistically: where, what, what's happening, and
isn't the shot nice? So, I think that that was something that I hadn't anticipated, because mainly the people that show up to those things are mostly
Anglos. So anyway, it made me really figure out—What was I doing?"[18]

Ben followed his first attempt at outreach with a collaboration in 1984
that led to the Electronic Café and Gumbo House.[19] This facility connected

five locations around Los Angeles and introduced Ben and others to the capabilities of the Internet and video and teleconferencing.[20] In response he began to develop an idea to produce a documentary on youth titled *I Fresh*.[21] This film was to be a significant look at the contribution by black youth to culture. But first Ben had to confront several issues.

So another filmmaker and I started on a script with it. We had all kinds of fights because he hated hiphop you know, and I was advocating for it. So, but the whole thing was—you know it wasn't adversarial—it was more like it was artistically pushing and pulling. Because he would, he would play the devil's advocate for a lot of the things like, just, "OK why do you like those, those, those uh . . . ghetto blasting trucks and stuff? Why do you want that to be a part of them? What's so good about that Ben man? You can hear it, you know as blind! You can hear it two blocks up!" And, I say, "And that's part of the beauty of it man." You know the— so we'd be going like that and I would be saying that it was noise graffiti. And you know it was a way that, that, that graffiti happens within what they're doing it at all the levels of their life. They're imposing themselves on communities even through their music.

I said I used to think that myself. I would be around the—like in the army, if I was all around nothing but just white guys who were real evil and not nice, I'd put on this soul music and just make this—envelope the music around me. That just caused me to feel this a little, another way that I could just sit there and no matter what in the hell they were doing to bug me. I think that's what the kids are doing. And I, you know, so me and, and Ajay would call it noise graffiti, you know. So we were dealing with that and so, that's how the kids are and, and so we'd argue about little, things like that. And so we structurally put it on film a nice group together, about a young man coming of age and, and it was supposed to take place around a facility like our building.

Ben Caldwell began to think beyond the documentary projects that were his passion, and he began to consider factors contributing to the social, political, and cultural world of young people—and how his love of art and film related to their world. He states that he adopted an approach from Bertolt Brecht in the hope that the relationship between art, film, and politics could evolve organically by collaborating with youth. He then considered his involvement within various structures and projects. He considered his professional struggles to determine a particular artistic project to be a part of his work with youth and an important aspect in the overall development of KAOS.

I felt the best way for me to help those kids was to help kids who could be helped—that these kids were in a war zone similar to what I had seen in 'Nam. And that they had malnutrition. They were just, they were like what I, what I always told my wife was just like they're the axle grease of the society they were like, they, they were just making the wheels turn, you know. It's like their blood and guts and stuff are,—We're the axle grease of the society and, being that close to it, you have to participate with being the axle grease yourself. It's pretty hard to get that close to the axle grease and not be a part of it. And so, I said: "Well, so now, what I'm going to want to do is just focus on not the, W. E. B. Du Bois concept of the cream, but to just focus on what the kids really want to do. And I'm not defining those as cream, and I don't care where they come from. It's just as long as they have a power and fight within them as an artist. Then those are the ones that I want to work with no matter what kind of art they want to do.

Thus for Ben Caldwell and many others like him, conflicts over getting a group of professionals to work with youth includes insight on how he considers art and music to be political and representative. He listened to the young people and began incorporating their ideas into his plans. In the end, his work with youth changed both him and his plans.

I think that I touch more than I thought I ever could—was how much, um, we touch the young people. Or I've been able to touch the young people that are in— that have passed through here this, the last fifteen years, sixteen years, you know. And, to see kids that have gone from junior high and then see them as twenty-five now, you know, and, uh to see, how just little bugs in the ear—of towards some ideas of how that grows into major movements, and concepts, that even people don't even know sometimes. You know, I always believed things happen through whispers, you know like from one ear to another ear to another ear to another ear. And it really to me proves that in a lot of ways—'cause you just like, the kids are here, and I'm like, well gee that's little James Brown? You know, or George Clinton, you know, you know and then, you know, they sample that and then it becomes, The Dog! You know, it becomes the stuff that they love and they copy, and copy it and copy it. And, I whisper it and then, other people like us whisper it, and, and it, it ends up being a pervading mood that really encompasses the youth and then they don't even know from whence it came but it came from us whispering it as far as I'm concerned.

So those are the kinds of things that I'm the most amazed at. And so, uh—and I think that the power of media shows in that sense, what it can do and so . . . And that is my academic goal. My reason for being in the media in the first place was to see how persuasive a little camera can be toward changing people's goals and ideas, you know. And, and for it to be a good pill, you know, not of an empty, an empty pill, but to be a kind of like forcing people to say OK here is some good spiral—you just need it. Your body needs it. You don't know it. And, it doesn't taste as bad as an aspirin, but it's better for you, you know. And, and that kind of, of a goal was what I was dealing with. And . . . so that's, those are the basic precepts I guess I'm answering, even though this isn't the end that's still, what I started with. I mean it's not the end, but this is where I am up to this point, and that's the same goals I started with are kind of the same things that, that, that are still exciting me about the project.[22]

Charletta Johnson
Thugs Have Heart

Charletta Johnson began teaching at a high school in Orange County, California, and then moved to an inner-city high school in Los Angeles and then to a high school in the Compton area. She says, "I was born to teach. You know when I was a child I was teaching my sisters. I was always appreciating. I was just a kid and I always wanted to teach." Yet, a love for teaching could not prepare her for the gang takeover of Compton and other high schools and the wearing of gang colors. At first, she compared the change in dress among students to the change she participated in the 1960s. When she was in high school, hairstyles changed from straight to Afro, and clothing moved to African-influenced styles. These changes had a political meaning, and schools resisted them and even punished students for having natural hairstyles. These changes, however, were not the same that Charletta Johnson experienced in the 1960s. As a teacher she was suddenly faced with students who, instead of pushing political and social change, pushed domination and fear. She was incredulous. "It used to amaze me that these things, guys! You know, coming up in the sixties you know the thing was like the school. And they were just the opposite!— Red tennis shoes red, red! Oh, oh, what is it? A belt—red! And they go walking through the city, in enemy territory?" For her it was both devastating and unbelievable.

As a high school teacher she attempted to support students in their interests, and she experienced firsthand the effects on youth of the decay of their communities. Teachers like Charletta Johnson had been on the

Charletta Johnson, late 1990s.
Photo courtesy of Charletta Johnson.

front lines of the Black Power Movement and yet now witnessed the rise of the takeover of schools by gangs. It was urgent that these teachers develop new ways to communicate with their students and support them. At the same time, they had to prepare their students to deal with the weekly deaths of their classmates by gang violence. They had to try to help them with skills to avoid gang warfare and police brutality. And, somehow, they had to teach hope. Charletta Johnson considered hiphop to be the only thing her students respected, and thus as the place where there was any hope at all. She introduced many of her students to KAOS Network as she began to understand the importance of hiphop in their lives. She brought students to Ben during the *I Fresh* period and then when Project Blowed began.

I was always open enough to let the kids just rap what they wanted to. And there was one person, well she wasn't in my class, that was Yolanda Whitacker who was Yo-Yo. She worked in the main office and she would come and give—you know whenever she would have these ah go around to the classes to submit reports—and I would say you know Yo-Yo just rap. You know she would just rap and oh the kids would just—they thought she was wonderful! I didn't have any idea she was good and so I sent her to Ben and he knew immediately, you know he said there was something about her. So that's how it really started. And so I let the kids rap because I had access to all these kids, you know. So I began not really understanding, but just letting them be themselves because to me it was a form of, you know, poetry. And I would just allow them to do it, just as a way of, just trying to get into their world—not even trying to get into their world—just trying to allow them to create using the kind of language that they were, you know accustomed to. And that's how it really started, and that's how I was able to refer so many kids. Because I would—I always felt that if they weren't interested in my class I just wanted them to be interested in something.

While it is certain that Charletta Johnson would have tried anything to connect with her students, like Ben Caldwell and many others she did not immediately understand what was involved in being an MC and how lyrical skill was evaluated. In fact, in the beginning she did not like hiphop at all.

And it would just amaze me. He [Ben] was really interested in rap and hip-hop. I really wasn't interested in it at that time, because, they were just talking about tennis shoes, you know the stuff that came out of New York. He was talking to me. I said, "What How stupid is this?" You know, My Adidas and Run DMC! I— this is some stupid music, you know but I wanted something that had a little more edge.

And so, he was working on the film and he asked me if I needed new students. And not that I did, I really wasn't interested in the music, that the kids would rap. I couldn't get a hold of most of the words in the dictionary. Before those raps, they would do that. I would do that. I would say "Gee this is tough you know. This is just really, really tough!" So that's how I really got interested in rap. But I must say it really wasn't until I worked at Centennial, that I got really interested in rap. And it was, it would be young gangster rap and so it was oh, when I think about all the good stuff that had gone on before! I was just sending people to Ben that I, people that the kids would tell me oh they were good. And you know it was a way for them to express themselves in an English class, but I wasn't into it much at Centennial because Compton was gangster rap.

Johnson's appreciation for the music grew when she noticed the work that went into writing raps, such as searching the dictionary for new words, writing and rewriting, and peer critique of both writing and performance. However, the MC style was gangsta' and she did not have an appreciation for it. At Centennial, two students who were involved in gang activity, BJ and Zenith, found their way to Johnson.[23] They convinced her to listen to gangsta' rap, and she agreed to do so if they would work with her to reduce their gang involvement. In doing so she received criticism from other teachers. As she describes it, "The assistant principal says why do you spend time with him? He's a thug!" She responded, "I like him! I like thugs, the thugs have a heart. Thugs have a heart."

And I was just trying to tell them this was a whole new different experience. I'm just trying to figure out a way how I'm going to get to these kids at all. And it was through BJ. . BJ was one of my students, and that's how I became interested in gangster rap. He told me, and I listened and I was horrified. But I was so happy because that was the time that I really connected to the kids. Because, if you listen to the music, they tell you about the despair and their anger and the pain and it's all there! It's the history. It's right there. But we're not going to listen to it you know, because of the profanity and the obvious vulgarity.

Another, one of my other former students is is living with me now. She was telling me all about Goodie Mob and come and see The Goodie Mob. You've gotta have a lot of respect for those guys, you know. Because they changed the music—you know, wouldn't take nothing off of anybody! And, you know, because that whole underground—and they were able to lay it on—you know, their own record labels. I said that is just wonderful, they caused a whole lot of people to make money. It went on the whole mainstream. All these R & B artists they had, they owe a lot to those rappers, those thugs. You have to give them the props so I loved that. And then I was able to see how it was just continued how it would, you know, be related to jazz, and the improv, and the freestyle and it was all the same and then of course to really um, um, you know appreciate the rap. Those guys are really serious. They are really connected too. They know more about all the old R & B and now they're mixing it with the jazz. And that's wonderful.

Both Ben Caldwell and Charletta Johnson became involved with hiphop as they pursued their chosen areas and worked in the professions they loved. They are not youth workers, and they are not committed to other organizations outside of their work. Instead, their association with young people was part of their everyday life and activities and not a separate and independent commitment. Their work and their commitment are both what they do and who they are. According to Ben Caldwell, a good filmmaker connects with his or her subject in every way. For Charletta Johnson a good teacher reaches out to and connects with her students wherever they are. To stop doing what they do is to cease pursuing their own lives and dreams. This is not to suggest that those who work with youth professionally are not as committed to helping them as are Ben Caldwell and Charletta Johnson. The point is that the strong and consistent support for youth is a part of how the adults live their lives. As the following chapters show, the support by both Ben Caldwell and Charletta Johnson was not only in the form of offering space and moral support. They also shared their artistic, cultural, political, and historical perspectives and experiences. They describe themselves as people who listen, follow, and try to provide examples for others. Their influence, along with the city of LA and the black community, served as a foundation for those interested in underground hiphop. This foundation was one based on linguistic theory, cultural socialization, practice, artistic creativity, and evaluation of skill.

Welcome to the Underground

You Wouldn't Understand the Ghetto
Framing Hiphop Culture

HIPHOP CULTURE DID not come out of the blue. The youth who created the Hiphop Nation and Project Blowed came from the core of African American communities and culture where there are established and well-known social and political practices that critique and work to change the American system of justice (cf. Perry 2004; Shelby 2005). In African American communities, resistance against oppression and movements for equality have included physical protests as well as critical narratives, political movements, creative art movements, verbal genres, and more. The youth who fashioned hiphop art, culture, and politics—whether from the Bronx, the Caribbean, Atlanta, Chicago, South Carolina,

You ever seen a rapper with fire in
   his eyes
Wired up off the smoke tryin' to
   fly?
Rap, rap, rappin', rhyme, rhyme,
   rhyme
Leimert Park and 43rd turn into a
   landmine
B-boy's tryin' to flow they rhymes,
   and b-girls
Lookin' oh so fine
My man Badru gots the fresh
   designs
And Cheatham got the sound set
   bangin' from behind
5000 boomin' watts, KAOS network state of the art
Audio-video, filmin' and editin',
   capoeira and meditations
Computers and telebeams, at the
   workshop every Thursday night
Where we give the new definition
   to open mic
I hope y'all don't mistake glitter
   for gold
While we doin' it, and puttin' it
   down at the Project Blowed

ACEYALONE, "Project Blowed"

CHAPTER TWO

New York, New Jersey, or Los Angeles—were reared on endless tales of the American dream versus the American nightmare. These tales serve as examples of how each individual must develop a sense of self-worth, overcome obstacles, and continue to fight for freedom and equality. For example, black youth learned early on that the Black Muslim leader Malcolm X was told by his high school counselor that he should not aim too high "for his own good"; that the police seem to serve and protect others; and that justice is directed at "just us." As urban youths tossed cardboard boxes onto the streets of the Bronx, relaced and unlaced their sneakers, refashioned their dress, reconstructed sound systems, and redefined synthesizers and mixers they did so within two cultural contexts. One was a dominant culture that had discarded and demonized them; the other was an African American culture that had a tradition of confronting prejudice and injustice.[1] Through their resolve, they created more than hiphop.

Though hiphop's influence on African American youth is often overstated, in some respects it has done more to crystallize a young, urban African American and American youth identity than has any other recent event in history or politics. Moreover, it has managed to do this while highlighting unique and culturally valued aspects of different societies and communities. Its familiar slogan "Get in where you fit in" claims inclusion as the foundation of hiphop ideology, but within parameters. While the focus in African American culture is on justice, freedom, and equal representation and inclusion in the wider society, hiphop's argument is for the inclusion of everyone who respects hiphop, irrespective of race, class, gender, religion, nation, and so on. Through both commercial and underground media forms, the art, dance, music, and words of hiphop transcend language, neighborhoods, cities, and national boundaries, thereby resulting in international varieties where marginalized groups and political parties appropriate hiphop as a symbol of resistance and where ethnic, religious, and regional disputes are renegotiated (Mitchell 2001; Sunaina 1999; Rap Pages 2000). Simultaneously, hiphop fights for local and national identity and against the marginalization of any group that comes together around hiphop's edicts. In 1992, when the group Public Enemy toured Europe with the rock group U2, their charge to hiphop's nation of millions was "Fight the power!" This slogan began to appear on walls in England, Poland, Italy, and elsewhere. In fact, a worldwide audience quickly gravitated to hiphop's unrelenting critique of society, as well as its notion of community, recognition, and representation, because it fit within already established international local and national movements for justice, education, rights, and independence (cf. Sansone 2003; Skelton and Valentine 1998; Scott 1990).

The notion that everyone has the right to be represented affects every aspect of hiphop culture, and while the idea is an inclusive one it does not necessarily guarantee a harmonious result (see chapter 5). In particular, this notion does not necessarily protect and respect the ideas of cultural and societal norms and values held by earlier generations. In fact, hiphop's notion of black identity is often criticized as a disruption in black political and social history that does not acknowledge earlier relevant social, cultural, and artistic movements that preceded hiphop (cf. Reed 1992; Kitwana 2002). Yet, while the civil rights and Black Power struggles of the 1950s, 1960s, and 1970s may have introduced the myth of a united, politically and socially homogeneous African American community, hiphop members boldly and brazenly argue for the "real" in relation to national, as well as regional and local, identities and loyalties. This rupture may have occurred because hiphop considers racism to be part of a system of beliefs and attitudes that include social class privilege, sexism, discrimination against youth, xenophobia, religious preferences, and so on. Thus hiphop youth are likely to attack an organization over its lack of support of youth while also supporting them in their fight against racism. In this sense the appearance of fracture, which is examined in detail in chapter 5, may represent a change in discourse about the African American and minority American experience rather than the destruction of the African American community.

In spite of the situation described above, from a cultural perspective it is surprising that some African American adults should consider hiphop aesthetics and politics to be at odds with earlier artistic, cultural, and political movements. Many of the adults became aware of hiphop when they recognized their own generation's music and expressions sampled in hiphop songs. For them, hiphop recalled their youth when groups of young men on the block harmonized and recited tall tales while keeping time by hitting their legs and snapping their fingers to "The Signifying Monkey," "Shine," and numerous other black folk rhymes that filled the urban landscape. These were periods of talk-sing, rhyme, and poetry by performers like the Last Poets, Watts Poets, Gill Scott-Heron, and Isaac Hayes, or by those like the Ohio Players who crooned and chanted "I Wanna Be Free" over slow-driving funk beats.

During the late 1960s, groups like Martha Reeves and the Vandellas claimed that dancing really did occur in the streets, where music blasted through speakers at impromptu block parties that "borrowed" their electricity from unsuspecting patrons.[2] Urban areas were treated to an insurgence of public art as leaders and contributors to African American culture, previously erased and ignored in American history, were uncompromisingly resurrected to demand their rightful place in American history. Suddenly, massive pictorials appeared as writing on the urban canvas in the form of "walls of respect," where the newly articulated movements for black pride and black respect exploded in vivid living colors.[3] At the same time black fraternities, marching bands, and drill teams executed their elaborate steps, body movements, poses, and acrobatics with precision and attitude—to the delight of captivated audiences. Many of the performers were unaware that their various step rituals continued a custom of incorporating African traditional dance. All of the artistic movement occurred under the watchful eye of the deejays, who ruled the nightlife as the tireless dancers created dance after dance in tribute to their favorite music and the deejay's ability to rock the party into the night. These "mixmasters" created a musical landscape that recognized the thriving beat and musical history necessary to move bodies in a continuous flow. In response the singers sang their praises, anointed them "Mr. Deejay," and recognized them as lifesavers, and in so doing gave them a much-needed reason to live night after night.

The abundant and infectious musical, cultural, and social traditions of hiphop's prehistory were integrated into the daily lives of African Americans. People breathed Marvin Gaye's political critique of the Vietnam War and the peace movement in "What's Goin On," and later in his expression of desire and passion in "Let's Get It On," as they lived, worked, raised families, and wrestled with what it meant to be living in America as what Curtis Mayfield called "We people, blacker than blue." Musical, verbal, and artistic expressions were not museum artifacts of African American culture but rather its very fabric. In fact, musical innovation and creativity accompanied virtually every social movement of Americans of African descent (cf. Lipsitz 1994; Keyes 2002; Dawson 2001).

The Great Migration of African Americans from the South to the North was accompanied by the screaming of the blues and the shift from spirituals to gospel musical. When they arrived in urban areas, African Americans of the 1920s and 1930s were greeted by the big bands of Cab Calloway, Duke Ellington, and Count Basie. As African Americans became more urban and working class, they did so to the sound of the more personal, introspective, and critical wailing of the jazz trumpet and saxophone that blew sweetness, bitterness, pain, regret, injustice, and chaos into the urban landscape. The civil rights movement progressed slowly at first—to the pulse of the spirituals and freedom songs. Soon Motown and Stax and Chess Records stepped in and do-wopped and crooned for Black Power and all the sit-ins, marches, demonstrations, and civil disobedience that the masses could muster. Virtually every political, social, historical, artistic, and cultural move that African Americans made was to a pulsing beat, a song, a dance, a poem, a story. Because music, dance, art, and poetry were so ingrained in African American life, in some respects hiphop's beginning seemed unremarkable. However, though hiphop appeared to be integral to the social and political life of the African American and the Latina and Latino communities on the East Coast, it was in many ways unique and represented a significant departure from the earlier movements that occurred within African American musical traditions.

While each aspect of art and performance was powerful in and of itself, in the late 1970s verbal genres, dance, music, and art as well as political, cultural, and social critique joined forces and congealed in the South Bronx as hiphop. Instead of art and music accompanying and reflecting a political and social condition, hiphop became the movement itself. Hiphop incorporated the artistic elements, traditions, and cultural practices that previously coexisted and only occasionally bonded together, and then it decisively united them into a powerful "workforce" of art. Hiphop's devotees fashioned a creative expression comprising the genre's four artistic elements— the deejay and the turntable, the delivery and lyricism of rapping and the MC, break dancing, and graffiti art and writing. As I noted earlier, these elements are all sustained through evolving cultural standards for expression and representation and endless critique and assessment.

The DJ Made Me Do It

While hiphop culture is based on African American cultural practices, it is also influenced by practices throughout the African Diaspora, especially the Caribbean. Hiphop developed within the traditions of Jamaican party DJs and African American radio DJs.[4] In African American communities DJs are not minor players in urban social and political development;

rather, they have been at the core of cultural and political movements. Prior to the introduction of black-themed radio, communication about local and national issues regarding African Americans was highly regulated, and it was only found in the few black newspaper publications of the time. While in some respects the radio served to manipulate and regulate the music being played, it also was a resource in a situation of segregation and injustice. With the massive migrations of African Americans from the South to the North in 1940s, radio DJs both controlled the music marketed to blacks and mediated information about community events and interests, culture, art, and political and social movements (Barlow 1999; Keyes 2002).[5] Suddenly, black-themed radio became the community's "newspaper, mayor and minister" (Black Radio 1996). News and opinions from DJs meant that those with minimal education and literacy skills had access to information about issues related to their experience and how their lives related to other regions of the United States.

As blacks migrated from the southern parts of the United States to the North, they could learn from DJs how to navigate their new environments, including which locations were safe and which were not, where necessities could be found, and where they could locate their culture and art. In fact in the 1960s some DJs would interrupt their music programs to devote parts of their broadcast to discussions about the civil rights movement.[6] The role of the DJ was a national one, and by the 1980s people of African decent in urban areas who participated in the secular world moved to the same musical and social beat as their radio night DJs who segued into programming of *The Quiet Storm, Midnight Groove, Slow Jam,* and more. It was they who first created the possibility of "one nation under a groove."

When the Bronx party DJs of the late 1970s began their rise, they did so with the local knowledge of both the clubs and radio they claimed as their own—Caribbean and African American (Hebdige 1987; Hinds 2002; Chang 2005). The traditions of Jamaican DJ style combined seamlessly with black American styles. Not only did Jamaican DJs traditionally serve as alternative new sources to formal radio broadcasts that ignored and did not reflect most of Jamaica's population, the DJ also introduced the tradition of the toasting competitions, remix, dub, and so on (Hebdige 1987; Brewster and Broughton 1999). The Jamaican creation of a sound system with the DJ pushing the crowd as well as delivering the news brought a new flavor to DJ tradition. To paraphrase the musician George Clinton, the DJ's skills not only made you move, it removed you and healed you. Hiphop DJs inherited the role of playing music that reflected the beat and mindset of a generation as well as the responsibility of providing a voice and information within a system of oppression and misrepresentation. They manipulated local sounds and sensibilities as well as demonstrated a musical sense of time, timing, and memory that embraced and provided shout-outs to the globe. Soon, DJs discovered national, international, and local musical genres, as well as traditional and popular artists, and they consumed the histories and cultures of the people they discovered. The DJ traditions merged so that not only did one get a rocking sound system, but also word (worldwide) about "the system" and "the man." It was clearly time to turn over the mic to those who could handle delivering the word full time.

I Go to Work

While DJs provided the foundation for hiphop culture, as hiphop grew the MCs became the focus. In their work they introduced stories of hiphop's beginnings, struggles, personalities, spaces, and places, and they also highlighted local associations by describing and naming neighborhoods, public transportation systems, schools, and highways. The focus on place and space resulted in narratives that transformed urban landscapes into shared places based on the desire to represent particular communities and connect them to each other (Lefebvre 1991). As Sun Ra suggests in his 1974 movie *Space Is the Place*, the search for a safe home that naturally incorporates artistic, racial, cultural, class, and spiritual difference and creativity requires a salvation narrative of mythological proportions. Similarly, artists often insist that where they were born is also where God and the gods roamed. The transformation of the land of the ghetto into the land of myth and the future has resulted in what Murray Forman calls "the extreme local" (2002, xvii). It is constructed in relation to local culture and history that is seen as particular, but through which other neighborhoods and the world are also evaluated.

Since the East Coast was the birthplace of hiphop, its urban terrain became synonymous with hiphop's very existence. Through hiphop artistry, the local descriptions of East Coast areas were a demographer and cartographer's dream. Not only did young people throughout the United States learn about the Bronx, Bedford Stuyvesant (Bed-Stuy), and Harlem, but also Brooklyn (BK), Hollis and Jamaica (in New York), Queens (the

Bridge), Staten Island (Shaolin), and New York housing projects like the Marcy Projects and city avenues and streets like Houston in New York City and Hollis Avenue in Queens. Territorial wars developed over what neighborhood had the right to different aspects of the hiphop foundation narrative. The Bronx won the rights to the DJ history through constant repetition of the first time that DJ Kool Herc connected his sound system and mixed records. Yet it was quickly clear that battles over local rights to the first time for hiphop's other elements would never settle a claim. Instead, battles over who first created b-boy moves, graffiti styles, DJ techniques, and lyrical and production styles fueled excitement, purpose, an audience, and sense of local community.[7] They also generate income and an increase in skills and therefore a heightened sense of the necessity of hiphop in young people's lives.

As DJs perfected their skills and MCs began controlling their mics, hiphop's audience grew along with its producers and the entourage of the recording studio. While African American producers previously had worked within the confines of the record industry and its well-defined market demands, the hiphop producer was the authority of the market for the music and thus reconfigured the relationship between those involved in the art (especially the MC and DJ), the record company, and the support system. The hiphop producer worked within the competitive system of hiphop representation. The MCs and DJs began to use styles that represented the entire team. In addition, individual producers expanded their business and influence into related and unrelated marketing ventures. Suddenly, a hiphop artist did not simply represent a community or what is real, but a brand and product. Production teams and the honing of particular styles led to a more predictable and formulaic hiphop. In turn, this expansion of the role of the producer led to the widespread popularity of hiphop, and it opened the entire country and the world to its potential. At the same time, regional labels also developed. Nelson George (1992) describes this period as going national and regional (see also Forman 2002).

While production crews focused on a revamped notion of "the business," those who were hiphop's founding generation began to lobby for intense scrutiny of the real—real skills, real life, and real hiphop. The constant agitation from hiphop's founding generation was answered by the emerging generation of youth who had grown up in what was now hiphop culture. They reinvigorated the hiphop nation by constantly reassessing and developing their skill, knowledge, creativity, and systems of evaluation regarding the representation of the four elements. While hiphop skills have evolved, they have done so as part of a generation of youth who grew up submerged in hiphop.

Young people are socialized into hiphop through elaborate ritualized practices and activities. It is only when they have gone through some aspect of this socialization that they can "represent" hiphop. It is at this point that followers of hiphop achieve the fifth element of hiphop culture: knowledge. Membership in the community is instantiated and mediated through audience corroboration and collaboration (cf. Duranti and Brenneis 1986). The right to represent the hiphop nation is substantiated by its members' purchase and copying of recordings, memorization of rap lyrics, practice and freestyle performance, loyalty to crews and individuals, and participating in some aspects of hiphop's elements and in evaluation of artists' skills. Activities surrounding these five aspects of participation are ritualized and repetitive. They often result in the emergence of two groups that represent and protect hiphop and express a commitment to hiphop culture: the *core* and *long-term (LT)* members.

The Core
Just Wannabe Represented

Ever since the first MC held a mic and caused onlookers to both move their bodies and listen with their minds (domes), the hiphop audience has been composed of critics whose mission is to protect hiphop and keep it "real" and fresh. They have extensive knowledge of many aspects of verbal and artistic and performance skills, including shifts in aesthetics. These audience members begin as adolescents who have an uncompromising expectation that an MC should be exceptional and be able to accept severe criticism. They develop their methods and values of critique—and how to handle critique—through an elaborate process. The core audience of the hiphop nation is formed by adolescent males and females between twelve and seventeen years of age who listen to, memorize, and write raps (cf. Wheeler 1992), dress in the current hiphop style, keep up with the current dances, and tag or at least practice graffiti writing. The core regenerates in five-year spans and its members often believe that true hiphop began when they came of age. They only recognize earlier moments in hiphop when they become long-term members. The younger group members also practice freestyle and compete with each other over the best rap, delivery, style, and so forth. The core members of hiphop usually discover that they are part of the hiphop generation when they are in school and as they play with classmates and practice drawing and tagging their names and dancing and memorizing lyrics. They don't describe their commitment to hiphop as being "jumped in" in reference to violent gang initiation, but rather of having been charmed into hiphop culture. Theirs is also a story of being mesmerized by the excitement associated with being vividly represented in music, art, and dress, and realizing that hiphop is one way to describe who they are and what they feel and experience.

Khia, who is twenty years old and from Boston, remembers that she began participating in hiphop dance competitions and exhibitions around the age of ten. She and her friends would just "break into formation and dance hiphop styles wherever people were hanging around." Khia said she often tagged her name and was introduced to "those big phat markers" through her brother.[8] She then began tagging walls. She explained that the first song her group of friends memorized was "Choice Is Yours" by Black Sheep (1991). She quickly launches into the rap.

> You can get with this,
> Or you can get with that.
> (three times)
> I think you'll get with this,
> Cuz this is where it's at.
>
> You can get with this,
> Or you can get with that.
> (three times)
> I think you'll get with this,
> 'Cause this is kinda phat.
>
> Engine, Engine, Number Nine,
> On the New York transit line,
> If my train goes off the track,
> Pick it up! Pick it up! Pick it up!

Karyn, a twenty-five-year-old student who grew up in Chicago, was also drawn to hiphop culture. In an animated tone, she refers to several different artists during her passage into adulthood:

56

See, DJ Jazzy Jeff and the Fresh Prince—he doesn't use that name anymore, it's Will Smith—but I use to love his—Ooooh I LOVED "Parents Just Don't Understand" ((launches into lyrics)). We didn't have nobody to represent ((us)) when I came up. So when I was young I listened to A Tribe Called Quest, especially "I Left My Wallet in El Segundo" and "Bonita Applebum" (1990). Oooh I use to just love it. I still know it, see:

> Hey Bonita, glad to meet ya
> For the kind of stunning newness, I must have foreseen ya
> Hey, being with you is a top priority
> Ain't no need to question the authority
> Chairman of the board, the chief of affections
> You got mine's to swing in your direction
> Hey, you're like a hiphop song, you know?
> Bonita Applebum, you gotta put me on

And then I liked "Scenario," "Buddy" by De La Soul and then I got older and got into everybody else—you know, Busta, Nas, and I even like LL.[9]

The core audience members, whether artists or enthusiasts, develop through at least five overlapping stages that train and socialize them into hiphop culture and the evaluation of skills in the four elements of hiphop.[10]

Stage 1: Boys in this stage draw action figures—transformers on pieces of paper —they have others draw on the same page and they exchange pages as well. Girls may begin with writing names—their name, their friend's names, and those they like romantically. Both boys and girls then begin to write their names as action figures and in 3D. It is at this point that they begin to think of their names potentially as tags and a graffiti personal identity.

Stage 2: Both boys and girls repeat lyrics along with their favorite artists and memorize their favorite songs. They play CDs and listen to hiphop on the radio in cars and in bedrooms across the country. These core members may not know the meaning of the lyrics and when they suspect that a reference may be regional or purposefully indirect, they consider it their mandate to determine what the word means and then to strategically employ it. They discover meanings by scanning websites, listening to interviews, and talking to friends, cousins, and others from other parts of the country.

Stage 3: Core participants may graduate to owning artist's drawing books called piece books—where they continue to tag their names but also experiment more with shading, color, mediums, and potential throw-ups (graffiti art). Piece books are passed around and people comment on the tag and whether the style is appealing, innovative, unique, or bitten (stolen) from someone else. These books generally move within and among groups. It is common to own or hold many books that the owner or holder has written in but did not start. These books may include writers who are unknown to the owner.

Stage 4: Participants begin tagging the route to school. At this point a developed tag is for friends and neighborhoods. It is an act of pure love. It is saying "Hello, have a good commute—See, look at my name, isn't it pretty?" This stage may also be marked by inventiveness using markers and spray nozzles and the late-night writing of elaborate pieces and in competition with other crews. It may eventually result in attention from law enforcement.

Stage 5: It is common for core members to participate in all four elements of hiphop. By this stage members begin to practice and focus on what they enjoy the most. The revelation that they are more than consumers of hiphop is often accompanied by evidence of emerging critics as the young recite, at length, lyrics to their favorite childhood raps and describe their dance and graffiti styles.

Participation in these stages (especially stage 4) may also lead to professional drawing and lettering work and attention from parents and teachers, as well as enrollment in art classes. Badru, a graffiti artist in LA, described his entry into hiphop culture as the realization that his classmates and neighborhood friends knew who he was because they saw his tagged name everywhere. "I *had* to write my name. Just to see it! On the bus, on the walls, on the freeway sign, on the bench—everywhere you went, especially on the way to school! At first I didn't tell that it was me. Then people started saying that they saw my name—and I liked it!"[11] These core members also have endless arguments with their parents and schools over the clothes, shoes, hairstyles, and jewelry worn by their favorite artists.[12] They also talk about obtaining recording and deejay equipment, computer programs, and vinyl recordings of favorite artists, and they have personal music players, piece books, earphones on their ears, and the delight in knowing that neither their parents nor school officials are able to translate and understand their music. While the core members purchase the most recordings and are essential to hiphop's stability as an artistic form, they have not and may not develop a critical perspective on hiphop artistry and representation—prerequisites to actively participate in hiphop culture. It is unusual to see core members in the underground unless they are with adult relatives and friends. Because the underground requires knowledge of hiphop, local and national history and politics, popular culture, and so on, the core's older counterparts outnumber them in the underground.

Long-Term Members
Building Conscious Ciphers

As core members move from ritualized activities, they increase their participation in evaluation and, if highly skilled, artistic practice. They quickly assume the role of the hiphop critic—the guardians of hiphop culture. The most influential segment of the hiphop nation is formed of young people in their late teens to middle twenties. These long-term (LT) members consciously participate in hiphop culture, populate the underground, become critics, and search out haters,[13] and they may also practice freestyle, participate in local and underground open mic performances and competitions, and identify with particular rap genres or crews. This segment of hiphop often writes letters of praise or complaint to various hiphop publications and gives *props* (respect) to artists. Long-term members display their knowledge and also serve as nation builders and often offer political and historical commentary and context to current hiphop styles and artists.

The LTs often begin their hiphop critic passion as core members where they learn to evaluate MC skills during hiphop circles or ciphers. A cipher usually consists of rhyming MCs and onlookers who form a circle and evaluate the overall lyrical skill of participants (Keyes 2002; Peterson 2003). The center of the cipher can be occupied by MCs demanding an audience, competition, and critical evaluation. The skills necessary to participate as an MC and as audience members incorporate a broad understanding and reverence for all levels of knowledge and all people. Ciphers are considered to be the heart of the underground because all styles, values, norms, and beliefs of hiphop must come together in order for an MC to represent. The levels of knowledge include popular and public culture, history, politics, art, music, language, philosophy, literature, religion, and more. To participate, one must be able to creatively *play* with all of the knowledge sets in a competitive manner. The MCs then freestyle— that is, produce imaginative rhymes instantaneously or deliver prepared rhymes in inventive ways. It is also in the cipher that MCs develop their battling skills and their ability to provide and accept critique. Some MCs adapt a variety of personas and flow with many styles within and across ciphers to demonstrate their knowledge and the proof that they control the mic (Krims 2000).

Knowledge of lyrical styles also means that, if necessary, one can signify on another style or person. In fact, there are a variety of hiphop styles including old school, hard core, gangster, gospel, social and political consciousness, and others. Both men and women practice these styles as they are not fixed and can occur across a performance turn or be a few lines within a long rhyme. The LTs are aware of all of the styles and evaluate MC skills accordingly. Whether one gains financial success is not a serious issue, unless the community members perceive that the artist ignored their core hiphop audience in order to achieve it. Achievement in hiphop is related to the creative and relevant forms of sound, writing, style, music, and delivery that resonate with the audience.

The role of the LT audience as critic is based on African American cultural practices, especially call and response. Geneva Smitherman describes call and response as "spontaneous verbal and nonverbal interaction between speaker and listener in which all of the speaker's statements ('calls') are punctuated by expressions ('responses') from the listener" (1977, 104). Call and response has also been referred to as the "amen corner" because it also occurs in religions sermons. Hiphop incorporates a somewhat different spin on call and response in that it considers affirmation to be a process of critique. The LT serves as the social and cultural critic that assesses every aspect of the performer, including his and her body, movement and adornment, language and message. The audience assesses critically the social face and persona of an artist and the audience members (those who are a part of the crew) who support him and her as well. These critics describe, broadcast, and evaluate the background of the artist, predict what the future has in store, and challenge anyone to prove them wrong.

In the case of Project Blowed, the audience members affirm the MC by bobbing their heads, moving their shoulders in quick succession, throwing their hands up with their fingers in the shape of the letter W, or even forcing the MC off the mic by yelling repeatedly "please pass the mic." The critic can be loving, caring, an ally, an enemy, or all of the above. Friendly yet fierce battles concerning the criteria of evaluation and facts are often waged between critics, often in the presence of hearers, willing audiences, and passersby who acknowledge the victor at every turn. In fact, at times the artist is also the critic—evaluating his or her performance as well as that of others. Other than the mandate that hiphop is to represent the social, cultural, and political life of youth, the hiphop community is not bound by conventional attempts to codify and standardize its value system and artistic codes. Rather, artists must reflect a frenetic energy that mirrors the unpredictable nature and uncertainty of urban youth culture. They do this by introducing their listeners to their lives, language expressions, neighborhood, childhood, problems, personal flaws, strengths, dreams, and conflicts.

If the LT audience rejects the artist because the words, referents, experiences, and symbols evoked do not reflect the reality of the streets (or *their* community), then suburbia will eventually reject him or her. In this regard, Bill Adler's famous quotation that hiphop "is adored by millions in the streets and reviled by hundreds in the suites" (1991, xv) is only a hint of the real relationship between the streets and suites. Few artists can navigate the scrutiny and pressure of a crossover hit since this form of success results in the LTs' intense reevaluation of the artist for cultural, social, and creative authenticity and standards. Suburbia's uncritical acceptance might signify that the artist is a "perpetrator," a term that is the equivalent of a spy and the antithesis of what hiphop symbolizes.

Joan Morgan illustrates the "wrong" that the suite brings to hiphop in her discussion of the reaction by some critics to Arrested Development, a group that reigned in 1992 and 1993 but could not garner strong support for their second album. Their debut album, *3 Years, 5 Months and 2 Days in the Life Of . . .*, was released in 1992 and sold over five million copies. In 1993, Arrested Development won Grammy awards for the best rap song and best new artist. Critics outside of hiphop described them as contented southern Negroes, "naive" and blissfully "unaware that anything is wrong." There is no question that the admiration and support of establishment purveyors of culture and art contributed to Arrested Development's undoing. Moreover, they were one of the first major hiphop groups that did not come out of an urban area and that represented the South.[14] Arrested Development's lead MC, Speech, attempted to defend the group by arguing that they also have hardcore elements: "I'm not a violent person, but I don't think this album is nonviolent. I say, 'Brothers with their AKs and their 9mms need to learn how to shoot them correctly. I'm talking about *bum-rushing* the system'" (quoted in Morgan 1992). Yet, in spite of Speech's insistence that Arrested Development is critical of dominant culture, and in spite of the support and admiration of a number of political, social, and cultural figures, there was little anyone could do to convince fans that a group who enjoyed the tremendous crossover success of Arrested Development was really loyal to describing and defending the black youth experience and hiphop.[15] Their second release was a colossal failure.

Lyrical flow is one of the few MC attributes that can save a commercially popular MC from relentless scrutiny by hiphop's critical audience. The height of creativity and proof of leadership is to demonstrate that they can "rock the mic," take things to the "next level," and "flow." It is not easy for an MC to receive this recognition. Accordingly, when audiences and other artists recognize an MC for his or her ability to flow, they acknowledge that the MC is a leader and dominant lyrical force irrespective of popularity. To flow is the standard for determining superior MC skill. Anywhere in the world where there is hiphop, there is the demand that MCs be able to flow in order that their country, community, and crew are represented as part of the hiphop nation. The ability to flow is based on incorporating language ideology and philosophies in a creative way that represents local, social, and dominant language varieties as well as hiphop language and discourse styles.

Said It—Meant It
Word

The power of the Word is not a new concept and has been discussed throughout academic writing on hiphop. The Word brings hiphop into being as an art, a culture, a space and place, and a people with a history, ideology, and much more. However, it is not mere words and expressions that create a bond among hiphop followers throughout the world. Rather, it is based on African American language ideology where the words signify multiple meaning and critique power. Hiphop presents African American English (AAE) as a symbolic and politicized dialect where speakers are aware of complex and contradictory processes of stigmatization, valorization, and social control. The hiphop speech community is not necessarily linguistically and physically located but rather bound by this shared language ideology as part of politics, culture, social conditions, and norms, values, and attitude.

For hiphop, everyday language creativity requires knowledge of a linguistic system as well as how language is used to represent power. It uses language rules to mediate and construct a present, which considers the social and historicized moment as both a transitory place and a stable one. In this respect, hiphop represents the height of fruition of discursive and symbolic theories of identity and representation. It incorporates symbols and references based on shared local knowledge, and it produces a frenetic dialectic by interspersing and juxtaposing conventions and norms in the form of language and dialect varieties (Morgan 2002, 2001, 1998). Hiphop, then, introduces contention and contrast by creating ambiguity and a constant shift between knowledge of practices and of symbols. Thus, while the hiphop nation is constructed around an ideology that representations and references (signs and symbols) are indexical and create institutional practices, what the signs and symbols index in relation to power remains fluid and prismatic rather than fixed. The use of a famous phrase or line is not enough to claim the Word as an ideology. Rather than be imitative, the objective is to be creative within an existing ideological system. For example, Jacqueline Urla (1997, 2001) in her discussion of the construction of Basque nationalism in Spain includes an analysis of the use of African American expressions and cultural references by the music group Negu Gorriak. The mere use of these references by the group helped represent and symbolize a Basque identity and nationalism that could be understood by anyone in the world. The expressions linked their struggle to the civil rights and Black Power movements in the United States—a struggle known worldwide as one for basic civil and human rights. Consequently, Negu Gorriak's usage of African American linguistic and cultural references and expressions found in black films and music served not simply to imitate U.S. and African American culture but to represent the Basque nationalism struggle as a righteous one.

Those involved in Japanese hiphop also faced the challenge of how to reference and use African American language and symbols in ways that are not imitative but instead representative of Japanese hiphop. In fact, the early participation in hiphop by the Japanese was viewed as mimicry. According to Dawn Elissa Fischer, "verses were constructed in ways that either actually used AAE and/or Hiphop language phrases or AAE sentences were translated into Japanese and then performed over beats" (2007, 25). In response, Japanese fans of hiphop who lived abroad registered their embarrassment of the practice, as did African American and African National residents and visitors to Japan, and thus MCS began to manipulate the Japanese language to achieve rhyme and rhythmic flow. In fact, Ian Condry reports that "the skepticism was transposed from the formally dominant discourse of hip-hop's association with African-Americans and the English language (in contrast to Japan's ethnic and linguistic setting) to a new discourse challenging Japanese hip-hop's authenticity on the grounds that it was 'simply commercialized (komasharu) pop music'" (2006, 13). Fischer writes that "in the 1990s, emcees like K Dub Shine and producers like DJ Yutaka brought cultural and linguistic knowledge of Hiphop style to crews in metropolitan areas like Tokyo . . . In addition, emcees, in line with the Hiphop mantra of 'keeping it real' began to incorporate dialects and narrative traditions (such as Osaka-ben and Osaka comedy)" (2007, 3). The messages by the artists began to take on subjects important to Japan's youth, including the education system, the sex industry, the teenage bullying victims who turned into schoolyard murderers, and even America's handling of the war on terror (cf. Condry 2006; Fischer 2006). Similarly, in Germany the language ideology of AAE also prevails (Brown 2006; Richardson 2006). As Elaine Richardson notes, "Hiphop carries with it a paradigm, an aesthetic, and ideologies brought about through culture-specific sociopolitical and economic realities" (2006, 95).

In many respects, hiphop's language ideology addresses attempts to resolve how individuals interpret utterances, referents, and meanings while simultaneously recognizing that there are different senses and therefore possible interpretations of referents (see Frege, Geach, and Black 1977; Austin 1962). But it goes even further. Young people recognize that their voices are routinely marginalized, and thus their language ideology is one that assumes that agency and power reside in the ability to produce this discourse as proof of hiphop's existence and its ability to infiltrate and interfere with dominant culture. Young people are not concerned with sustaining a system hidden from dominant culture but rather one that is a strategic in-your-face antilanguage.[16] Those in hiphop consider this language to be visible yet unattainable unless one respects hiphop's language ideology. It is the barely perceptible antilanguage (Halliday 1978) and counterlanguage (Morgan 2002) that produce potentially dangerous discourses with power. That is, African American youth respond to society's attempt to stigmatize and marginalize AAE usage by their continued innovations within the norms of both dialects (Morgan 2002).

64

Consequently, discourse styles, verbal genres, and dialect and language contrasts become tools to not only represent African American culture but also youth alienation, defiance, and injustice in general.

The importance of creativity regarding counterlanguage and language contrast is obvious in the following hiphop lyric that, at first glance, appears to be nonsense.

> Bum stiggedy bum stiggedy bum, hon,
> I got the old pa-rum-pum-pum-pum
> But I can fe-fi-fo-fum, diddly-bum, here I come

In these lines from "They Want EFX," the group Das EFX both exemplifies and signifies on what it means to be a relevant hiphop MC. Their *nonsense* became one of the most distinctive and influential lyrical styles of the 1990s and was generally described as a new style of tongue-twisting lyrical gymnastics. That is, the wordplay, with its pop cultural and childhood references, focused on the potential of "words at play."[17] Suddenly, no sound was meaningless, and any sound, even when associated with cartoons, could have a new meaning when placed in a social and political context. Dressed in army-style fatigues with dreadlock hair and serious expressions, every syllable that Das EFX delivered exploded with attitude, critique, and a cry to battle. With phrasing, pronunciation, and grammar, Das EFX made it clear that in order to identify serious ideas (what is really going on), one must interpret what the speaker means and intends because of and beyond the words used in order to capture and understand the force and power of the Word.

Fighting to "Keep It Real"

As discussed above, one aspect of hiphop culture's complexity, and an aspect of its language ideology, is that it insists that members be informed and knowledgeable of potential meaning. Yet it is impossible to know all potential meanings since some are popular, regional, historical, and context dependent and may require prior knowledge. Nonetheless, an incorrect interpretation of what someone says guarantees a loss of social standing. It is this interplay of certainty and uncertainty about meaning and intention that brings play and seriousness into hiphop. The interplay that comes from indirectness is an integral part of this system. This is particularly true when it comes to making meaning in conversations about topics that may be avoided and considered taboo in some speech communities, while common and embraced by other speech communities.

In hiphop the individual participates in, works, and manipulates the communication process in order to set the stage for what Erving Goffman calls a kind of information game—"a potentially infinite cycle of concealment, discovery, false revelation, and rediscovery" (1959, 8). In this type of interaction, "the witness has the advantage over the actor" (9). In many respects, the business of hiphop culture is to continuously challenge and change the information game in order to get to the truth and to what is real. For many, especially those who express their "true" and "real" attitudes and beliefs in social contexts that are hostile to their beliefs, indirectness becomes an indispensable discourse strategy.[18]

Indirectness occurs with discourse that incorporates audience collaboration, and it is weighted in terms of both speaker intent and audience inference and interpretation. It occurs when someone says something that may have multiple meanings and referents. One must decide and interpret speaker intention and what is really being said. Indirect discourse must therefore be analyzed and read using many forms of knowledge. In this respect, whether premeditated or not, indirectness is interpreted as a conscious act and a performative, relying on speech community norms. Consequently, the use of indirectness is interpreted as reflecting the speaker's "true" and "real" identity and intention. This means that one must respect and be observant of others as one constantly listens, learns, and tries to keep abreast of what is going on. This practice is adapted from African American speech communities where interpreting a speaker's intentions is a culturally symbolic and mediated activity. One can be severely reprimanded for "reading someone's mind"—that is, attributing someone's intentions outside of social context.[19]

In the annals of African American history, only two types of people are depicted as believing that they know what someone intends. The first type is the mothers, who often *do* know what a child is thinking. The second type is the white supremacists, who actually believed that they were intellectually and emotionally superior to blacks and could enforce their belief about what was on a black person's mind, irrespective of what a black person said about what he or she intended. Consequently, the act of stating what another person thinks is so potentially tenuous that one is regularly reprimanded for speaking for another adult. Even if the person is not present, it is seen as assuming the person being spoken for is incapable of representing his or her own intentions (Morgan 1996). Irrespective of which case one uses as a model, to speak for someone else is treating them as a child. It is the ultimate put-down.

In hiphop another important aspect of word play is to not only uproot conventional signs (e.g., Grice 1957, 1975; Searle 1969, 1983, 1995) but also to change what is actually meant by the conventional by forcing the listener to pay attention to (or develop knowledge about) the said and the unsaid, and the marked and the unmarked, meanings and references.[20] For example, the MC Notorious B.I.G. (Biggie) in his 1994 hit song "Juicy" deftly manipulated multiple levels of meaning and signifiers to speak to his audience and let them know that his message was exclusively for them. He answered the question of who he is and what he means by dedicating his rhyme to the teachers who taught him nothing, the neighbors who prevented him from hustling, as well as to those who, like him, were trying to make ends meet. Biggie then represents the fantasies of those who lived during the early hiphop years.

> It was all a dream
> I used to read Word Up magazine
> Salt-n-Pepa and Heavy D up in the limousine
> Hangin' pictures on my wall
> Every Saturday Rap Attack, Mr. Magic, Marley Marl . . .
> And if you don't know, now you know. . . .

Throughout the song, Biggie paints a detailed picture of poverty and teenage hiphop dreams and desire against involvement in petty crimes with his refrain "And if you don't know, now you know." Through phrases, images, references, and symbols, Biggie not only establishes his hiphop credibility; he provides a narrative that recuperates the "founding nation time" of hiphop. He dedicates the song to those "in the struggle," mentioning one of the first hiphop magazines (*Word Up*) and the beginning of hiphop radio programs (*Rap Attack*) with the DJs Mr. Magic and Marley Marl. He "shouts out" the names of Salt-n-Pepa and Heavy D, two respected and popular artists from the 1980s. Later in the rhyme he recognizes racism and injustice while expressing hope: "Stereotypes of a black male misunderstood—and it's still all good." He again calls out to casual listeners and cultural outsiders who may not be aware of the extent of racism in his life: "And if you don't know—now you know." All of these often indirect yet symbolically rich rhymes occur through the sampled refrain of Mtume's (1983) soulful "slow jam" hit "Juicy Fruit."[21]

> You know very well who you are
> Don't let 'em hold you down, reach for the stars
> You had a go, but not that many
> 'Cause you're the only one—
> I'll give you good and plenty
> Juicy

Biggie's use of symbols, expressions, language, references, memories, and music creates a sweeping whirlwind of a fully realized present that evokes not only the black cultural community but one mediated by a hiphop ideology that signifies on others and on itself as well.[22]

While Das EFX's lyrical strategy focused on the fact that speakers have intentions that can be represented outside of immediately identifiable sounds and symbols, Biggie illustrates the relationship between intention and choosing identifying symbols that represent a particular ideology. As an accomplished hiphop artist, he also takes into consideration the values of interconnecting and sometimes hostile communities and symbols. The system they both employ is one where references and symbols must be regularly evaluated and reconsidered in order to represent "what is really going on." This particular skill of mediating the construction and representation of meaning and intentionality and specific reference is a relentless pursuit in hiphop culture. The expression "Said it—Meant it" recognizes this pursuit and that the artist and speaker intends and accepts responsibility for how he or she is interpreted. But Word is more than how an artist represents intention and meaning; it is also about language ideology itself.

Hiphop Philosophy
(Common) Sense and Reference

Another African American speech community notion that is embedded in hiphop ideology is a philosophy about common sense. In order to understand power and interactions, it is common sense that there is no such thing as a stable symbol and referent and everything is open to reassessment and can be reframed. It is common sense that those in power can exercise a certain type of control over participants in interactions. It is also common sense that those in power may not be aware that those over whom they have control are critiquing them. In this case, the idea that those without power reassess presumably stable symbols is part of a verbal art form unto itself. The comedian Dave Chappelle, known for both his comedic genius and support and involvement in hiphop, adeptly represents this notion.

Chappelle plays with the notion that there are innocuous, innocent, unmarked words and symbols (see Das EFX above) as well as the notion that one can claim to know a speaker's intentionality without assessing social context and "what is really going on." Chappelle explores the complexity of determining intentionality and "reading someone's mind" when he asks the questions: "When is someone being racist? How do you know what someone really thinks?"[23] Chappelle then goes on to display the complex symbols embedded in interpreting intentionality through a bitingly indirect narrative about a service encounter: "Have you ever had something happen that was sooo racist, that you didn't even get mad? You was just like: '**Goddamn! That was—that was racist!**' I mean, it was sooo blatant you were just like—'**Wow**!' Like—it's almost like it didn't happen to you? It was like a fucking movie? Like you was watching *Mississippi Burning*? '**Wow!**' ((audience laughs))." According to Chappelle's account, his experience was so racist that he had to check with himself to make sure it was both an extreme act—and that it actually happened. He weaves through many levels of local and popular knowledge as he develops a recursive routine where one act produces another and also turns into itself as he reflects on it. He successfully requires the audience to collaborate with him using three reciprocal questions about the endemic yet subtle nature of racism: "Isn't it crazy?" "Am I crazy?" "Did something crazy just happen?"

Chappelle's treatise on everyday racist notions that blacks are not intelligent enough to make their own objective decisions begins with his reference to the 1988 movie *Mississippi Burning*. At one level *Mississippi Burning* is about the 1964 murders of three civil rights workers (Andrew Goodman, James Chaney, and Michael Schwerner). However, what is ironic is that the movie is not mainly a portrayal of racism in the South and the fight against racism in the United States in general but rather it is a historically inaccurate cop drama about the sacrifices and conflicts of white FBI agents and their bravery and positive contributions to the civil rights movement.[24] Thus the movie, and Chappelle's reference to it, is about racism as a brutal physical act (the killing of the civil rights workers). It is also about the discursive act of changing the story of how the FBI cooperated with white supremacists and did not protect black civil rights workers. Suddenly, the *real* story is about how whites and FBI agents save, know, and understand what black people really want, think, and need—better than they know it themselves.

After setting the social context of Mississippi and the movie, Chappelle explains what specifically happened to him that he considers equivalent or comparable to the civil and voting rights injustices in Mississippi.

I was in Mississippi doing a show. And I go to the restaurant to order some food. and I say to the guy, I say, "I'd like to have"—and before I even end my sentence, he says—"THE CHICKEN!" Wha? Huh? I could **not** believe it! I could **not** believe that shit. This man was absolutely **right**! How did he **know** that I was going to get some chicken? I asked him. I said how did you **know** that? How did you **know** that I was going to get some chicken? He looked at me like I was crazy!

"Come on buddy. Come on buddy. Now everybody knew soon as you walked through the goddamn door, you were going to get some chicken. It is no secret down here that blacks—and chickens—are quite fond of one another."

Then I finally understood what he was saying and I got upset. I wasn't even **mad**. I was just **up**set. I wasn't ready to **hear that shit**. All these years I thought I liked chicken because it was delicious. Turns out I'm genetically predisposed to liking chicken. **That shit is wack!** I got no say in the matter. That guy ruined chicken for me! Now I'm scared to eat it in public.

Chappelle's routine makes explicit some of the strategies used to determine "what is really going on." He first establishes a concrete case of racism (murdering civil rights workers) and a less obvious case in the retelling of the story of Mississippi civil rights struggle. In the movie version, those who were most involved and credited for the civil rights of blacks are not black people themselves but mainly government agents. He then moves to a typical encounter that suggests that racism continues to exist in that some whites believe that blacks can't think for themselves. Chappelle reasons that if that is true, the completion of his statement and his thought—"THE CHICKEN"—is likely a racial insult—even if he did, in fact, want fried chicken. What he focuses on is that not only is racism a basic day-to-day reality but its symbols are treated as unmarked and natural in simple encounters. He has unpacked and deconstructed the presupposition of the statement. One cannot even refer to chicken without dealing with racism.

So far we have dealt with nonsense words, nostalgic local references, and chicken. Further elaboration of the complexity of identifying the range of possible meanings and intentionality occurs when an actual word or expression is created and reclaimed as a hiphop symbol and reference. One such case, particular to Los Angeles, is "ghetto bird"—a term used extensively in the black communities in LA and known throughout hiphop culture. It refers to police helicopters that are mainly deployed for surveillance of poor communities. They are equipped with, among other things, high-powered light beams that follow suspects and are often directed into homes when those residing there are eating dinner, watching television, etc. (I have personally experienced this.) The ability of the police to track a community is comparable to Foucault's (1972) analysis of the panopticon, where in prison one can be seen by those in power without the prisoners seeing the guards see them. One knows one is being watched, but not when and by whom. With ghetto birds, instead of those in power being the only ones who know when surveillance is occurring, there is a constant reminder in the community that surveillance is everywhere, everyday, and every hour: 24/7. Yet the discourse about the ghetto bird is so powerfully subversive that it also exposes the weakness and brazenness of power.

The name "ghetto bird" at first simply seems a creative acknowledgment of the police helicopter's purpose. It also suggests that these helicopters, like birds, fill the sky—gliding and flapping-whirling their wings-blades over urban areas. Unlike birds, however, they do not reflect beauty, nature, or freedom. They are dominant society at its most blatant and cynical. Those in power were generous enough to support LA's black community by giving them something that might improve the quality of their life. After all, it flies like a bird! In fact, the Los Angeles police argue that it is necessary to protect the community. In its renaming of police helicopters, the black community has turned the protective nature of the ghetto bird into a signifier that represents their sense of what the government thinks of their community and what the ghetto is entitled to have. Birds designed to hunt down any black person. They hover, wait, and anticipate that something will happen as one eats dinner. In this sense, the renaming of police helicopters as ghetto birds is a scathing critique of power while simultaneously playing with popular media-driven notions of black youth as prey and a menace to society. The ghetto bird becomes the signifier of a police state because that is the reality in the community where they operate.

Hiphop's early refrain *represent, recognize, come correct* gives value to artist's and participant's work to identify, define, and refine their notion of truth and reality. It does this by critiquing dominant culture, by rescuing aspects of urban life that have been denigrated, and by reframing them within the sensibilities, hopes, and desires of those communities. An important instance of this reframing occurs in the representation of neighborhood, home, and place.

To *represent* in hiphop is not simply to identify with a city, neighborhood, school, and so on. It is also a discursive turn—it is the symbols, memory, participants, and objects and details that together produce art of the space and time. Representing rebuilds and reinvigorates the space by making it hiphop. Representation is accomplished through a fantastical and complex system of indexicality—literally pointing to and shouting out places, people, and events when an interaction is framed around important referential symbols and contexts. In this case, shout-outs index and remind us of contextual layers that then invoke related contexts and ideologies (Peirce 1995; Lee 1997). Through this system of representation, hiphop endorses its cultural insiders and the particular set of interpretative beliefs and practices that are in play. This is especially true when describing identity and the ideology of space and place.

While city government and the business district may identify a city in terms of its commerce and affluent communities, in hiphop a city is defined by its neighborhoods, quality or lack of services, transportation lines, people, sounds, smells, and places where youths congregate. It is one of the few places where they can "keep it real." Aceyalone, one of the lead MCs from Project Blowed, illustrates how his neighborhood is actually a sacred place on earth.

> Project Blowed what's the code
> I been rockin' mics since I was 12 years old
> I was born in the Jungle, the concrete slab
> Where people take any and everything that they can grab
> Some niggas chilled on the block, but I chilled in the lab
> My project was to blow you up and break you off a slab
> People are strange, and people are bad
> But the gift of gabbier was something beautiful to have

It started at the Good Life, house of the first sightin'
We snatched raps out of they mouths when they were biting
There was nothing more exciting than to serve and perform
On Crenshaw and Exposition God was born
He said please pass the mic to whomever is tight
Me and the Fellowship took it and we held it for dear life
The Inner City Griots, the wild, the style, the crew
The ones they got their styles from, but claimed
They never knew

Aceyalone recognizes and "gives shout-outs" to some of the groups and interests that support the Project Blowed artists. He also represents through the space and location of Project Blowed as well as recognition of where they and God were born—at the Good Life—their first underground venue on Crenshaw Avenue near Exposition Boulevard.[25] While this version of the neighborhood may be viewed as counterhegemonic and a critique of the dominant discourse, it is still their neighborhood, their corner, their home, and where their families and friends live, love, dream, and die. As Robin Kelley argues, "While some aspects of black expressive cultures certainly help inner city residents deal with and even resist ghetto conditions, most of the literature ignores what these cultural forces mean for the practitioners. Few scholars acknowledge that what might also be at stake here are aesthetics, style, and pleasure" (1997, 17).

It is not surprising then that in hiphop to represent is not simply to identify with a neighborhood, school, and so on. To represent is also to express and expose one's belief, background, knowledge, and so forth regarding how society views and treats those who share youth's experience and background. It is an indictment of society that a black teenager who is sullen and intentionally intimidating as well as one who is rhetorically sophisticated and socially conscious are both viewed as a threat and resistant in relation to the dominant stereotypes of black teens. In contrast, in African American culture either style of self-presentation is considered typical and a predictable aspect of teenage angst and expression, and thus hardly worth comment as a particular type of behavior. To represent is a discursive turn—it is the symbols, memory, participants, and objects and details that together produce art of the space and time. To do this not only disrupts many classical disciplines and approaches but also challenges theories of modernity in that it publicly holds these approaches in contempt. In this case indexicality incorporates contextual layers that invoke related contexts and ideologies so that those who know the reference can manage to understand what is being said in the present and in a refreshed framework of the hiphop social, cultural, local, political, imagined, and artistic world (Peirce 1955; Hanks 1996; Silverstein 2004). Indexicality may not only reveal and display cultural knowledge, beliefs, and practices, but also it may serve as an endorsement to cultural insiders that a particular set of interpretative beliefs and practices are in play. In terms of "ideal" middle-class American city dreams, the area at Crenshaw and Exposition is not, as Aceyalone claims, where "God was born" or where the "House of the First Sighting" stood. Rather, it is only the ghetto.

To *recognize* hiphop culture challenges participants both to contribute their skills and analyses within this value system and to acknowledge that there is a dominant method of evaluation that is hostile to and suspicious of hiphop's system of fair play. One also recognizes by knowing and publicly presenting the local and national history of hiphop—the contributions that specific individuals have made to art, culture, and social history—and by encouraging participation from anyone who respects the values of hiphop. Similarly, to *come correct* requires constant artistic and personal development, study, analysis, and evaluation. It highlights personal social face and responsibility. One must both represent and recognize while demonstrating respect for hiphop through the execution of skills that can only be achieved through practice, study, self-discipline, and respect for hiphop. The motives are to achieve at the highest level (cf. Turner 1982, 1987).

Hiphop's endurance is dependent on a counterpublic sphere and a counterlanguage that, to paraphrase Michael Dawson, is a product of *both* the historically imposed subordination of the working class, women, blacks, and other minorities from whites throughout most of American history and the embracing of the autonomy of each group as both an institutional principle and an ideological orientation (2001, 27). However, the nonstop emphasis on "keeping it real" and "what is really going on?" is not necessarily evidence of progressive intentions—though they may be interpreted as such. Indeed, adolescent behaviors are often impulsive and not readily identifiable in relation to personal, social, cultural, and political motivation. That is, they are framed within a consistent set of core characteristics and standards that are simultaneously sensitive to the complexities of place, time, and generation (Forman 2002; Rose 1994; George 1998). It is participation and socialization into hiphop's culture and value system that provides youth the option and framework with which to engage society. It is in this sense that hiphop culture aggressively confronts what Cornel West (1999) calls the "ignoble paradox of modernity (that) has yielded deep black allegiance to the promises of American democracy" (1999, 51). It calls into being, through words, sounds, and style of discourse a matrix of tropes that connect and reframe cultural, historical, social, and political contexts that reintroduce not only events but narratives about activities and attitudes that existed as part of the past event.

Artists express agency, constantly undergo change, and inevitably express the right of all youth who participate in hiphop culture to assert identities that incorporate race, gender, social class, location, and philosophy. So instead of being fixed, hiphop identities are resolute. Instead of being fluid, they flow. In turn, each hiphop era is marked by philosophical battles over the nature of representing and identity, the notion of recognizing and truth and sense and reference, and the notion of coming correct and intentionality and power. Similarly, the hiphop mantra "keeping it real" represents the quest for the coalescence and interface of ever-shifting art, politics, representation, performance, and individual accountability that reflects all aspects of youth experience.

Yet irrespective of the ideology, philosophy, and lyrical battle, the Word rules as supreme. Yet the Word is only as powerful as the linguistic system it represents, promotes, and exploits.

Slanging Linguistics
How You Like My Dialect Now?

While the discussion in the pages above concerns the ideology and philosophy around the Word, principles of linguistics are also at the heart of hiphop MC lyricism. The ability to flow is based on the power of the Word, which is the bible, the law, and a source of worship and competition. It is the core of the hiphop nation, the power, trope, message, and market all in one. As mentioned earlier, by the 1990s AAE language and discourse had become a symbol of both truth-realism and disaffection among young people throughout the country. Urban youth recognized, co-opted, and capitalized on directness and indirectness, dialect contrast, and signifying, and incorporated these elements in dress, body, and art. It is in this respect that hiphop represents the integration of the African American experience within American culture. Black urban youth and others have taken counterlanguage and in turn exploited it by focusing on the following tenets: sounds, objects, and concepts embody and index memory, community, and social world; choices of language and dialect can signify status, beliefs, values, and specific speakers; and all meaning is co-constructed (co-authored).

The first tenet refers to the importance of signifiers or indices and emblems of black urban life. These may include the use of and references to AAE, general English, proverbs, popular television and children's television, kung fu movies, neighborhoods, streets, public transportation systems, prisons, police stations, and the issues youth must deal with. However, the value of these items may change quickly. Thus it is not only the popular items that have exchange value for youth culture but also how they function within a system of markedness where the notion of normal, expected, and stable are disrupted by forms, references, expressions, and so on that question what is considered normal and accepted. Moreover, a system of markedness functions within popular and local trademarks and brands (cf. Coombe 1998; Bucholtz and Hall 2004), and youth may use the system to mark the same symbol as both positive and negative in any given moment.

The second position is concerned with identity, ideology, power, and attitudes toward language use. It directly refers to the possibility of altering symbols and trademarks as a means to exploit and subvert them. As Stuart Hall says, "Identities are . . . constituted within, not outside, of representation . . . within, not outside, discourse, and constructed through, not outside, difference" (1996, 4). It seems that Hall may have had young people in mind when he described identity as the changing same (see Gilroy 1994), and "not the return to roots, but the coming-to-terms-with our 'routes'" (4). Young people expose and "flash" their routes all the time—on their way to asserting their difference as well as their sameness and recognizing the power in the expression of their identity. Adolescent social identity is one that experiments and thus fuses crucial identity issues into play and back again. What's more, identity is viewed through referential and indexical language use where the discourse evokes times, places, experiences, and ideologies that accentuate not only the terminology itself but also the power of the discourse ideology.

The third and final point makes obvious that neither the youth nor the artist stands alone as an independent, disconnected, and decontextualized individual. Rather, the ties to the audience-generation, speech community, and urban youth bring him or her into existence. In this sense an artist is a composite of the audience—representing experiences that are shared—and the audience determines whether the artist can assume that role. The artist must represent where he or she is from, irrespective of how distant it may seem to others.

To move through linguistic minefields requires skill and knowledge of various dialects and standards. In word formation and morphology, a morpheme is the smallest unit of sound or sound sequence of a particular language that has meaning. They are the foundation of words and the lexicon. In hiphop in general and Project Blowed in particular, morphemes like the prefix *dis*, which does not typically exist as a freestanding word, becomes the free form *diss* with a negative meaning similar to its use in words like *disrespect, dispose, disdain,* and so on. It is also highlighted as a negative within words where it is not a prefix and when it is pronounced with heavy stress in words like *meDISsinal (medicinal), preDISposition,* and so on. Thus the new meaningful word *dis* takes on further significance as it is manipulated within the system of hiphop language ideology.

As discussed earlier, hiphop's language ideology, while mediated through the tenets discussed above, is also concerned with the play and pleasure inherent in contrasting and perfecting one's knowledge of many aspects of linguistics. When MCs believe that they have extraordinary linguistic ability and are connoisseurs of word formation, they may refer to their word choice as slang. This is especially true for the manipulation of lexical and morphological norms. Hiphop artists constantly change word classes and meanings, resulting in a sense of chaos, movement, and urgency. The value of lexical items rises and falls for reasons that range from poor artistic and musical expression to uncritical appropriation by suburban youth. This turmoil is often accomplished through semantic inversion, extension, and the reclamation of General English (GE) and AAE forms. Semantic extension emphasizes one aspect of an English word definition and extends or changes the focus of the word's meaning. Thus the word "wack," which means unbelievably inept, inadequate, and deficient (Smitherman 1994), is from the adjective "wacky," which means absurd or irrational. In cases of semantic inversion (Holt 1972; Smitherman 1994), an AAE word means the opposite of at least one definition of the word in dominant culture. For example, the word "down" can have a positive meaning of support in the sentence "*I want to be down with you.*" It can also be used as part of a locative with the word "low" to mean secretive as in *"Keep it on the down low (DL)."* In the early nineties the stressed term *STUPID* meant good, though its usage is archaic in hiphop today.

The process of expansion has evolved in hiphop so that a word can be extended from GE and then inverted once it has stabilized as a hiphop word. For example, the hiphop word *ill* can include verbal usage (Stavsky, Mozeson, and Reyes Mozeson 1995; Atoon 1992–99) and can mean extremely positive, though initially its meaning was categorically negative (e.g., Fab 5 Freddy 1992).[26] Moreover, the verb *come* is often called a camouflaged form because in AAE it expresses the speaker's indignation about an action while in general grammar it refers to motion. As a result, the hiphop statement "You better come correct" is a warning that the person's attitude must be one that represents and recognizes and shows respect for hiphop.

Some words have competing etymologies. For example, the word *ratchet,* used around New Orleans and Shreveport, Louisiana, in 2006, is defined as in bad shape, or negative in some way (e.g., Lil' Boosie of Shreveport says: "The president, he ratchet, and Saddam"). *Ratchet* could be from the verb that means to force the rise or fall of something (e.g., "They ratcheted up their argument when she asked where he hid the money"). It is also a noun and the name of a lifting device that permits motion in one direction. But it is most likely derived from the word *wretched,* which shares a similar meaning and differs only at the level of vowel sound.[27] This latter argument appears more persuasive since the words share similar meanings as well as pronunciation.

In conversation, performances, and recordings, hiphop members can also expand the meaning of a word by using multiple applications of AAE features. For example, grammatical classes and meaning are routinely shifted so that the verb "fly" also functions as an adjective in hiphop that embellishes the noun as in: "Those boots sure are fly" and "Jennifer Lopez was one of the fly girls in the television program *In Living Color.*" The verb "floss," as in "Do you want to floss with us?" has an extremely positive meaning that incorporates coolness and focuses on the attitude and intentionality of the subject. It follows the norms of non-state verbs (e.g., floss/ flossed/ flossing). Artists also form new words by moving affixes (bound morphemes) into independent lexical items. It also exists as a verb that marks tense and aspect (diss/dissed/dissing). Another striking aspect of hiphop language style is the regularization of verbs. For example, the verb *converse* has been replaced with the verb *conversate*, including its nonfinite form *conversating* (e.g., conversate/conversated/conversating): "They just be conversating with me all the time" (Smitherman 1994). Moreover, hiphop has popularized a process of suffixation common among working-class and poor African American communities.

Hiphop has also reclaimed classic American childhood language games like pig Latin and transformed them to fit hiphop's language playground. Pig Latin is a basic game where the initial syllable (morpheme) or consonant sound of a word is moved to the final position of the word and followed by *ay*, which serves as a suffix and bound morpheme. There are variations for words that begin with vowels where one can place the *ay* suffix at the end of the word or include a *y* at the beginning of a word as well. Thus, *catch* would be *atchkay*, *stop* is *opstay* and *on* is *onyay*. At the same time, African American speech communities began to play with a type of talk attributed to pimps and hustlers. This form of discourse was popularized during the 1970s black exploitation era in films that featured unlawful lifestyles and starred comedians like Richard Pryor. There, the barely articulate hustler spoke in a stream of vocalics and vowel sounds with rising and falling intonation occasionally interspersed with sibilants: *s, z, sh*. This form of talk was barely comprehensible and considered hilarious. Later, the combination of vowels and sibilants was popularized in the dance club song "Double Dutch Bus" (Smith 1981). There, Frankie Smith played with the *z* (vocalic sibilant) sound between syllables and produced such variants as girls/gazirls, and the famous line "wilza isa pilza in dizouble, dizuch, dizouble dizuch, dizouble dizuch." Artists like Snoop Dogg revitalized the genre by introducing context into the interpretation. His famous line "Fo' shizzle my nizzle" revealed a system where instead of the movement of syllables the focus is on initial consonant sounds that are pronounced followed by izzle (sure is shizzle) and can be incorporated at any point in the syllable structure (Mitchell is michizzle). This form of play requires that one know the possible words that fit the context, for there are seldom any clues as to the vowel sound of the original word. Words that begin with vowels are not treated as unique items, though words that have frequent use may be. Thus the word *shit* is *ish*.

Contrary to norms of general English usage, American working-class grammatical and phonological norms, especially consonant simplification and vowel length, are used to establish regional identities. Thus the shortening of vowels, an increase in glottal stops, and the reduction of consonants marks the East Coast. In contrast, vowel lengthening marks the West Coast. The different use of vowels in the West and consonants in the East is related to musical influences as well as social class allegiances. Thus the word *didn't* and *ghetto* are often pronounced *di'n* and *ge'o* on the East Coast and *di:n* and *ge:do* on the West Coast. Both the East Coast and the West Coast are heavily influenced by a variety of musical styles, though fast-paced Jamaican Dance Hall music is central to East Coast rap, and funk rhythms are central to the West Coast.

New words refer to words that are not directly derived from free morphemes. They may also reflect a change in the meaning, usage, and grammatical category of a word previously occurring in GE or AAE.[28] For example, *dis* (discussed above) is not only a bound morpheme but is used to form a new word that means to reject, ignore, and embarrass (see also Smitherman 1994). Hiphop language ideology also favors adding bound morphemes (affixes and suffixes) to highlight an already established meaning or a change in meaning. Other favored bound morphemes include *est, ous/ious, er, ic,* and *un/in*. Thus the words *mack* and *mack daddy,* though fitting within hiphop language style, would not be counted as new words since they have existed in AAE with the same meaning of someone who exploits or hustles for sexual favors (Major 1994; Smitherman 1994).

Spelling

Though each category is important unto itself, it is the relationship between categories that make words significant within urban hiphop youth culture. Spelling in hiphop is critical because many young people write the lyrics as they memorize them. For the most part, artists and writers did not make their lyrics available until the late 1990s. In fact it was a badge of honor to be able to correctly interpret, write, and spell the words of a favorite artist. As a result, the audience (LTS) developed many of the early spelling conventions.[29]

Hiphop spelling conventions can represent ideology, and the use of certain letters can introduce and critique identities. New spellings follow English consonant-vowel (CVCV) form and are an important signifier in hiphop wording.[30] New spellings often accompany a change in word meaning and reflect AAE and hiphop pronunciation, knowledge of the subversion of GE spelling rules, and alphabet symbol ideology. For instance, when writing about America's negative treatment of urban youth, it is common to find it spelled Ameri*kkk*a, using the initials for the white supremacist group the Ku Klux Klan (KKK). New spellings also focus on English irregular spelling rules. So to give a compliment about an activity or object one might say that it is *phat* (pronounced "fat"). Virtually every word that exceeds two syllables and ends with the *er* suffix is vocalized and spelled *a, uh,* or *ah* is in *brothah* (brother) and *sucka* (sucker). Similarly, words ending in *ing* are written as *in/un* as in *sumthin* for something and *thumpun* for thumping. Spelling also reflects syllable reduction and vowel assimilation with rhotics and semi-vowels; thus *all right* is spelled *aight*. As reported by John Rickford (1999) and elsewhere, *I'm gonna /I'm going to* is written *Ima,* reflecting the deletion of *d* and *g*. Finally, *gots* is frequently used in place of *got/have* in order to highlight urgency, unfairness, power, and at times necessity.

Reclaiming Words

Reclaimed Words may be a small category of hiphop terminology, but their occurrence often signifies knowledge of film, politics, history, music, and historical events. Thus words such as *mack* and *gat,* found in gangster movies in the 1950s and in the black exploitation movies of the 1970s, are reintroduced to the younger generation.[31] Ice Cube used the word *gaffled:* "I was hassled and gaffled in the back seat." According to *The Rap Diction-ary* (Atoon 1992–99) gaffle refers to harassment by the police, while its earlier usage was in reference to an ordeal. The example of ratchet/ wretched mentioned above is also a case of an archaic word being re-introduced. Words that are not considered part of the younger genera-tion's vocabulary can also be reintroduced through a change of word class. This type of change often reflects potential grammaticalized forms of words that have a high frequency of usage. As with *ill* described above, many words share more than one grammatical category in GE but are used as one category in hiphop. Though one might say *"I ain't mad at ya,"* it is also common during rhymes to hear an emcee say *"I drop madd rhymes"* where mad is both a quantifier and an adjective that means crazy and extreme.

Another type of word reclamation is associated with the reduction of sounds and syllables. Unsurprisingly, the most common reductions (also recognized in spelling, as noted above) are morphophonemic. They often serve to represent regional affiliation. Thus *didn't,* written as *didin* or *did'n,* actually represents the voicing of stops before nasals (West Coast) and the glottalization of voiceless stops before nasals (East Coast).

Hiphop artists revel in the creative representation and recognition of the discourse and linguistic skills described throughout this chapter. It is their playground and their place of serious business. Creativity in hiphop is a celebration and recognition of well-developed skills that are relentlessly and incessantly practiced and evaluated. For many, especially in Los Angeles, the underground was where they went to perfect their skills, learn about their culture, and become unwavering members of the hiphop community. They step to the mic with a cultural and linguistic arsenal ready to battle and execute their flow for their community, culture, and themselves.

Unauthorized Biography
Power Flows in the Counterpublic

When an artist flows, the achievement is both acknowledged and shared by the knowledgeable audience of LTs. Yet part of the pleasure of achieving the level of flow may be embedded in the contested collaboration that also marks the state. When artists reach the level of flow, they often appear domineering and conceited and the audience is admiring and challenging. This may be forgiven, since they have mastered numerous skills and been judged by their peers for years. To flow in hiphop refers to an MC consciously producing lyrics within a system of representation and fragmentation, dislocation and symmetry, disruption and order, and contradiction and unity. An artist communicates what he or she means, intends, and represents, through symbols, style, and contrasting aspects of artistic and linguistic skill and social life. Flow exists at multiple levels and includes stylistic rhyming, symbolic representation, and linguistic manipulation coupled with attitude and social standing. Thus the achievement of flow demands that resources of language and discourse be employed in recognition of the complexity of social and public life.

Flow in hiphop is unique when compared to other discussions of artistic flow because it cannot be attained unless the audience and other performers acknowledge that this level of artistry has been achieved. Thus it must be ratified in some way. In this respect, attaining lyrical excellence is not an individual, private experience or one that may be considered cultured, privileged, and exclusive. Instead, it is based on the notion of hard work and study, accessibility and respect, and inclusion and fearlessness. Technically, most cases of such achievement in hiphop include spontaneous rhyming known as freestyle, as well as the ability to relentlessly focus on topics, symbols, and various language structures and word forms. All of these elements combine to not only represent the artist's ideas but also his or her philosophy about the world, community, and the space and place where he or she currently inhabit.

Once the "real" and socially critical context is established, artists may enter a flow state (cf. Csikszentmihalyi 1975; Csikszentmihalyi and Csikszentmihalyi 1992) and what hiphop artists call "the next level," as they reach a state of pleasure, limbo, and complete immersion in the performance. The MCS achieve this state as part of a battle, real and imagined. They play the role of leader, martyr, dictator, and god. The audience shows their affection by bobbing their heads and throwing their hands in the air to the rhythm of the delivery and beats. This moment of "great satisfaction" is also part of a system of social corroboration and is tied to social and community-building values (Turner 1969, 1982; Goffman 1967). In this way, hiphop's ritual of respect and collaboration often appears as stalking, boasting, and deriding. In 1989 EPMD declared their prominence and meticulous style on the album *Unfinished Business*. After many verses that flowed using language, social and political contexts, popular references, and symbols of space, place, and identity EPMD punctuates their lyrical effusiveness by announcing, "Another rapper was hit, by Mister Slow Flow."

The founding Project Blowed artists Aceyalone, Medusa, and Abstract Rude also proudly claim and demand that flow be the highest level of achievement and a space that must be defended and respected.

> Anywhere you go
> I am going to find you
> And every time you flow
> I'll be right behind you
> Just to let you know
> And constantly remind you
> You can never be as dope as I am
> Goddamn (Aceyalone 2001)
>
> It's about flows, not ho's (Medusa 2005)

Like mobbers were marching that Malcolm X-type pain
Fill out the carcass with heavy blood flow, slain
Gotta rhyme for each kind in your crew
or any other solo appearance you might do (Abstract Rude 1999)

MCs cannot be insecure when they step to the mic. They enter the chaos, battle, and cipher to display the hiphop mantras—*represent, recognize, and come correct*—in order to establish a socially critical context. They have their linguistics, their culture, their artistry, their knowledge, their ancestors, their lessons, and their skill. They are ready to take on any and all powerful elements in the universe. The MC begins his or her flow fully absorbed in the activity, art, and audience. Although they seek approval, it is only sought from those who have also paid their dues and are ready to experience the real hiphop.

Thursday Night
at Project Blowed

Well the party's jumpin'—the
  Blowed is packed.
And when a crowd's like this, I'm
  ready to rap.
But before I can bust a rhyme on
  the mic,
I gotta serve you in a cipher just
  to earn my stripes.
The scared battle dog, with the
  underground catalogue
Fuck it, tryin' to make the world a
  better place
Instead of duckin', still tryin' to
  make the duckets
Make the knowledge rain down in
  buckets
Make a little somethin', and tuck
  it—just to give it away
Build a work shop round where
  I stay.
Some people got the love, but
  they don't know the way.
Some people know the way, but
  they don't know what to say.
And I'm the sensei I greet 'em
  from far and near
Better watch the light in your eyes,
  a star's in here
Leimert Park's very own
  Aceyalone
The one who made the whole
  world come off the dome
Up at the Blowed

ACEYALONE, "Project Blowed"

IN THE EARLY EVENING on any given Thursday in the late 1990s, an array of people are walking around Leimert Park, looking at Afrocentric greeting cards, jewelry, art; digging in bins for old jazz and R&B records and other memorabilia; and getting a bite of soul food, health food, Jamaican, or Mexican. Most of the people are in their early thirties, though there are also many seniors greeting their friends. Some of the poets who perform at the World Stage on Wednesday are sitting at the outdoor tables of the 5th Street Dicks, listening to the jazz billow from the coffee shop and watching the old men play chess. The mood is relaxed and inviting as babies are passed around and people greet each

CHAPTER THREE

other as if they are not strangers. The blend of people, politics, religions, and social classes coheres seamlessly as everyone enjoys the ambiance.

The entrance to KAOS Network is at the northwest corner of 43rd and Leimert. On late Thursday afternoon, KAOS is filled with about twenty-five people from a research project that includes high school students from two inner-city high schools and several University of Southern California graduate students and their professors. The project, cosponsored with the University of Southern California and the California Institute of the Arts, uses satellite technology and video conferencing to bring diverse students together. Participants sit in chairs in circles and at tables with video cameras rolling. Some are at the camera broadcasting to other students at satellite schools. It is a bustle of activity, and one can see the majority white upper-middle-class students from the private school twenty miles away on the television screen. These private school students see a group of black, Latino, and Filipino students from LA's public schools involved in activities that are similar to those they engage in.[1] Everyone disperses by 6 PM as students head back to their respective communities. Once the program winds down, Ben Caldwell locks the building, gets a late lunch or an early dinner, and picks up his daughter from school. Leimert continues to flow with its jazz and Afrocentric rhythms. Around 7 PM, however, everything begins to change.

At 7:30 Project Blowed's soundman, Cheatham, stops his car on the corner of 43rd and Leimert, gets out, and surveys the scene. He usually sighs deeply, crosses his arms, furrows his brow, and takes inventory of every detail around the establishment. The mellow jazz sounds produced by 5th Street Dicks are noted, and as someone waves at him he barely nods his head in recognition, never changing expression. He looks disapprovingly at the trash on the sidewalk. He is of average height, clean head and cleanshaven, and slight yet muscular, wearing a white T-shirt tucked in his jeans, black boots, and a jacket. He is one of the most serious of the twenty-year-old brothers in Leimert Park, and there are two things he seldom does when he sets up the sound system: smile and talk.

As Cheatham begins to unload his equipment, other members of the Blowed ask if he wants their help. This is merely a ritual, because he always says, "No man, I got it." On average it takes twenty minutes to unload the car, especially since once inside Cheatham puts each piece of equipment near where he will finally place it. The actual installation usually takes about two hours. He measures cords with a tape measure and

The KAOS Network building at the corner of 43rd and Leimert. Photo by Tony B, courtesy of Project Blowed.

then tapes them to the floor when they are finally hooked up. He sets up turntables behind the speakers that are painstakingly placed on stands and propped up so that they are at a height of about five feet, which will result in sounds that carry throughout the room and through every muscle in the body as bass beats boom. Cheatham is meticulous, and the equipment is the basis for everything that happens on Thursday. If there is no music, the flow of the event is abruptly interrupted. This also gives the DJ (Wolf) ultimate power. He can, at any time, simply turn off the music and bring about just such an interruption. Rather than an act of sabotage, however, if the DJ turns off the sound it is often a test of the artist and whether they can flow without a beat. But that is the DJ's call.

The main entrance of KAOS opens into a large room with a raised landing directly across from the entrance and front windows. Later into the night, this area will serve as the stage. The walls are covered with original art and posters for Free Mumia and the play *For Colored Girls*. The back wall of the stage includes a large banner with KAOS written in enormous graf writing. The room contains two TV monitors. Behind the landing is a small room with state-of-the-art video equipment. On the left wall of the room is an open doorway leading into a long narrow room that has tables and a display case with albums, CDs, T-shirts, videos, and so on. The bathroom is also on this side. The front window is covered with blinds, and the door has bars.

Cheatham makes sure that the sound is balanced and the bass is in full effect. Once the system is perfectly situated and connected, he puts on a record that is full of percussion and intense bass beat. Sometimes it's reggae, or else African Music, jazz, or R&B funk. As the record plays, Cheatham walks into the middle of the room, arms folded, brow furrowed, head lowered—and he listens. He then walks from the middle of the room

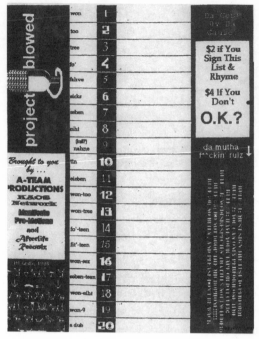

The sign-in sheet for Thursday nights at Project Blowed. Courtesy of Project Blowed.

to the stage and then to the side, each time standing tall with his arms folded and a discerning look. During this ritual, he often switches the music to break beats and MC recordings. Then finally, he returns to the middle of the room, folds his arms, listens, glances at the host or DJ, and simply nods and walks away.

Once Cheatham's work ritual is complete, the Project Blowed members begin their particular tasks in earnest. A video camera is placed in the back of the room, and members sweep the floor, set up the entrance and the moneybox, and remove the chairs and tables used by the LA Link project. Next, they go into another room and set up the refreshment and concession stands, where they unfurl T-shirts and prepare to sell the latest music. Ben Caldwell sets up three TV screens that show videos projected from each side of the room and behind the stage. When they run out of things to talk about, the MCs will freestyle based on the images on the video, which runs a loop. Blowed members also clean outside of the building, sweeping the sidewalk and removing the trash. The preparation is marked by a near complete absence of verbal communication—everyone knows what they're supposed to do and usually they just do it. At times, the Blowed members who come in to help with setup do ask questions; in response, Cheatham, Fish, and

88

Ben usually just look at them—suggesting that they should know the answer to their own questions.

Blowed members begin to enter the main room. The b-boys and b-girls greet and quickly move to the vacant floor space as the music plays. Various dance moves are shared and demonstrated. Different crews form one large circle as they compete and display their skills. Friends who accompany them are given keys, wallets, and lipstick to hold, since these objects will fall out of their pockets during capoeira[2] moves or if they do spins, butterflies, and other dance styles. The MCS move between the middle room, side room, and immediately outside. Friends are greeted and CDS and tapes are exchanged. The sound system is bangin', the DJ is mixing, the graf writers are comparing full art in their piece books, the door is covered, the sisters are at the concession stand, and the MCS and dancers are in the house. Project Blowed is in effect.

Taking over a Village

As the Blowed members work inside KAOS, young people slowly begin to congregate around 43rd and Leimert. Several groups cluster in front of what was once KAOS but is now the Blowed. They gather from the barred entrance to the concession area to the corner entrance of the Blowed building. The 5th Street Dicks is the beginning and cutoff point of the Blowed's official sidewalk. Youths often cluster tightly, and one must navigate a maze to pass through. Groups wander back and forth and practice their skills in ciphers—small circles where MCS rhyme and their crew praises or criticizes for brilliance and wackness. "Are you ready?" is the recurring question as Blowed members come out to field the energy from the moment the doors are anticipated to open. Cars pull up emptying more groups of mainly young men from throughout the city. They park at meters and sit with their windows open with hiphop bass beats pumping from their car stereos. They do not do this on the Degnan side because they would be confronted by the merchants: on Thursday nights the World Stage, sponsored by the late Billy Higgins, slowly gathers as people show up for the Thursday night jazz program. Hiphop bass beats do not mix well with the serious jazz crowd. In the park, several crews are practicing in ciphers. The park is also the place where deals are made, drugs are shared, and stories are told. Fierce practice battles occur in the park and most regulars and OGS (in this case, Original Good Lifers) stay on the sidewalk.

The crowd gathers outside Project Blowed on Thursday night. Photo by Tony B, courtesy of Project Blowed.

By 9 PM the side of Degnan bordering 43rd Place is teeming with youth. More arrive in groups. They are dressed in baggy pants, caps, hoodies, Tims (Timberland boots), and T-shirts. Many carry backpacks or have oversized jackets crammed with CDs and tapes. Leimert Park now belongs to the youth: it will be Project Blowed's place for a few hours, and they intend to make the most of it. At the entrance of Project Blowed is a sign. It is placed on the outside door and explains the rules of decorum. They include no alcohol and smoking, when MCs can compete, and that they have to be original and should not "bite" other people's styles. The sign also states that it is a black business in a black area, so the actions of those at Project Blowed must not get violent. It suggests, instead, that those who want to be violent go to the community of Westwood. The statement "Take that stuff to Westwood" refers to the affluent and commercial community near UCLA where in 1988 a group of youths created a disturbance and a young woman was fatally shot. The statement is a warning that this level of disrespect will not be tolerated at Project Blowed.

There is a second sign at the entrance table, which explains that MCs must sign up to represent on the mic as well as pay $2 to enter. If they do not sign up, they must pay $4. After paying, people congregate in the main room and the annex. In the main room, DJ Wolf is playing classic breaking beats and b-boys and b-girls are practicing their moves. Members of the LA

You Are Now About To Enter
project blowed
READ THIS FIRST!!!!!

✓ NO SMOKING OR DRINKING ALCOHOL IN HERE! The owner has "requested" that this be a no-alcohol, no-smoking business. Fa' sho'.

✓ THERE IS OPEN MIKE AT THE *BEGINNING* AND AT THE *END*. NO ONE WHO IS NOT CALLED FROM THE LIST BY THE HOST CAN GET ON STAGE *AT ANY OTHER TIME*! REMEMBER THAT!

✓ This is a Hip Hop Educational Seminar, where styles are shown so many can learn and grow. *DO NOT BITE STYLES*, BECAUSE YOU LEARN NOTHING! **DO NOT GET VIOLENT**, BECAUSE THIS IS A BLACK-OWNED, BLACK-OPERATED BUSINESS THAT CAN'T AFFORD TO HEAR THAT! **Take that stuff to WestWood**.

✓ Project Blowed is presented for the love of hip hop entirely by Black people. However, it **can't** get done if everybody's bills don't get paid, so we charge the "participants" TWO DOLLARS to practice their styles, and we charge FOUR DOLLARS to people who want to watch education at work. This pays for using the building, the sound, and keeping it going on - also known as THE CAUSE of keeping hip hop underground.

Read this first: the rules at Project Blowed. Courtesy of Project Blowed.

Breakers come through. In the annex, people pass around each other's piece books to be examined and to write in.

It is Thursday night on "the hippest corner in LA," Leimert and 43rd, and Project Blowed members are hyped for battle. In hiphop the battle is not about irrational and personal vendetta, though some may participate for that reason. Instead it is about the struggle for excellence, the righteous, and the believers. The main room, slightly beyond its maximum capacity of one hundred, is filled with youth dressed mainly in their underground gear—xxx T-shirts hanging down to their knees along with jerseys from sports teams and brand-named shoes draped over a range of bodies. While deejays mix beats, LA Breakers and b-boy and b-girl crews continue to break into their dance routines. The crowd gives them just enough space to form a tight circle so that they do not injure anyone when they suddenly uprock, pop lock, drop to the ground and spin, freeze, and bust into capoeria moves. There is no smoking inside the Blowed, though many people try to smoke and some seem to have smoked trapped inside their oversized jackets and hoodies. Instead of smoke, there is a haze that results from the heat of bodies at work as the dim spotlights illuminate the

Thursday night at Project Blowed. Photo by Tony B, courtesy of Project Blowed.

shadowed faces in the crowd. Most faces are framed by hoods and caps with brims pulled down to just above the eyes. And all eyes are riveted on the line on the stage of those who want to battle and to represent as emcees.

Outside there is even more action. Groups of young people are crowded around in their circles and ciphers to practice freestyle rhymes. Others are arguing about the state of hiphop and when they or their friends are going to "jump off." In the park itself, which is actually a small strip of sparse grass and low-cut trees, more groups are practicing freestyle, while the homeless, addicts, and bud sellers circle the groups looking for clients and anyone who might care about their hard-luck story. Circling in the distance and heard over the phat bass beats of the Blowed and practicing emcees is the sound of the LAPD's ghetto birds. Besides these ever-present helicopters, the LAPD (mainly from the infamous Rampart Division) are undercover at the Blowed and on the street as well as patroling the area in black and whites with the motto "serve and protect" marked on the side. In addition, some slowly ride by in unmarked cars as they all hover in wait for a reason to close down the underground. Everyone sees the cops, and in the midst of the serious practice sessions and staging of imaginary lyrical battles on the sidewalks and on patches of grass in the park, the LAPD seem menacingly buffoonish and completely out of sync with what is going on and—as one young man says—obsessed with working stereotypes.

Back inside the Blowed, a young man is on the mic. His knees bend and his upper body bobs so that his head rises on the downbeat as he spits his

CHAPTER THREE

Chu on the mic.
Photo by Tony B, courtesy
of Project Blowed.

lyrics and feigns freestyle skill. The crowd, moving their heads with similar movements, looks at the MC, who is rigid and fixated on the amateur. He shakes his head as though disappointed with the world and the audience raises their hands with their fingers formed as Ws, bobbing in opposite motion with the head and repeating "Pass the mic! Pass the mic!" The amateur continues and the MC, with his mic in hand, comes closer and lowers his face so that he can get under the brim of the amateur and look him in the eye.

Up at the Blowed

Around 10 PM the Blowed is usually in full force. The breakers have conceded the space to those there to partake in the MC battles. The DJ changes the beat from b-boy breaks to the rhythmic bass beats favored by MCs. Chu, who controls the mic for the Blowed, begins to speak. His job is to make sure the rules are clear and fair. He also reveals his feelings about the night and the list of people who have signed. He encourages others to sign up and explains that it is a workshop and everyone needs to practice. He says that people should come to Project Blowed to learn, and that it is a classroom where they should create rather than have to read about it in a book. Many people moving between the main room, outside, and the concession area constantly repeat phrases that they will use later in the night. In fact, it is nearly impossible to have a conversation that doesn't rhyme in some way with those who intend to go before the crowd later.

The flow of MCs depends on the ratio of beginners to seasoned MCs. The stage has at least two mics. Chu usually holds one and gives the other to the MC. That person then begins their rhymes with Chu standing near while listening and looking at the MC and the crowd. If Chu thinks the person is weak, he either begins rapping on top of their rap or looks at the crowd and says, in measured beats, "Please pass the mic." If the crowd strongly agrees, they repeat the refrain until the MC gives up the mic.

The crews and the individuals who were regulars at Project Blowed from 1994 to 2000 include:[3]

2 Mex

2000 Crows—Zagu, Faxx

Abstract Tribe Unique—Abstract Rude, Fat Jack, Zulu, Irie

Abstract Rude

Aceyalone

Afterlife

Ahmad

Aspect One

Awol One

Badru

Born Allah

Busdriver

Chillin Villain Empire (CVE)

Crooked

Customer Service

DJ Drez

DJ Fat Jack

DJ Rashida

Dumbfoundead

Faxx

Flako 7

Freestyle Fellowship—Mikah9, Self Jupiter, Aceyalone, P.E.A.C.E.

Haiku D'etat

Hines Buchanan

Hip Hop Clan—Crooked, Reckless

J Smooth

Jizzm High Definition

JUNE I

Jurassic 5 (combined Unity Committee and Rebels of Rhythm)—Zaakir (a.k.a. Soup), Akil, Shawnee Mack, Mark7, Nu-Mark, DJ Cut Chemist, Chali 2NA

Kenny Segal

Kinky Red

Longevity

Medusa

NgaFsh

Nobody

Omid

Open Mike

Pigeon John

Planet Asia

Pterrodacto

Raaka

Rebels of Rhythm—Zaakir, Akil

Riddlore

Rifleman/Ellay Khule

Self Jupiter

Subtitle

The Unity Committee—Marc7, Cut
    Chemist, Charlie Tuna

Tray-Loc

Trenseta

Wreccless

When MCS who are skilled come to the stage, they are recognized as such through the apt attention of the crowd and through the bobbing of heads, rhythmic body movements, and hands in the air, often with fingers forming *W*s. Chu normally commends a skilled MC as well, and he encourages all MCS to come up ready to represent and do battle. If the MCS' performance skill level is not up to par, they do not quit. Instead, they usually sign up again and go outside to the perimeter of the building or park to practice in a cipher with their crew. When they return, Chu acknowledges that they are back and he and the crowd listen closely. If there is improvement, it is acknowledged, though the crowd and Chu may still insist that the MC pass the mic if the performance skill is not at the level they think necessary.

Battles may occur for a number of reasons. For example, the stage might be taken by an MC who represents a crew with a long-standing rivalry with The Blowed. In that case, various MCS from the Blowed crew will follow (including Chu), and the battle can go back and forth for extended periods of time. Battles can also occur when an MC who represents from another area rocks the mic but also disses Project Blowed by including a bragging segment about having the strongest skills in the house. Battles do not develop with lone weak MCS no matter what they say. Instead, they are verbally *beat down* by Chu or the crowd. If there is an MC battle, Project Blowed members are expected to represent. If they fail to beat their opponent, they are censured in some way. Usually the punishment is banishment from the Blowed for a designated period during which he or she is expected to continue to develop his or her skills. Everyone is expected to practice and "rehearse the verse." It is a workshop "every Thursday night, where we give the new definition to open mic."

It is 10 PM on April 18, 1996. The bass beats designed by Cheatham, the sound man, flow outside the Blowed where over one hundred youths are gathered on a warm LA night. Some congregate in the middle of the sidewalk, just outside the main entrance of 3333 Leimert Boulevard. Their bodies seem to move as tightly connected rhythmic motions so that, in order to pass, one has to walk around a maze of bodies oblivious to those who do not recognize that they are trespassing. Most who approach the site greet the groups of young men with ritualized hand moves and shoulder holds. Other groups congregate along the curb, near parked cars, and across the street in the park. In the park and on the sidewalk some youths form ciphers, practicing their rhyming skills in tight circles as crews prepare to meet their competition. Those gathered inside and outside on the sidewalk can hear the music and voices on the mic coming from the stage at Project Blowed. Indoors on the stage is Chu, the night's MC, along with Fish, another Blowed member. They are freestyling, dissing, and urging the crowd to participate, evaluate, and acknowledge lyrical skills. Two television screens are playing the Charles Burnett art film *Killer of Sheep* with the volume turned off.[4] The crowd of onlookers is thin, and it includes about fifteen people who are standing and who occasionally mimic an MC in battle—crouched, head bobbing, and arms moving to the beat. Others occasionally begin a b-boy uprock or pop lock move. Just as quickly as they started, they stop and look again at the stage. DJ Wolf is on the ones and twos (turntables).

Everyone present is prepared for freestyling according to the workshop rules of Project Blowed; they also anticipate that there might be a real lyrical battle this night. While the rules of freestyle are well defined, the grounds for battle are not explicitly stated. Rather, they have been established through long-term socialization in hiphop skill development and assessment. The Project Blowed freestyle of rapid-fire, extemporaneous, articulate delivery is known throughout LA's underground. Members usually follow each other without missing a beat. Their style is the modification and reworking of the American English sound and word system—with Jamaican Creole and Mexican and Chicano Spanish thrown in for added measure. The Project Blowed style stands out in that it is a linguistic exercise in the juxtaposition of meaningful and meaningless sounds, words, and grammatical structures that create fissures that erupt into new meanings (see chapter 2).[5] The ethnomusicologist Anthony Krims (2000, 50) refers to this style as "speech effusive" because it uses unexpected sound symbolism and syllable creation while breaking down and subdividing the beat.

For example, the reigning African performer of much of underground hiphop is the late Nigerian musician Fela Kuti. He was a musician and composer, a pioneer of Afrobeat music, a human rights activist, and a political maverick who died of AIDS in 1997. The introduction of his Afrobeat rhythms usually inspires numerous MCs to run to the stage and grab the mic for the challenge and pleasure of delivering socially and politically relevant skillful rhymes over his beats. Similarly, though few of the MCs at Project Blowed have ever visited South Africa, I have heard U.S.-born MCs use click sounds in their rhymes similar to those used by the Xhosa people. This sound is not a phoneme of English and is not spoken in the United States.[6] The occurrence of the click sound in a rhyme can evoke and invoke Africa, an Afrocentric context, and sense of power and pride. Its usage by a skilled and respected artist requires that true fans search for and research the possible meaning and reference of the sound.

At Project Blowed, the lyrical delivery style may include five to ten words, syllables, or morphemes (meaningful sound segments) in one-second intervals and beats. Only a few members of Project Blowed use this style repeatedly, though they all possess the skills to do so and incorporate them into extended rhymes. The style itself represents the height of what is known as lyrical fitness. It is not enough to speak quickly, but one should also enunciate.[7] Moreover, the rhyme must be part of an elaborately interactive extemporaneous narrative, referential, and linguistic system.[8] This system includes but is not limited to the following: extemporaneous rhyming while building a coherent narrative; manipulation of a linguistic structure; strategic utilization of indexicality; precise articulation and manipulation of phonetic system; wit and sarcasm; system of identification (e.g., naming, place names, locality, etc.); reference to immediate audience; reference to hiphop history, style, and artists; reference to social and political context; reference to national and cultural history; knowledge of regional and historical rhyming and musical styles; and use of signifiers for representin', recognizin', and comin' correct.

While most of the system given above is self-explanatory, a few items require discussion. Spontaneous rhyming does not mean that the MC must begin his or her first word extemporaneously. An MC's greeting and identification is usually a well-practiced, ritualized introduction. Thus extemporaneous freestyle skill is demonstrated after the introduction and by referencing current objects, participants, events, and so on in a way that makes sense to those listening. Those present are aware of numerous hiphop phrases and styles of those MCs on the mic, and they listen carefully for repetition rather than innovation. The manipulation of the linguistic system is described in detail below. The main point is that a skilled MC must have basic linguistic knowledge and knowledge of the ideological system in order to both represent and manipulate these facets. Since hiphop requires that participants have knowledge beyond their community and particular culture, membership is repeatedly ratified through symbols that index people, places, things, and ideologies. Another aspect central to MC leadership is identification through styles of naming. The artist's name and his or her ability to refer to spaces and places elevates his and her standing in the community. The use of references and a system of indexicality guarantees that local knowledge and ideologies of power and representation are on display.

If someone attempts to participate who does not know the rules, they are reprimanded through both direct and indirect insult. The extent of the violation determines whether it can only be resolved with a lyrical battle. There are essentially two paths that may lead to battle. *Organized battling* may occur as a way for MCs to challenge each other over lyrical ability. This may arise because someone insists they are the reigning MC and onlookers must settle the dispute and make the judgment. It is judged by MCs who are present, and in some cases the audience also judges through applause and yelling. In contrast, *spontaneous battling* often erupts when someone does not respect (intentionally or unintentionally) discursive norms of the Blowed. Battling may occur when MCs refuse to participate according to the freestyle rules of Project Blowed as described above. It may begin when an MC ignores the norms that every artist greet the crowd by revealing his or her name and introduce his or her neighborhood, region, affiliation, and so on to those who have invited them into their space. The introduction serves to identify the participants, where they are from, who they represent in terms of crew and neighborhood, their philosophy, and so forth. It is a respectful greeting that provides information on crew affiliations and the participant's socialization into hiphop rhyming style. This is considered a disrespectful and aggressive posture and an attempt to corrupt and seize the Project Blowed mic.

Early on in the night, Chu introduces the Project Blowed rhyming philosophy and style within a mock battle as the other MCs filter into the venue. Boldface type indicates that the word is heavily stressed and each line represents the number of syllables and sound segments per second.[9]

1	CHU:	**What's** my name?
2		**Who** want to fuck my chain?[10]
3		**Who** say fuck Wu-Tang?
4		**I** know his game
5		What's wrong with this?
6		Ain't no shame
7		A wack no style
8		Look at our new style
9		Born as a prince child
10		What the fuck that about?
11		How you **like** me now?
12		This ain't no G?
13		This is that nigga fuck style
14		Pistol in the joint?
15		Boo I caught you
16		You better get the fuck up off of me
17		Huh, boom boom
18		Buck the boom, fuck the police
19		Yeah the fuck boom
20		1, 2, 3, 4
21		**No** I ain't gonna take it no more
22		Let's get it on rappin jazz
23		Back off yeah I buck bohs
24		Yeah I'm worth all
25		Yeah I work all?
26	FISH:	No you didn't

As members of Project Blowed, Chu and Fish are practicing as part of the workshop and modeling its rules, styles, and the like. They deliver their rhymes while weaving, circling, and bobbing in exaggerated moves, as though they are in a boxing match or martial arts competition. Fish begins his segment (line 26) on the beat after Chu lowers his mic and head. Prior to that, he is Chu's partner who is there to both support and represent. They are representing their crew—and their position is defensive. When members of the same crew represent in this way, the first task of the audience is to use all of its resources to determine what might have happened and what is being referenced and indexed.

The signs that Chu and Fish occupy a defensive position are evident in lines 1–2 when Chu begins by stressing his first three WH (what, who) questions (lines 1–3) and an accusation, framed as a rhetorical question, to which everyone knows the answer: "What's my name?" As mentioned earlier, in hiphop a name is not simply a reference to a person but also can represent someone's lyrical style, status, and that of his or her crew. It is also indexical and echoes a speech by Malcolm X where he constantly stresses, in a chanted slogan, "What's your name?"[11] In this speech Malcolm X illustrates that slavery destroyed the ability to know family names, and that the names given by masters to those of African descent represent slavery. Consequently, the question itself implies that the subjects are descendants of slaves, have been subjugated by white supremacy, are the object of bigotry, and so on. "Don't you know who you are?" "You're of African descent!" It is a fully loaded rhetorical question.

To name oneself is thus to claim an identity, an association with others, and to demonstrate knowledge of the power apparatus. It is to claim a past, a present, and a place. Any serious MC can answer the question "What's my name?" in many different ways. For example, as MC Lyte explains in *Lyte as a Rock* (1988): "Lyte as a Rock, or I should say a boulder—Rolling down your neck, pounding on your shoulders—Never shall I be an emcee, called a wannabe—I am the Lyte, L-Y-T-E." A name in hiphop indexes place, group affiliation, significant historical moments, material goods, and so on. A hiphop name is an identity statement that says: "This is who I am, what I'm about, where I'm from, and what I do." Thus MC Lyte is the hard light, truth, and vision glaring down and firmly smacking, not lightly touching, the world. She uses the word light/lyte because she is pointedly stressing that she is heavy—the opposite of light. She is "the light" and all-knowing, shining, and sharing knowledge and fighting against ignorance.[12] It is in this respect that a rhetorical question regarding naming, when directed at an opponent and competitor, allows an MC to identify who he and she is at many levels and to listeners who have varying levels of understanding. It signifies on those who don't know the answer and it allows the MC to represent the crew and space in a manner that is simultaneously aggressive, demanding, and indifferent. It also warns others that they "better recognize" and respect the MC's crew: anyone who matters knows my name.

The rhetorical question in hiphop not only states the obvious but also can function as a signifier on a target. Its use may represent a high level of skill because it requires that participants employ all aspects of the linguistic and ideological system. It requires hiphop knowledge and work. In contrast, a direct confrontation is a conversational strategy and may result in argument rather than lyrical battle; and it may lead to escalated dispute. The use of indirection is a dismissive and powerful discursive strategy because it requires collaboration from all of those present and does not allow the target a context for self-defense and face saving (Morgan 2002). Moreover, the collaboration is at the level of local knowledge shared by those active in hiphop and in Project Blowed in particular. It indirectly introduces the evaluation of an MC's right to speak and rhyme. An MC may raise it as a discursive strategy to illustrate his or her prowess and toward an opponent as a challenge. In the latter case, it is a form of disrespect that indexes that an MC might be weak, since at Project Blowed the dissing of artists often indexes a lack of skills on the part of an MC. In many respects, there is the prevailing philosophy that "those who rhyme—represent; those who lack game—complain."[13] Consequently, freestyle is not the time to criticize nonopponents. The only thing that matters is the ability to freestyle. Thus Chu's rhetorical question, "Who say fuck Wu-Tang?" in line 3 functions to dismiss (diss) the person (real or imagined) who made the statement that disrespected Wu-Tang. Everyone knows who said it, and to ask who did it indirectly chastises the person who criticized another MC group. Line 7 introduces Chu's diss of the MCs who are accused of being wack and lacking style. He confronts them in line 11 with another rhetorical question: "How you like me now?"[14] Chu then challenges the MC to stand and do battle.

Though all aspects of the freestyle system listed above are apparent in Chu's performance, several other important strategies are evident as well. These include the construction of the hiphop visionary and the juxtaposition of the linguistic system through the reading and interplay of dialect and style. The hiphop visionary is a mythical and legendary figure who has insight, knowledge, and street sense—and thus can survive in spite of the odds. He or she survives through the honest practice of skills and the search for knowledge. This figure is not necessarily morally heroic but rather has a higher level of understanding of "reality," as the MC does what his or her performance persona (i.e., name) must do to represent at the highest level. For instance, Chu identifies himself as "Born as a prince child" in line 9. Thus his vision as a prince who can see and foresee is also his destiny since he claims he was born into the role.

The use of stress to punctuate syllables as well as pauses, particular vowel sounds, and syllabic formation can also refer to the persona that the MC has developed. An MC may rhyme on vowels, consonants, or syllabic structure. Those who are particularly fluent at the juxtaposition of phonemes (meaningful sounds), morphemes (word units), or syllabic structure are thought to possess extraordinary skill. For example, Chu's use of the /ah/ sound in his pronunciation of the words: *style, child,* and *now* (lines 7–11) creates a rhythmic pattern of delivery. He also organizes his rhyme between long syllable sets when, in line 12, he says the letter G and then uses twenty-five syllables before he rhymes with the word "me" in line 16. He also employs subtle final consonant contrast in lines 24 and 25 when he contrasts the final consonants in "work" and "worth": "Yeah I'm worth all. Yeah I work all."

As noted above, in preparation for freestyle the MCs practice regularly in front of others in ciphers, where the participants listen as they also evaluate the skill level of the MC. When outside, an MC's crew severely evaluates his or her freestyle skills. Inside, an MC's crew acts both as a supportive audience as respected and as expert audience members who may have no allegiance to the competitor. In fact, on this night Chu continuously reminds everyone present that Project Blowed is not only a place to watch MCs perform but also a workshop for MCs. Members of the audience must participate. Those present are expected to take part as evaluators of skills, demonstrate their MC skills to be evaluated, or both. Everyone present is schooled and ready. In many respects, the stage represents graduation—the ultimate step in the workshop learning and the practice that is going on throughout the night, both inside and outside. On this night, Terra (Pterodactyl) rushes out of the Blowed and into the street, and he hones his skills when he sees someone holding a video camera:

1	TERRA:	Is the camera on?
2		Is the camera on?
3		Come here strong, top up with that
4		Fresh rap hiphop clan back, UH

5		I came here with the twenty seventy-eight
6		I was the agent,
7		Went up to the mack,
8		Came up with the rap
9		No I—don't go away from me
10		No don't look at that *((camera attempts to turn))*
11		I'm doin' phat
12		You know what I'm sayin'?
13		I'm where it's at
14	CAMERAMAN:	You the fuckin' bomb!

Terra's style is confrontational with the camera. His head juts back and forth as he asks and repeats the rhetorical question "Is the camera on?" The question is rhetorical because he can see that the video camera is on as he walks toward it. His preparation requires that he use the camera as an object from which to improvise within a coherent narrative. He chooses a two-syllable pronunciation instead of three for the word "camera" and repeats it. The repetition of lines can signal that extemporaneous rhyming is at play. Terra then rhymes the word "strong" with "on" in line 3. He identifies his legendary status in lines 4–8 where he describes himself as the agent who defeated a negative force (the mack) and was the victor because of his lyrical skills (line 8). As he practices, his goal is to find rhymes and a reason to rhyme in the development of his freestyle skill. It is his job to *represent* by rapping on any occasion—as though there is a competitor and using the style and references of Blowed—so that he represents the whole crew. He prepares himself to rhyme about anything— cameras, movement, and so on—as part of becoming adept at freestyle. In fact, every skill available to MCs is in effect on this night.

The Word Work

As discussed above, it is common for participants to move within Project Blowed's four spaces (park, sidewalk, side concession, and workshop/performance space) throughout the Thursday night venue, though crews in ciphers mainly congregate in the park. At the April 18 event, I reentered the performance space from the entrance/concession area at around 10:30 PM. People were mingling and furtively glancing at the stage. Several MCs from Project Blowed and another family crew, 2000 Crows, were looking around and claiming a turn at the mic. It was clear that someone had disrespected and challenged the Blowed in some way, and a battle was brewing. Nearly everyone from outside was in the room or crowded into the concession area, anticipating what would happen next.[15] The stage was packed mostly with Blowed members—many of whom were trying to grab one of the two mics. The crew members on the stage were shaking their heads. Then Aceyalone spoke before he started his rhymes. Once he began rhyming, two others followed without missing a beat. In the following transcripts I present the rhymes as they flowed that night, and my analysis of the protracted battle follows the transcripts.

The first MC appearing after Aceyalone, Terra, is a member of the Project Blowed crew. Prefect, a member of the crew that I will call Wood-west, follows Terra.[16] Members of the Woodwest crew have—presumably—disrespected the Blowed. This disrespect sets the conditions for battle into motion. A member of the Project Blowed family, MC Otherwise, follows Prefect.

1	ACEY:	*((speaking))* It's like, it's like, it's like, it's like.
2	CREW MEMBER:	Give me a beat. *((DJ begins beat))*
3	ACEY:	It's like the vice platoon with a lot of **ANGRY SOLDIERS**.
4	STAGE:	That's right!!
5	ACEY:	Sooner or later we have to **JUST CALM THOSE FOLKS DOWN!**
6		Hear what I'm **SAY**in'? **THAT'S** how we do it.
7		*((rhymes begin))*
8		The heat circulatin'
9		And the energy expose
10		To each and everybody
11		Through your clothes—and ya
12		If you feel enclosed
13		In Project Blowed
14		These four walls and that high-ass ceiling
15		Get you feelin' and reelin'
16		Cause it's to ya
17		By the way I do ya
18		By the way that I go through ya
19		I can listen to all of you

20		And see out to Leimert
21		Listen to my word-work,
22		Understand me now?
23	TERRA:	Well, You take **hiphop** too personal
24		We be puttin' up an arsenal
		((directed at another MC))
25		I'm first to flow
26		Step up
27		I'm Terror
28		Are you a **Blowed?**
29		Are you a **black man?**
30		Yeah, you straight brother
31		But you don't act like we came from the same mother
32		You don't act like you from the same bloodline
33		Or
34		Floodline
35		Always in your ear
36		I'm Terra **Boom**
37		I'm strikin' fear
38		On the microphone with lyrics
39		Lyrical spirits
40		I mean lyrics—I
41		Speaking to myself
42		But not speaking the lyrics
43		I'm pumped
44		All to myself
45		Free to come to the cipher
46		Without a wall I'm givin' Ws up
47		Y'all aint got enough Ws in your breath left?
48	PREFECT:	I'll throw a W
49		Way up in the air
50		And after that I be like
51		No, I don't believe
52		It there
53		I fuckin' smoke
54		But don't like brothers and sisters?
55		But this is shit education

56		No! Fuck that.
57		I don't need that.
58		I'll get me a 40
59		And after that
60		I kick raps
61		I'm pumped
62		Though
63		You might not call me naughty
64		But I be like
65		Be livin' it
66		And rippin' it
67		I'm skippin' it
68		I'm hoggin' it
69		And likin' it
70		I'm sleepin' it
71		And feelin' it
72		Like a bitch
73		I ain't off the hook
74		I ain't no crook
75		No I ain't no shook
76		I ain't no shit rhymer
77		From the east coast
78		It's the w-e-s-t
79		Representin' on the mic
80		At Project Blowed
81	OTHERWISE:	Well look me in my optical
82		As I hold you responsible
83		If you eliminate
84		Elements of intelligence
85		Only the logical's possible
86		Obstacles you thrust—I
87		Def with precision
88		Catch a glimpse of
89		Without centrifugal, peripheral vision
90		Corner of my cornea
91		Call it Corner of Brother obituary
92		You don't rhyme bitch, you scary

There is a break in the beats and the people on the stage are calm, but annoyed. Someone on the stage tries to begin spoken-word poetry, but he is prevented from doing so and told that this is freestyle only. Others argue or comment about unity as they wait for the beats to return.[17]

The differences in freestyle strategy are apparent at many levels. Both Acey and Terra average six syllables per second while Prefect averages four and a half. Otherwise averages nearly eight words per second. Though Blowed members tend to introduce more syllables per second, what is manifest in the diversity of style between the two crews is the use of sustained multiple syllabic rhyming. Acey slowly introduces the battle, using contrasting one-second segments of up to six syllables. Terra's segments are in bursts of lyrical fury where he has eighteen syllables in two seconds (lines 23–24), followed by five seconds where he uses a maximum of four syllables per second. This is followed by another burst where he delivers twenty-two syllables in two seconds (lines 31–32). Otherwise (line 81) also flows with multiple syllables and has only one one-second segment under four syllables. This contrasts with the syllabic style of Prefect (line 48) who averages four syllables per second but only has three continuous segments where he delivers more than five syllables per second (48–50, 54–55, 78–79).

Though the actual linguistic differences are noticeable, the more startling difference may be the actual portrayal of representation and respect. The narrative flow reveals several differences in terms of style and representation as well as the level of local and general hiphop knowledge necessary to battle. First Acey establishes the battle conditions as he defines the battle energy (angry soldiers), Blowed space, social context, and his position as an MC. He then describes the performative context (lines 8–22) and his skills, the room, the crowd's energy and facility to evaluate other MCs, and his own ability to work words (line 21). He completes his turn by reminding those present where they are and why they are at Project Blowed: *And see out to Leimert / Listen to my word-work / Understand me now?*

Terra immediately follows Acey's introductory flow with a direct attack on Prefect in line 23. Terra first exposes Prefect for not playing according to the rules outlined by Acey. He then sets up an incendiary rhetorical question in line 29: *"Are you a Black man?"* He answers the question himself on the next beat: "Yeah, you straight brother." *"Are you a Black man?"* is a particularly layered question because it masks as a rhetorical one but is only potentially so. To those who are part of the African American and hiphop experience, it is not only about racial identification but also about respect. The question suggests that Prefect is full of self-hate and self-loathing, and he cannot be trusted in general and in the presence of power in particular. He does not respect the rules of battle and thus does not respect the Blowed. The question also indexes black nationalist ideology, Africa, slavery, racism, injustice, and the like. Consequently, Prefect does not respect the black man and therefore himself.

Once the symbols and the social, political, and historical contexts have been indexed, Terra signifies on Prefect in line 30 when he describes him as a *"straight brother."* He is clearly signifying that Prefect is not real, and in line 31, Terra compounds the insult by suggesting that Prefect is not from the same mother as the black man—that is, Mother Africa. By saying that he is neither from the same bloodline or floodline (lines 32–34) Terra is denying Prefect any connection to Africa or a slave ship. After he has completed his scathing diss, Terra restates his name in line 36, "I'm Terra Boom," describes his style as spiritual and free, and then ends with a final diss to the Woodwest crew in line 47: *"Y'all aint got enough Ws in your breath left?"*

As Terra delivered his lines, the crowd moved their heads as though small electric jolts were going through their bodies. Some waved their hands in the form of the letter W for *Westsiiide!* Others just used profanity —"Oh shit. Da(aa)mn"—confirming that the diss was effective. The battle was on and someone had clearly been wounded.

The stages in Terra's strategy are as follows:

Terra vs. Prefect

1	Disses the MC	(disrespectful, self-hating, not black)
2	Rhetorical question	(Are you a Black Man?)
3	States name	(identifies and describes MC style)
4	Displays lyrical skills	(juxtaposition same word; *lyrics,* avg. 6 syllables)
5	Closing diss	(Y'all ain't got enough Ws)

In the context of a battle, the only option is to engage in the battle or acknowledge that you have lost it by lowering the mic and leaving the stage to the audience's screams of "pass the mic." Thus, it is no surprise that Prefect did not hesitate as he responded and that other members of his crew jumped onto the stage with him.

As the Woodwest crew begins, Prefect first claims that he belongs to the W (line 48). Then he directly addresses Terra's diss. First, he states his MC skills in line 53 by saying that his skills are exceptional to the point that he smokes or destroys other MCs. He then uses rising intonation to ask the rhetorical question "*But don't like brothers and sisters?*" He then uses the question as evidence that the Blowed should not be respected by referring to their workshop as "*shit education,*" and then he outright rejects the Blowed (line 56). He then describes his MC skills, which begin with a reference to 40-ounce malt liquor (line 58), and then provides examples of his lyrical skill within eight instances of four-syllable phrases that echo each other on the third and fourth syllables (. . . in' it). He then returns to the content of Terra's diss, claims he is legitimate and that he represents the West (lines 78–80), and therefore has the right to participate at Project Blowed. His sequence is as follows:

Prefect vs. Blowed

1	Has the right to represent	(throws Ws)
2	Rhetorical question	(don't like brothers and sisters?)
3	Disses the Blowed	(shit education)
4	Displays lyrical skills	(juxtaposition syllable/sound *in*, avg. 4 syllables)
5	Describes self	("I ain't no"; represent the West)

While Prefect responds to the attack on him and his crew, he does not do so within the norms established by Project Blowed. Though he is responding to an attack, he does not construct a creative and coherent narrative and argument that they are wrong and that he is a "real brother." Neither does he present a critique of "authentic" blackness to demonstrate both skill and knowledge. He does not creatively dismiss the Blowed position that they are better MCs through some direct representation of MCs. Instead of reframing the diss and stopping it in its tracks, he insists that he belongs. Yet he does this without stating a name, rhetorically or directly, and without aligning with a named crew. There is no clarity of his identity in terms of crew, region, and place. He does not come correct and represent. For those present, his response did not prove sufficient evidence that he respected the Blowed and that he should be in control of the mic.

Inside Project Blowed on Thursday night. Photo by Tony B, courtesy of Project Blowed.

Science

Because MCS evaluate a battle, and virtually every MC present at the Blowed is connected to a crew, it can be difficult to identify the definitive moment when one crew has silenced another. In spontaneous battles, crews do not routinely concede a loss unless the crowd has completely turned against them through chants of "pass the mic" and jeers. They are silenced, or shut down, through nonstop and hard-driving lyricism from another crew. When a crew believes that they are raising the stakes and producing the highest level of lyrical skills—showing their fitness—they are often said to be "dropping science." This expression refers to the result of combining numerous linguistic techniques with multilayered indexicality and social knowledge.

As the DJ begins again, Acey does not rhyme, but instead talks to the crowd.

1   Oh damn! This is the beat!
2   Y'all just simmer—settle down.
3   Get your rhymes together.
4   Know y'all thinkin' like: "Yeah I'm gon' come out like this!"
5   Oh damn! This is the beat!
6   I hear some **SCIENCE HERE DROP!**

Acey praises the beats chosen by DJ Wolf and produced by the CVE.[18] Acey encourages and challenges the MCs to get their rhymes together, and he shares what he believes they must be thinking about how they are going to present their rhymes and represent. He is again moved by the beat, and with head lowered he repeats: "This is the beat." In a reverential manner, he looks out and predicts that there will be some science in the house this night. As his words fade in an echo over the beat, MC Kinky Red (Project Blowed) addresses the battle and its warriors.

7	RED:	*((Talking))* Science building! On the side of the stage.
8		When Dynasties come in and they leave.
9		There's one more there to make you to turn the page.
10		Now full of **rage—ANGER**
11		What I mean to tell you is
12		Don't fuck with the Red opposite ranger.
13		What I mean to tell you is
14		*((Rhymes begin))* My science **DANGER**
15		When I walk into the cipher
16		I be the first to lead, to rearrange you—
17		Your body like
18		Mary love Jesus inside of the manger
19		Where's the hanger?
20		I want to hang some devils in here
21		Don't give a fuck when it comes to rhymes,
22		Cali 9's in your atmosphere.
23		Throw my hands up nine times,
24		Ws will trouble you, my rhymes
25		With all the intellect and intertwined
26		Y'all want beef, just resign
27		I beat yo ass nine times give you nine lines
28		In your anal ashes—a goddamn shame
29		Why that sissy's got no name?
30		You nameless
31		It's a goddamn shame
32		Its too many MCs be down to me
33		And all of them that want to come up here
34		And grab this M-I-C
35		Now do you wreck? Do you disrespect?

36		Diggin' in the spot with the new intellect?
37		With other brothers?
38		Do you know how to serve?
39		Do you know how to play the undercover?
40		Whoa! Cali 9 got the brain train in control.
41		Preach—Cali 9s—a casualty
42		Back up you can't compare to gravity
43	ACEY:	Gra:::vity, Gra:::vity,
44		*((Comments on liking the beats))*

Red identifies himself as member of the Cali 9 crew, a part of the Project Blowed family.[19] He is battling for the Blowed. He initially narrates his turn at the mic as though it is a prologue to an epic movie. It is a visionary tale of dynasties and rage when the hero arrives (line 15). The beat fills the room and his rhymes commence. Red is a speech-effusive syllabic MC who delivers an average of seven syllables per line. He foretells the damage he intends to do (line 16) and uses biblical references (line 18) to describe the kind of support Prefect will require to live with the crucifixion that Red intends to bestow on him. He is after devils and uses the planets (nines) and intellect to represent. The seriousness of the battle, and Red's stake in it, is revealed in lines 28–29 when he uses a derogative homosexual reference for Prefect (sissy) and accuses him of having no name. Project Blowed members tend not to use homophobic references, and excessive name calling is unusual and generally only used by weak MCs unless there has been a serious affront. There are often attempts to control stereotypical name calling since it is not within the norms of evaluation and is viewed as potential argument rather than lyrical skill. This use results in many turned heads and raised eyebrows, as though the battle had many layers. Red's diss of Prefect has the following components.

Red Prefect

1	Warns other MCs	(My science danger)
2	Identifies self and crew	(Cali 9's in your atmosphere)
3	Displays lyrical skills	(juxtaposition sound rhyme, syllable avg. 7 syllables)
4	Disses MC	(No name, no respect)
5	Rhetorical question	(Do you disrespect?)
6	Identifies crew	(Cali 9 got the brain train in control)
7	Closing diss	(Back up you can't compare to gravity)

According to many at Project Blowed, Red is a skilled MC and thus the attack on Prefect is viewed as personal rather than an indication of Red's lyrical skills. The crowd watched, and listened even more closely, as they sensed something was wrong.[20] From an MC perspective, the serious discursive insult is that Prefect is nameless—does not claim an identity. Moreover, because of Red's personal insult, it appears that Prefect may be connected to Red, who now feels betrayed. Red suggests that this is the case as he claims his position as a leader of MCs (line 32). He then asks successive rhetorical questions that are meant to be heard in the negative. Prefect does not respect, does not understand the new intellect. He does not know how to serve and play the undercover (lines 35–39). Kinky Red, representing the Cali 9 and Project Blowed, has slain an MC. He is heavy like gravity. Acey chimes in and confirms the gravity of the situation with a drawn out pronunciation of the word gravity. But it is not over. Either Prefect cannot concede or he simply will not—and begins his response.

45	PREFECT:	Here we go,
46		One more time
47		You have no right
48		To remain silent
49		When you grab
50		That mother
51		Fuckin' mic
52		Why do you kick
53		The precise
54		And claim
55		That you say you didn't
56		It's that mystical shit
57		That you kickin'
58		You're black
59		You think that
60		When I attack
61		With this W
62		I'm here to trouble you
63		No time to react—
64		Brother you
65		I'm gonna strap you
66		Right in your track

67	I Hit you with
68	a different style of
69	100%
70	When I act.
71	So sit your ass down
72	Get taught
73	Right about now
74	When I kick you
75	No questions
76	Is crossed over
77	That W
78	with the 2 twisted
79	In the middle
80	Like my riddles
81	Despicable prophet
82	The typical minds
83	Imani Osiris
84	Resurrection goddess
85	Ruler of the upper world.
86	Fuck these tricks
87	Who claim they bitches.
88	6–6–4 switches.
89	What is this really all about?
90	Silly ho.
91	I bet you sound like
92	R. Kelly's videos.
93	**I DID THIS TO YOU.**
94	It's the motherfuckin'
95	W Crew!
96	So where you at!
97	Sit your ass
98	Way in the back!
99	You can't even rap
100	You motherfuckin' lyrical actor—
101	Actress.
102	I'ma slam the door
103	In your face.
104	You're the one I'm looking for!

105	You'll plead for sure!
106	So grab this microphone
107	If you can.
108	I got the target runnin'
109	Before my joint is when I aim.
110	So get it together
111	Partner. *((menacing dance-hall style))*
112	You need somethin' else!
113	No wait, wait—
114	You need some *((sings raga style))* JoJo bouncer
115	To get active
116	Actor and actor rich.
117	I'ma grab this microphone
118	And talk like a 4–4 split.
119	And if anybody want to battle,
120	I'm with the W
121	But if you want to battle me,
122	But I have to trouble you and
123	And what you can in concrete ·
124	So you can get to—

Prefect's flow is long and deliberate. It is distinctive in that Prefect still does not identify himself in terms of name or vision. Nor does he establish his location, neighborhood, crew, or any other typical symbol of affiliation. Instead, he instantly addresses Red in the battle. His style is not speech effusive but rather laid-back with an average of four syllables per second. He begins by literally reading Red his legal MC rights: *You have no right / To remain silent / When you grab / That mother / Fuckin' mic* (lines 47–51), as if Red were apprehended for perpetrating a fraud.

Prefect vs. Red

1	Warns MC	(You have no right to remain silent)
2	Question	(Why do you kick the precise? / What is this really about?)
3	Diss MC	(It's that mystical shit)
4	Threatens MC	(I'm gonna strap you)
5	Displays lyrical skills	(juxtaposition syllable, avg. 4 syllables)
6	Closing diss	(I did this to you / I got the target runnin')

Until now, the battle has clearly focused on what transpired in real time, but Prefect's choice of words introduces the notion that he is indexing a previous context and conversation to which those present aren't privy. Why does he say Red had no right to remain silent when Red wasn't silent about what he thought? Prefect uses confusing terminology to make this claim as he struggles to create a meaningful narrative. For example, Prefect says that Red was precise and that Red denied it (lines 52–55). But that does not make narrative sense. The MCs on stage and in the audience shake their heads at the missteps in Prefect's flow. Though the extent of their disagreement is not clear, Prefect is unambiguous in his criticism of Red's black nationalism, referring to it as mystical (line 56). Prefect also suggests that Red's form of nationalism is completely dishonest. Though Prefect claims allegiances to Ws, an attack on Red is an attack on the Project Blowed crew. Prefect actually admits this when he says he intends to cause trouble (line 62) and he insists that he also represents the W, though he suggests that Red's W is twisted (wrong, confused, crazy). But Prefect seems to confuse his references in line 65 when he refers to Imani Osiris as a goddess of resurrection. Virtually every MC surrounding him on the stage frowned and looked at each other with disbelief. While Imani is an African name and an Egyptian/Nubian name that means faith, Osiris is an Egyptian/Nubian god of the dead! Moreover, Osiris is regularly paired with Isis. Prefect then compares Red to the women in R&B singer's R. Kelly's videos, whose sole purpose is to perform sex acts for the singer. He then proclaims that he is successful when he says, "**I DID THIS TO YOU.**" And he identifies himself as representing the W Crew. He then begins his diss sequence. Once again, he does not present a name, vision, location, crew, or coherent narrative, yet he does not concede but instead passes the mic on to Acey who rhymes:

125	ACEY:	Well I don't have a punch line
126		But I still stand in a lunch line
127		And I still get busy
128		When it's crunch time
129		My style may take me
130		On a loop—loop-t-loop
131		Style so bigger than a hula-hoop
132		Goin' around your whole frame
133		You're frameless, nameless

134	We don't want to know your name
135	Why you came and so strange
136	To the MCs in the house
137	Lookin' hazy,
138	Some lookin' more like
139	Little mouses,
140	Or little mice, mice to men
141	You just a nice friend
142	Who tried to come in and gin the Project Blowed
143	And try to blend
144	But you cannot blend in
145	With the style that will never win you
146	Defending the wrong purpose
147	Your style is so surface
148	Then it's so shallow
149	You'll get to swallow—
150	((*speaks*)) I'm done

Acey's rhymes begin with a biting diss of Prefect and his style, which he describes as a series of punch lines. Acey has an analysis of Prefect's problem: he is nameless (actually, *"frameless, nameless"*) and does not have an identity to represent. In contrast, Acey describes himself as a humble MC who continues to practice, as he is willing to stand in lunch lines and is ready *"When it's crunch time."*

Acey vs. Prefect

1	Diss	(Well I don't have a punch line / You're frameless nameless)
2	Lyrical skills	(Juxtaposition of same words, rhyme, syllables; 6 syllables)
3	Question	(Why you came so strange?)
4	Answer	(Who tried to come in and gin Project Blowed. / You cannot blend)
5	Diss	(Defending the wrong purpose, style is surface, shallow)

According to Acey, Prefect is neither representing or recognizing and thus has no purpose. He has identified the problem, and he is disgusted. Acey simply stops. Prefect is not playing according to the rules of the real hiphop. There is only one reasonable response remaining.

Acey ends his rhymes as the beats fade. The DJ has taken an unannounced break. Someone asks if there is a beat box—someone who can make percussive sounds with their vocal apparatus—but no one volunteers. The extent of Acey's diss of Prefect slowly seeps into the Woodwest Crew as everyone waits for the beats to begin. By all rights they are defeated, having been fully exposed, humiliated, and beaten, but they will not respect the rules of engagement. The Project Blowed crew quickly amasses in full force, and they jump to the stage and begin with Misfit. But Prefect does not step down and allow Misfit his turn to flow. Instead, Prefect wrestles back control of his mic and signifies (disses) within Misfit's rhymes by overlapping within Misfit's turn (brackets [ ] show the areas of overlap).

151	MISFIT:	Born between
152		Like planet to [earth]
153	PREFECT:	[That's not Ea::::rth.]
154		Shit be your turf
155	MISFIT:	Another nigga be pushin'
156	MISFIT:	A lot of [shit to your mind
157	PREFECT:	[Fuck what you hea::rd
158	MISFIT:	Then you find out you were [fuckin' wit'
159	PREFECT:	[Fuck what you heard]
160	MISFIT:	The wrong nigga that you heard
161		I heard that a nigga slash
162		Give a slack give it back
163		You're not the man
164		Sugarland. You think I'm worthless
165		I heard this before
166		Nigga step to me
167		Niggas get served—the Lord
168		Got rhymes stored for you
169		Niggas take a view down my walk
170		Niggas talk the holy walk
171		And talk the walk
172		And I the hawk
173		Nigga I open banks
174		And thank me for bringin' the dank

175	I swang in the air
176	And sling by the trees nigga
177	See the breeze
178	And it comes easily, easily.
179	I serve MCs and heed me
180	I sweep niggas off they feet
181	Real sweetly
182	Fuckin' around
183	'Cause 2000 Crows put it down.
184	How ya like this now?
185	West Coast underground.

As Misfit begins, Prefect overlaps and attempts to disrupt Misfit's flow on the word *earth*. His interruption takes two seconds, twice as long as the line Misfit delivers. The Project Blowed crew hovers as this happens and allows Misfit to represent. Prefect first disputes Misfit's description of earth and Misfit, who is stunned that Prefect is rapping over his rhymes, allows Prefect another clear verbal space to claim that Misfit's earth is worthless (*Shit be your turf* [line 154]). Misfit responds by indirectly saying Prefect is a nigga with manure on his mind (line 156). Oddly, earth, shit, and fuck become words and symbols of the battle over target, reference, and index. Misfit wrestles control of the mic through a series of indexical references. The lyrics: *"You think I'm worthless—I heard it before"* (lines 164–65) constructs Misfit as a prophet and sage. Not only is the image of dominant culture claiming youth of color to be worthless a staple of conservative commentary in the United States, it is also regularly depicted in stories of high school counselors discouraging youth from their dreams, and hiphop tales of trying to succeed while adult authorities repeat that they are worthless. Misfit's use of "I heard it before" is the perfect index and brings the entire crowd to his side. We have all heard this before. He will get served and will serve the Lord (line 167). His style is holy. He cannot only walk the walk, but talk it. Moreover, he can rob and give (*"open banks and thank me for bringin' the dank"*). He can traverse through and save the jungle—with no effort so that what he does is done so beautifully it is seen as sweet. He recognizes his crew, 2000 Crows, and asks how Prefect and his crew feel about the rhetorical question: *How ya like this now?* This question indexes one of the classic old school hiphop battles between Kool Moe Dee and LL Cool J. Kool Moe Dee (1987) accused LL

Cool J of copying (biting) his lyrical style and among his many verses he includes:

It irked my nerve / When I heard / A sucker rapper that I know I'll serve / Run around town sayin' he is the best / Is that a test? / I'm not impressed/Get real, you're nothin' but a toy / Don't ya know I'll serve that boy? / Just like a waiter / Hit 'em with a plate of / These fresh rhymes and / Make sure that he / Pays the bill, and leave him standin' still / When he's had enough, hit him with a refill / And for dessert it won't be no ice cream / I'm just gonna splatter and shatter his pipe dream /Make him feel the wrath, beat him and laugh / Then when I finish them, I'm gonna ask him / Who's the bests, and if he don't say Moe Dee / I'll take my whip and make him call himself Toby / Put him on punishment just like a child, then ask / How ya like me now?

Misfit delivered the flavor and the flow of West Coast underground. As he utters his last word, he is followed by Zagu, another member of his crew, who feels the flow.

186	ZAGU:	2000 Crows underground
187		When we come around we clown
188		Like Homey Don't play that.
189		How dare you say that.
190		You better pay that due To Who?
191		Big bad Babu Brown
192		Drag you down.
193		Six feet underground
194		I put a lot of dirt
195		'Cause I do mass work
196		For to shake the spot like you ass hurt
197		To pompom drop that bomb bomb
198		Rhyme rhymes all the time time.
199		For the top of the mind underline—
200		'Cause my shit be divine.
201		And Oh—Oh What?
202		And Oh,
203		These is just one of those kinda buts,
204		And whether this rhyme's true
205		And Babu
206		Plus this nigga's not herb?

207	And not true
208	Triple those
209	2000 Crows and Project Blowed
210	Now back to the blunt session
211	That was in prior progression.

After Zagu introduces himself, he quickly and indirectly dismisses the Woodwest crew through African American popular culture references. To say that 2000 Crows clown, like *"Homey don't play that,"* is to state emphatically that they know when they're playing—and it's not now. Homey the Clown is in reference to a character played by Damon Wayans in the 1990s television program *In Living Color.* Homey is a convicted felon who was forced to become a children's clown as part of a parole agreement. At birthday parties, if the kids say racist, snobby, or other disrespectful things he hits them with his stuffed sock and says "Homey don't play that." So the Woodwest crew has to pay their dues to people who work hard. Zagu then moves to double word rhymes and asks a rhetorical question (line 190). Chu then comes forward to make certain that the Woodwest crew and Prefect have completely surrendered the mic.

212	CHU:	Its like uh,
213		You at the centerfold
214		Uh Really don't know
215		But it's kinda cold out here with the Eskimos
216		But I'm with the best pros
217		From the West Coast
218		Where I dress the most
219		With the number one I be the host
220		The leader of the high post
221		Like Olajuwan I'm drop the bomb
222		Comin' up here like Vietnam
223		Look at this real calm
224		At the psalm in the palm of my hand
225		Can you witness when you do like
226		My man stretch to the catch, fetch, like a dog
227		Go get it Rover. You get it with the ball.
228		A small can't do,
229		Can't see through your rear view
230		Now this nigga ain't true now

231	Comin' like a zoo keeper
232	Got my guns and my sweeper
233	Come and get the creeper, beeper
234	At your expense
235	Switch-bitch
236	Do you come around here making no sense
237	Got self-defense for your government
238	And lovin' it, rubbin' it Flubbin' it
239	I'm a skeet huuh?
240	Every time I teach you sleep, but you crease your skin
241	Niggas can't win
242	What's up now Irv?
243	You 'bout to curve into my serve—
244	You think anyway
245	What nerve,
246	I swerve, I pitch
247	Wait a minute bitch
248	What is this? *And it's you together ((sings))*
249	And wait a minute
250	Your whole crew
251	*Is gonna be a little felt better ((sings))*
252	Now that you will know what to do
253	I'm gonna send you
254	A walk to the venue
255	Its menu—
256	Trick, trick, trick—get off my dick
257	'Cause you got hit upside the head with a doogie stick
258	Yeah, it's 2000 Crows and the Project Blows
259	Yeah, it's 2000 Crows and the Project Blows

Chu finally unleashes an arsenal of linguistic and discursive strategies. He acknowledges that Prefect is in the cold and that Project Blowed are the visionaries and that Chu is a leader. His leadership is as high as the nearly seven-foot-tall basketball player Hakeem Olajuwan who comes careening down on his opponents. He is righteous and holds psalms in his hand for Woodwest to witness and then he directly insults them. Chu then refers to Prefect as shameful, a pet dog, zoo keeper, and liar (lines 226–31). He also interprets Prefect's remark as an accusation that he is a weak man when he asks a question to highlight his right to defend himself and his crew (*"I'm a skeet huh?"* [line 239]). He responds by highlighting the absurdity of the accusation and uses boxing, basketball, and baseball language to describe what he is doing to them, and then he sings his rhymes to both Prefect and his crew as the ultimate insult. He then shows them the door that provides the exit from the venue, describes for a final time the extent of the verbal beat-down that has just occurred, and then closes with "It's 2000 Crows and the Project Blows."

Project Blowed (Misfit, Zagu, Chu) vs. Prefect

1	Diss	(You I heard it before)
		(Homey don't play that)
		(It's like you at the centerfold— really don't know)
2	Visionary	(Niggas get served—the Lord / Got rhymes stored for you)
		(Cause my shit be divine)
		(I'm with the best pro)
3	Direct	(How you like me now?)
		(This nigga's not true)
		(Now this nigga ain't true)
		(I'm gonna send you /A walk to the venue)
4	Names crew	(2000 Crows and Project Blowed)

Throughout Project Blowed's blitz, members dispensed with rhetorical questions. Instead, they aggressively battled and represented their right and claim to their space by creating a barrage of attacks. They referred to the days of white supremacy with references to "I heard this before," and they recalled classic hiphop battles through the phrase "How ya like me now?" They also reminded the crowd of the popular TV character Homey the Clown, who hated the disrespect of the black man and would end each segment with a song: "Homey the clown, don't mess around. Even though the Man, try to keep him down. One day Homey will, break all the chains. Then he'll fly away, but until that day. Homey don't play." They finally bring in Jamaican rhythms and Rastafarian word order (see chapter 5). They have made their claim as righteous warriors.

It is unbelievable, but though the Woodwest Crew has been defeated they still refuse to respect the rules of Project Blowed and surrender the mic. There is a long break as members of crews discuss what to do. Physical confrontation within the Blowed is not an option. Besides, Project Blowed members have established that they have helped a number of the MCS on this crew and are sick of their disrespect. The only ones who believe they have not lost are the Woodwest crew! Other MCS have signed up to participate and it is important that they get an opportunity to come to the stage and demonstrate their skills. Terra is on the stage and confronts another member of the Woodwest crew, Sox, whom they suspect is behind the problems with Woodwest.[21] Terra juts his chin back and forth, flattens his hand, and moves it rapidly about three inches from Sox's face.

260	TERRA:	What happened to your apology?
261		It's time for a little sermontology
262		That's hypocrisy
263		You jump to the microphone
264		But you ain't knockin' me
265		You stepping up to poetry
266		Yeah, you know it's me
267		Yeah it's Terror
268		Terra whatever you want to call me
269		In any section
270		I'm not battlin' you
271		I'm looking for something bigger
272		You need to be trudgin'
273		In some other corner of the globe
274		Some other corner of this episode

Sox then interrupts Terra's flow as Terra glares menacingly at him. Before Terra is interrupted, he asks, "What happened to your apology?" Because no one from the crew apologizes, Terra sermonizes, juxtaposing and imposing identical word endings (ology—bound morphemes). Terra declares that Sox cannot touch his poetry, he states his name and states his refusal to battle (lines 267–70). He then dismisses Sox (lines 271–72).

275	SOX:	*((talks))* Do you want to share?
276		Do you want to share?
277		*((rhymes))* Cause I'm the leader
278		Of the pack
279		Nigga
280		So step back
281		Nigga
282		For who is large
283		ain't no room
284		for a slack
285		[Nigga
286	TERRA:	[Nigga
287	SOX:	I throw a brick
288		Nigga
289		Since you'se a prick
290		[Nigga
291	TERRA:	[Nigga
292	SOX:	My bitch hits harder than you
293		You little snitch
294		Nigga
295		You thought I switched
296		Nigga
297		But you'se a
298		Bi-atch
299		Nigga
300		BIU only slut
301		Nigga

Terra overlaps and signifies on Sox with the word Nigga. This is treated here as a true insult and Terra's eyes dart and his face is scrunched in anger. By overlapping, Terra is directly returning the insult to Sox. Sox attempts to continue his diss of Terra but after name calling, he relents and lowers the mike. Without missing a beat Terra hits back.

302	TERRA:	Well that's too many Niggas
303		You need to switch up your style
304		You coming with a little gangster
305		Sound like its doo doo coming out your mouth

306		Talking out your zoot suit
307		You need to salute a soldier
308		A warrior I told yah
309		This story was a little bit older
310		When you told it, it was told down in your family
311		You must examine it
312		This microphone
313		When I was cramming you
314		In this little box like Mitches?
315		On channel 11 on Saturday Night
316		At 8 o'clock, oh knock
317	SOX:	(talks) I thought it was freestyle.
318		But if you want to battle I'll come right back
319	CHU:	It was freestyling

Though Terra has been freestyling throughout the segment, Sox does not recognize it as such. Sox is wrong. Terra has directly attacked Sox and rhymed an average of eight words per second. He derides him for using the word Nigga excessively, an indication that Sox does not have real skills. He critiques his style (line 303), questions whether he is really gangster. He then treats Sox as though Terra is teacher. When Sox says "I thought it was freestyle" in line 317, Terra gives him an incredulous look. Then he just walks off the stage. Sox then begins his rhymes.

320	SOX:	East Side
321		West coast
322		Nigga
323		that's what I'm claiming
324		Leaving Niggas hanging
325		by their fuckin dangalang
326		This is for my enemy
327		Who soon be a memory
328		'Cause my fucking crew
329		is gonna cause you
330		so much misery
331		Come on get your crutches?
332		And MCs I be lunchin
333		About to have a house party
334		Like Johnnie London,

335	What Nigga talking 'bout,
336	get riding like some cattle
337	I'm serving MCs
338	like from New York to Seattle
339	Now what's up Nigga
340	what you wanna do,
341	you can't fuck—
342	mess with me or my crew
343	I'm coming with the freestyle
344	off my mind
345	Come back
346	so you can bust
347	one more rhyme
348	Whas up Red—
349	I won
350	Whas up
351	you're gonna
352	get done
353	By the shot bang gun
354	It seems like
355	This Nigga made it clear,
356	The wack MC
357	Just disappeared
358	From inside of here
359	A Nigga jazz
360	Represent your SVL
361	The Niggas swerving
362	You about to catch wordin
363	Cause my Niggas . . .

Sox insults Terra and the Project Blowed crew, but there is no real crew listening. Those who are still left in the room are talking to each other, laughing and so on. His words do not have an audience. He takes the mic into the audience as he raps in order to keep their attention. People laugh. Then Prefect begins.

364	PREFECT:	(Alright now check this out)
365		Some MCs
366		Who wanna give MCs props

367	But I'm from the rock
368	Hiphop
369	Pop and the hard rock
370	It's all about hiphop rock . . .

But no one is listening. The rhymes are inviting and have a melodic flow, but the Woodwest crew is weakened because they cannot and do not directly address the battle.

They resort to name calling. Project Blowed MCs have walked away from them! They did this when there was no risk that the crowd would insist: "please pass the mic." They disrespected Woodwest and feared no reprisals. In underground hiphop, the claim of winning is collaborative. An MC can't say "I won!" The MC must be supported, but there is no support for the Woodwest crew. Prefect tries to call out Red again, who is restrained by other members to allow the events to play out.

Woodwest (Sox) vs. Project Blowed (Terra)

1	Visionary	(I'm the leader of the pack)
2	Name calling	(nigga, you a prick)
3	Bragging	(leaving niggas by they fucking dangalang/serving MCs)

The crowd moves into sections of the main room and the concession area. Chu remains visible, but he does not actively try to prevent anything from happening or make anything happen. The Woodwest crew is through for the night. They have no one to pass the mic to and they cannot continue to create rhymes. As they begin to recycle their punch lines, they are completely exposed. They hand over the mics. Chu looks at the crowd, shakes his head, and says: "See, I told you."

Build a Workshop 'Round Where I Stay

Once the Woodwest crew departs the stage and surrenders the mic, Project Blowed takes over and the audience gathers in the room. The mood is playful. Chu mentions that this is a workshop as he peruses the MC signup list and calls the next MC to the stage to present their skills this night. Those who have lost the battle continue to mingle, though many in attendance give furtive glances and keep their distance. The seasoned artists listen intensely and offer support and criticism of the stream of MCs who take their turn at the mic. As the night winds down around midnight, MCS take to the stage and entertain each other and the crowd. The Woodwest crew remains between the audience space and the stage perimeter. If they intend to participate again, they must show that they respect the process of evaluation and the effort everyone made to provide a critical evaluation of their skills. Eventually, a member of their crew actually joins the Project Blowed MCS as they play and perform.

Tonight's battle has introduced God and gods, bitches and queens, and named spaces and places. It was a battle over skills and who you are and "where you at." It was the power of the Word and still it was much more. They battled for real hiphop where one represents, recognizes, and comes correct. The Woodwest crew had humiliated themselves and had to accept it. The Project Blowed crew had represented real hiphop and worked to maintain the principles they believe make up underground hiphop. And they clearly believe that hiphop won this night.

The LTS linger as lights are turned on and Blowed members begin to clean the space. Ben Caldwell is talking to groups of young men as the cleanup begins. The people working the door have taken the cash box, counted the money, and put away the tables and chairs. Those working the concession stands sell their last vinyl and T-shirt and close out the cash register. The beats of the DJ are still flowing as Chu comes to the stage and says the final rhyme:

"You ain't got to go home, but you got to get the fuck outta here."

(Ph)eminists of the New School

REAL WOMEN, TOUGH POLITICS, AND FEMALE SCIENCE

AFTER SCHOOL, *on Saturdays, and on week-days in the summer, Leimert Park is teeming with neighborhood youths who are taking classes in dance, writing, and music. Throughout the area, and while shopping in stores, it is also possible to drop in on spoken word and poetry work-shops and to hear the pulsating beat of West African drumming and voice and music lessons. Many of the participants in these activities are young girls sizing up each other's bodies and dreams. They are not focused on what the boys say and think about girls, but rather on express-ing who they are and what they are learning about life through art. They compare height, weight, hair, skin tone, breasts, feet, hands, smiles, eyes, pulses, stories, dreams, and every other bit of themselves.*

CHAPTER FOUR

As the dance drumming intensifies, crowds of family, friends, and passers-by congregate outside a door on Degnan in Leimert Park. Inside, girls are rhythmically moving, jumping, gesticulating, and making occasional yelps as advised by their teachers who have them dance the African rituals for gathering harvests, picking yams, representing animals, and so on. Sometimes they switch to Katherine Dunham's modern dance moves, which are integrated with techniques of ballet and African and Caribbean fluid styles of movement. Their long brown bodies flow as they move from their firmly planted feet or pointed toes and up the legs and spine through pulsating hips and outstretched arms, and end with quivering hands whose fingers are stretched open as though in turmoil over the emotion of the rhythm. The young dancers execute these moves with serious expressions and with steady sweat pouring down their bodies in celebration of the lives of their ancestors and in acknowledgment of their joy, pain, and sorrow. They have done the dances of Africa, of crossing oceans through the middle passage, of slave ships, plantations; the dance of rape by masters, the dance of endless slave work, the dance of loss of children, the abandonment of men. They dance the black women's history, life, and passion. They are so young, and their dance is strong.

> Don't hate me for being all that.
> Don't be mad baby—
> 'Cause I'm more than this
> And I proudly uphold the title of—
> One Bad Sista
>
> MEDUSA, "One Bad Sista"

Throughout Thursday night Chu, the Project Blowed MC, continuously peruses the list of names of those who have signed up to compete, represent their skills, and take their turn to rhyme on the mic. On most Thursdays the names are those of male MCs, and so Chu furtively shouts, "Are any sisters in the house? Any females?" Some members of the crowd look around but no one responds, and he moves on and announces the name of the next male MC. Though the women MCs do not come forward, they are present—and they are no more (or less) battle shy than their male counterparts. They are not absent, invisible, or erased, contrary to popular perceptions.

Some of the young women are outside participating in hiphop ciphers where they display their lyrical skills by battling and evaluating with those around them. Others are enjoying the rhymes, mingling with friends, and working at the door or sales area. Still others are busy searching for new talent as they pursue their dreams of becoming a hiphop manager and mogul. Yet in the late-night throes of the powerful and intense lyrical MC battles on stage, their absence speaks volumes. Chu's request for female MCs is not an insincere gesture. Rather, it is a recognition that an important voice is not represented and has chosen to be quiet—and Project Blowed knows the women have made that choice. This choice is not simply about letting black men have the stage. Hiphop is dominated by young men hoping to become grown men, and in this setting every issue of masculinity and male sexuality is in play. For them, it is a space of power and control—if only for one night. As Tasha, a long-time (LT) member of Project Blowed explains, in its early days, Project Blowed was like the rest of hiphop: "OK, there weren't really a lot of females around. It was Medusa that was there as an artist. It was another person, her name was Tomigo, she goes by Sapha now, and she was an MC-poet. There was Vixen, who comes around from time to time. I can count, maybe, five to ten females that would come through."[1] Sometimes, a woman rocks the mic and the men step back and give her her due. More often than not, women simply decide to pursue another method of participation for the night in a space that suits them. The sheer number of young men present on Thursday nights guarantees that males usually control the mic, but the criteria for power and control is actually based much more on lyrical skills than on gender. Females who control the mic in the underground are few, but when they come forward there is one thing that is certain. They have outstanding skills.

This chapter explores the symbols, signs, and practices of women in the underground who carve out a female identity that, for them, embodies the emotional complexity and humanity of black women (Morgan and Bennett 2006). When women battle and represent in the underground, their lyrical weapons include an arsenal of symbols and information about being a black woman in American society. Their participation in underground hiphop as a female implies at least two things. First, their participation confirms their knowledge of the history of racism in the United States, the implications of social class in terms of services, rights, health, policing, education, and so on, knowledge about sexism and feminism, and knowledge about traditional notions of subservient "good" women. To demonstrate this knowledge, they constantly refer to and index women singers, song lyrics, and movie lines, as well as cultural and political figures. Second, they expect their notion of a female perspective to be evaluated as part of their lyrical skill. They represent and are proud of it. The widespread expectation is that female MCs have this knowledge irrespective of their educational or class background. It is crucial that these women not be viewed as naive but rather informed and empowered. The skill necessary to uncover and present the truth about life as a woman in spite of distortions about and attacks on women is referred to as science (e.g., feline science). I spell feminism as pheminism with *ph* in order to emphasize the notion that presenting a young woman's perspective requires a high level of skill and commitment to the science of hiphop.

Female MCs can devour and set to rhyme the black women's history, social life, and dreams of being treated with respect as women in America. The stories that they tell in their rhymes generally focus on the importance of love and care for themselves and the future of their community, children, family, lovers, and so forth. They tend to address these areas through five archetypal themes: their passion(s); what all women share as mothers and as caretakers; women in relationships with men; black women's relationship to white men; and black women's relationship to white women.[2]

When Project Blowed opened its doors as an underground workshop in 1994, the first Thursday night MC was a young woman named Medusa. She was chosen to control Thursday nights because of both her leadership and her lyrical skills. Medusa, who is often called the Angela Davis of hiphop and the queen and high priestess of the underground, connects generations of black women's struggles and of women's struggles as a whole, and the struggles of the black community in general. Her freestyle skills are legend, having won many battles with both men and women.[3] She infuses her rhymes with her sexuality and politics. She is friend, sistah, gangsta, lesbian, lover, mother, and all women. In her work "It's a Gift" (1999) she proudly proclaims her persona and answers the question of who she is and her role in the history of the world:

> Turning MCs to stone with every breath I take
> Afros transform into dreadlocks
> Historically mistaken for snakes.

Not only does Medusa represent, she is explicit about why she is, who she is, and how and why she has made her choices.[4] She takes great delight in explaining the significance of her name and the notion that those with straight and limp hair would view her long, unyielding, tangled, twisted

Medusa at the mic at Project Blowed. Photo by Tony B, courtesy of Project Blowed.

African hair as threatening snakes that can strike without warning. Her interpretation of the Medusa myth is not as an unpredictable, crazed woman but one that wrestles with images of women and "all generations" by interpreting lives and the social and political conditions of black women.

Of course not all underground female MCs are as versed as Medusa in the details of the treatment of black women in the United States. Still, many critics and scholars of hiphop agree that women MCs, in the words of Tricia Rose, "interpret and articulate the fears, pleasures and promises of young black women who have been relegated to the margins (1994, 146)."[5] While women may participate "for the love of hiphop," it is not clear how they develop the determination to participate and represent themselves within and against patriarchal ideologies and social contexts. They willingly participate and are evaluated in a male-dominated genre where they compete with men, regularly dispute male perspectives, and endure sexist and misogynist comments about women while representing an array of female perspectives and defending their right to do so. As women have continued their involvement in hiphop, they have been met with skepticism from a variety of sources.

In the midst of hiphop's rise into America's consciousness, concern over the representation and role of women often has been in the form of scandal, moral panic, and cultural and political hysteria. Since the mid-1990s, politicians and public figures have harshly derided hiphop artists and fans for what they deem to be widespread misogyny and violence in lyrics and in video and staged performances.[6] Scholars and many feminists criticize hiphop's violent imagery and misogyny. Yet while some of these critiques are encouraging, neither the public debate nor the debate in academia improves the day-to-day life of the young woman hiphop fan and artist. Her reality remains fraught with numerous threats and stereotypical media images of young urban women who are frequently cast in sexist, racist, paternalistic, and contested and convoluted notions of the black woman as strong, angry, promiscuous, ball busting, child bearing, crazy, and wild. Moreover, the representations of these notions of young urban women occur within a barrage of discursive practices and symbols of womanhood, motherhood, sexuality, authority, race, influence, and desire.

While it is clear that women in hiphop occupy a complex position and must struggle to be heard, they do not think that misogyny exists because men don't understand the situation of women—and of black women in particular. In spite of the difficulty of growing up in impoverished communities and having to deal with society's racist views, many women in hiphop are raised in protective extended families that include strong female influences, such as the mothers, grandmothers, and aunts who introduce them (and their brothers) to women's lives and struggles. Men growing up in African American communities are not oblivious to the social and political history of black women. Both the men and the women of hiphop know these facts about each other. Thus it is not uncommon for male artists to produce songs in tribute to their mothers, their children's mothers, and to the plight of black women in general. Tupac Shakur in "Dear Mama" (1995), for example, recognizes the sacrifice and love of black women as he repeats the refrain: "And there's no way I can pay you back. But my plan is to show you that I understand. You are appreciated." Many women in hiphop suggest that men disrespect them because it mirrors dominant culture's attitudes, and also simply because they *can* do it and get paid off handsomely at the same time—and all at black women's expense. The young women who participate in Project Blowed are aware of the contradictions and hypercritical representations of their generation. They are also invested in affecting change in popular culture and among their peers through understanding the social, political, and musical history of women of color, and black women in particular, that led to these representations. They link gender, sexuality, race, and class and argue that women cannot achieve parity without including all aspects of oppression as well as all aspects of their lives.[7] Moreover, they believe that their existence—who and what they represent—constitutes a threat to society in general and that they in turn are threatened by these stereotypes.

While it is apparent that women in underground hiphop consider the underground a liberating space, they are not naive and idealistic about their role in hiphop culture. However, they argue that compared to the rest of society, hiphop has the potential for parity because everyone must recognize when someone has skills—for which they must be respected and rewarded even if they are female, poor, and black. Mystic, an esteemed female underground MC from northern California, underscores the significance of this point in an interview with the radio host Garth Trinidad in 2001:

> I've always been a writer . . . first and foremost because it allows me to heal myself . . . hiphop is just a microcosm of the world. The same things that happen everywhere else happen in hiphop. . . . As a woman working on the 9 to 5 job on a day-to-day basis, you can bang your head on the glass ceiling for your entire life and never get anywhere. And something that's beautiful for me about being an artist is that I get up on stage, and if I put on a dope twenty-minute show, when I walk off— I have my respect. I have my honor. I have support and you can't really deny it. And everyone who was there saw it.

GARTH: "Bearing witness."[8]

The knowledge held by underground female MCs regarding the multilayered black woman's experience does not occur magically. They are taught the difference between unaware women and naive ones, and they are informed that they cannot afford to be either. As young women, they undergo this complex socialization and are taught about the harmful stereotypes of women, black women, and black men, as well as those other cultures and ethnic peoples.[9] They are also taught about behavior that is valued and rewarded by dominant society. They are expected to learn hard lessons and yet thrive with dignity and wit, and with a critique that results in deft skills. They must emerge as strong black women. Understanding the socialization that they undergo before and during their participation in the underground, especially how race, gender, and class are presented in relation to art, explains how and why they continue to represent in performances and lyrical battles.

I Cram to Understand U

In any society, the socialization of children involves making them aware of their role in society and culture, especially concerning expectations about the behavior of themselves and others.[10] Until the late 1990s, socialization for young black girls also included a focus on personal responsibility, on respect for one's body, and on the ability of women to support themselves and their family. During their teenage years, young black women in urban areas are often taught about the history of black women through numerous community, educational, and church programs for adolescent girls. This is not a program of anti-male teaching, but rather an ideology of self-reliance and self-respect. If these young women are directly involved in the arts, it is part of their socialization. If they are middle class and born in the United States, they may learn about it in feminist courses, but they will definitely learn the history of black women in the United States in African American studies courses. Knowledge of these struggles is also provided in family and community discussions and stories of slavery, in the depiction of slavery in movies, and in reading novels by authors like Toni Morrison, Alice Walker, and others. Young African American girls are provided with anecdotes, examples, and instances of how racism and sexism means that black women must set values and goals for their own dignity and not sacrifice their womanhood in the process.

The socialization process occurs, in part, through musical traditions that often connect younger generations to mothers, women, workers, singers, activists, and organizers who have struggled to place the lives and values of black working-class women within general American and African American culture (Davis 1998; Dawson 2001; Rose 1994; Bennett 2003). For women involved in underground hiphop, the lives of women performers cover both the secular and the sacred worlds, as well as the conflicting views about gender, romance, and sexuality that are seldom discussed within families. The lives of blues and jazz artists provided open and essential information about the world, women, and black life that was not available to most of the black population until the late 1960s. Women like Ma Rainey, Dinah Washington, and Bessie Smith were living proof that bad luck and trouble could be survived; the life of Billie Holiday was proof that it could also destroy you through drug use. The mere existence of these performers is testament not to what could happen to you if you were a black woman, but what did happen to black women with regularity. Blues singers took the old saying "All you have to do is stay black and die" to illustrate the deeply layered meanings and webs of irony, betrayal, bitterness, and longing that comprised staying black in America.

These women blues and jazz artists presented an identity that included critiques of middle-class idealism regarding wives, husbands, and the home. These comments were often contrasted with working-class realities, a longing for power regarding sexual relations, and knowledge of both the white and black world's attitude and treatment of women. Yet like hiphop, the world of blues performance was a man's world, and men sang of loss, injustice, irony, power, heartbreak, and the need to keep moving away from their hard luck and trouble. They sang about being a black man in a white man's world. Women blues singers, and later the jazz singers, sang about that same man's world where they try to please their men who are subjugated—and who also regularly abandoned them. They were often audacious in their depictions of a woman's life where romantic love was the equivalent of abuse and heartbreak and the only happy ending was getting out with a little dignity and "some of what you came with." They knew that their men's notion of a better world was to have the same power of white men, and they knew that that notion of power included the subjugation of women. Blues women chronicled the occurrences of patriarchal ideology with accounts of physical and sexual abuse and financial ruin. The Dinah Washington refrain "Ain't it a mean old man's world" is part of the irony of being a black woman in a land where a woman must constantly struggle against patriarchal oppression.

It is not surprising then, that the discourse of women in hiphop includes a recognition of the woman whose identity is tied to men, as well as a critique of the clueless and naive woman who lacks agency, who does not speak up or examine patriarchy or respect her sexuality, and who does not consider class, race, or culture. They also mock the dominant sexual ideologies of the modest, controlled, and charming white female versus the overtly sexual black female (Carby 1987). Hiphop artists build from the blues and then broaden their notion of womanhood to incorporate hiphop's female science and negotiate womanhood in a male-dominated setting. For instance, the lyrics of blues women often focused on cheating lovers, relationships, domestic violence, and the "ephemerality of many sexual partners" (Davis 1998). Yet hiphop underground women are intent on building a community and world that is fair minded and inclusive. Thus while women in underground hiphop include similar topics as did those in the blues (cf. Rose 1994; Pough 2004), they also articulate a position that is both individual and related to the collective good. Likewise, hiphop artists value lyrical skill and make a conscious effort to provide a full assessment and critique of racism and sexism, while offering alternatives that explicitly explore social class as well as desire, emotion, power, and patriarchy. Talented hiphop women toil alongside men when they want or need to (whether the men like it or not), and in so doing they challenge both patriarchy and prescribed notions of feminism. Hiphop women insist that they be valued and that their men and members of their community respect, defend, and love themselves and their women.

Four Women
The Subject of My Objectification

In urban communities there are numerous art, music, and dance programs designed to teach artistic skill and cultural knowledge, as well as to teach young women to know "their worth." In the summer these arts programs proliferate, and they generally include a season finale of entertainment for the community. A common theme in these programs is the history of racism and sexism relating to black women. This theme is treated as an artistic and socializing experience for young women, and it often occurs with the interpretation and performance of Nina Simone's seminal "Four Women" (1966)—a recording that has introduced many young African American women and men to the realities of racism and sexism.[11] In this work Simone describes four corporeal types of black women and then inextricably binds them to each other through their relationship to patriarchy, sexism, racism, and whiteness. "Four Women" is particularly significant because it is presented in first person, as though it is Simone's life. In this sense Simone is all four women.

Because the use of "Four Women" in dance programs for young African American girls is well known, it also became a subject of a hiphop recording by Talib Kweli (2000), a male hiphop artist who is popular with the underground. Kweli, like many underground male hiphop artists, was raised and influenced by his mother and other women in his community who had a feminist perspective.[12] I include it in this discussion because it reflects his interpretation of what he was taught about the black women's experience and because many young women hiphop fans consider it both creative and corresponding to their experiences.[13] Kweli's recording, called "For Women," is in discourse with the four black women canonized by Simone. It also reflects the hiphop generation's modern perspective on what the lyrics represent in terms of gender, race, and class. In many respects he represents the crowd of onlookers who applaud the young women who dance to Simone's sorrowful song in communities throughout black America.

The first woman that Simone introduces is Aunt Sarah. Her name indicates that she has no control of her own identity and life because it is an archetypal name given to slaves (and servants) by whites. The young woman who dances and interprets Aunt Sarah is usually dressed in the tattered clothes of a slave and often wears a headscarf knotted in the back. When Simone says the name Aunt Sarah, she almost whispers it with forlorn sadness, as if in grief. It is a name that depicts the black woman's role as servant and caregiver—the one who raises "other people's children." In the South, where the system of respectful address for women is Miss or Mrs., the term aunt or auntie is a sign of disrespect when used by whites toward blacks. It is Aunt Sarah who cleans, feeds, and raises the master's family.[14] Under slavery, this work comprises her entire worth. As Simone explains:

> My skin is black
> My arms are long
> My hair is woolly
> My back is strong
> Strong enough to take the pain
> Inflicted again and again
> What do they call me
> My name is Aunt Sarah
> My name is Aunt Sarah

Talib Kweli revisits Aunt Sarah in the year 2000 when she is 107 years old, riding on public transportation in Brooklyn. He describes her as a woman with strong memories, whose skin is black and who has *"lived from nigger / to colored / to Negro / to black / to Afro / then African American / and right back—to nigger."* He retells the story of why Simone wrote the song: "She said it was inspired by, you know, down South. In the South, they used to call her Mother Antie. She said, 'No Mrs.—just Antie.' She [Simone] said if anybody ever called her Antie she'd burn the whole goddamn place down." Kweli then says he is "overpast that" and marvels that the woman he meets in the Brooklyn subway is strong and determined rather than bitter. However, this bleak story of Aunt Sarah is also one of strength to those in hiphop. Kweli recasts her as powerful when it comes to caring for and protecting her own children instead of other people's children. He ends his story of Aunt Sarah with women softly singing/ moaning in the background as he says:

> Her back is strong and she far from a vagabond
> This is the back the master's whip used to crack upon
> Strong enough to take all the pain, that's been
> Inflicted again and again and again and again and flipped it
> To the love for her children—nothing else matters
> What do they call her? They call her Aunt Sarah.

The second woman in Simone's work, Safronia, also has a descriptive name. Unlike Aunt Sarah, whose name is associated with slavery and the white naming practices of black women, Safronia is a name within African American naming traditions. She is the color of saffron and her name identifies her conception as the result of rape by her mother's white master. Simone speaks the name Safronia while enunciating each syllable as though rather than being ashamed of her background, she is defiant proof of subjugation of black woman.[15] When a dancer represents Safronia, they usually begin with jerky, furtive moves. Her hands are outstretched and flailing in the air, as if in search of something.

> My skin is yellow
> My hair is long
> Between two worlds
> I do belong
> My father was rich and white
> He forced my mother late one night
> What do they call me
> My name is Safronia
> My name is Safronia

Talib Kweli places his interpretation of Safronia's existence within modern America where she is phenotypically white and still the product of the rape of her black mother. Rather than sorrowful, she is confused about her identity and filled with self-hate and spite. Unlike Nina Simone's Safronia, the product of slavery, she must make choices about who she is, as Kweli explains: *"People askin' her what she'll do when it comes time to choose sides."* Her inability to choose is seen as a weakness that leaves her powerless and vulnerable. Safronia concludes as a vulnerable woman who does not recognize her power and reconcile identity as she is left pleading eight times —*"Don't, don't, don't hurt me again."*

> Yo, her skin is yellow, it's like her face is blond—word is bond
> And her hair is long and straight just like sleeping beauty
> See, she truly feels like she belong in two worlds
> And that she can't relate to other girls.
> Her father was rich and white still livin' with his wife
> But he forced himself on her mother late one night
> They call it rape—that's right
> And now she take flight
> Through life with hate and spite inside her mind
> That keeps her up to the break of light a lot of times
> "I gotta find myself, I gotta find myself, I gotta find myself"
> She had to remind herself
> They called her Safronia the unwanted seed
> Blood still blue in her vein—and still red when she bleeds
> ((Don't, don't, don't hurt me again))

The third woman in Simone's tale is simply named *Sweet Thing*. Her naming is directly associated with the absence of family who might claim her and anyone who cares about her existence. Her purpose is to provide men pleasure, and Simone sings her name as both sorrowful and sensual. She enters the stage swaying her hips, smiling, and clearly aiming to please.

> My skin is tan
> My hair is fine
> My hips invite you
> My mouth like wine
> Whose little girl am I?
> Anyone who has money to buy
> What do they call me
> My name is Sweet Thing
> My name is Sweet Thing

In Kweli's hands, Sweet Thing bears the legacy of abandoned and unwanted girls everywhere. Their search for someone who cares often leads to pregnancy and further abandonment. They come to believe that the only option for young womanhood is to trade their body for money. For Kweli, Sweet Thing has the least possibility of hope.

> *My skin is tan like the front of your hand*
> *And my hair . . . Well my hair's alright*
> *Whatever way I want to fix it, It's alright it's fine.*
> *But my hips, these sweet hips of mine invite you, daddy.*
> *And when I fix my lips, my mouth is like wine.*
> *Take a sip. Don't be shy. Tonight I wanna be your lady*
> *I ain't too good for your Mercedes, but first you got to pay me*
> *You better quit with all the question, sugar. Who's little girl am I?*
> *Why I'm yours—if you got enough money to buy.*
> *You better stop with the compliments, we running out of time,*
> *You wanna talk whatever we could do that it's your dime*
> *From Harlem's from where I came. Don't worry about my name,*
> *Up on one-two-five they call me Sweet Thang.*
> *((sound of DJ scratches and women singing and moaning*
>   *in the background))*

The fourth woman in Simone's song is named Peaches, which is a nickname often given to headstrong young women who have conflicts with authority and who are often combative and do not suffer fools gladly. Many view the name Peaches as one that is about the "inside" of a person —that is, a sweet soul encased by a hostile and brittle exterior. Simone sings—shouts out—the name with outrage! When girls dance this part, they routinely enter the stage with clenched fists, ready to fight, defend, and stand for all women!

> My skin is brown
> My manner is tough
> I'll kill the first mother I see
> My life has been too rough
> I'm awfully bitter these days
> Because my parents were slaves
> What do they call me

My name is Peaches
My name is Peaches

Kweli uses the symbol of Peaches to describe the history of African American women as one of struggle, pride, defiance, and prevailing. Even more, he constructs her as the future of the black community because it is her children who will be protected from domination and who will prevail.

> But me, my skin is brown and my manner is tough,
> Like the love I give my babies when the rainbow's enuff,
> I'll kill the first muthafucka that mess with me, I never bluff
> I ain't got time to lie, my life has been much too rough,
> Still running with barefeet, I ain't got nothin' but my soul,
> Freedom is the ultimate goal,
> Life and death is small on the whole, in many ways
> I'm awfully bitter these days
> 'Cuz the only parents God gave me, they were slaves,
> And it crippled me, I got the destiny of a casualty,
> But I live through my babies and I change my reality
> Maybe one day I'll ride back to Georgia on a train,
> Folks 'round there call me Peaches, I guess that's my name.

In the songs of "Four Women," skin color is not a thing of beauty but rather one that represents the history and horrors of objectifying women. Hair is not an object but a symbol of ancestry and rape. The body is for working, child bearing, sexual pleasure, and a source of strength and power. The bodies of the four women are set for young women to retell the story and talk about womanhood, race, sexuality, family, relationships, love, sexism, life, and community. Nina Simone provides us with the hardworking slave woman, the child of a white male and a raped woman, the motherless and fatherless woman-whore, and the angry female child of a slave.

Hiphop gives us the modern version of Nina Simone's four women where Aunt Sarah defiantly claims her children, Safronia must resolve her identity, Sweet Thing exploits her sexuality, and Peaches, while damaged by slavery, has won the fight for the next generation. They are all black women who are negotiating the same sexist, social, and racial terrain. As Simone weaves their lives into hers, they become iconic symbols of the shades of womanhood and the shared subjugation, irrespective of skin color and parenthood, of the black woman. These women, their stories, and what they symbolize are learned as everyday experiences for many black women and women of color. As hiphop rediscovers and reframes these women to represent their generation, they are faced with how to continue as responsible black women and men. The lesson from the jazz and blues singers is clear. Black women have to take care of themselves and claim their own womanhood.

The Battle for "Real" (Ph)eminism
My Mamma Raised a G

Do the ladies love and birth our brothers?
(yeah, yeah)
Now love me back
Have my back
Support me black
Like I'm the MC and you the track
Nothing beats a failure but a try . . . you can make it if you try
Pave the, pave the
I promise to use mine
I promise to use mine
Pave the, pave the, pave the way

MEDUSA, "Nothing Beats a Failure but a Try"

Considering the socialization practices experienced by hiphop women, one of the more vexing criticisms they confront is that they don't consistently condemn misogyny from male hiphop artists and fans. Of course the question assumes that the women do nothing, as well as the more fundamental irony that American society is not misogynistic as well. The right to talk and represent oneself and one's community is a fundamental aspect of citizenship. Black women in particular have talked their way into visibility and worked to reframe family, womanhood, relationship, and sexuality to guarantee their right to represent women within American life. Yet no matter what image or ideology a hiphop woman represents, she operates within a male-dominated adolescent world where identities, roles, and status are constantly being explored and where participants are convinced that everything is at stake and everything is about them.

The hiphop nation's insistence on noncensorship and the representation of frank honesty and realism means that virtually any activity or opinion that exists can be reflected and critiqued. Within this system, silencing is an unacceptable practice since ideological censorship is viewed as the work of hegemonic forces attempting to co-opt and corrupt hiphop. But the hiphop community does not provide a platform for all views since it can be fanatically heterosexist. This is exacerbated by the conflicts and excesses that result from negotiating adolescent desire (and rejection), from the emerging and conflicting gender identities and roles, and from racism in a society that produces, avoids, and silences public discourse on sex and sexuality and the objectification of women in general. The misogynist representations of male desire—where any woman who does not support or like a man who likes her is by definition dishonest, scheming, unfaithful, or a lesbian—is one outcome of this situation (cf. Kelley 1995).

Considering the powerful language of male discourse and the overall protection that it receives, it is not surprising that research on teenage-girl identity finds that adolescent girls confidently reject constructs of feminism in favor of the "benign versions of masculinity that allowed them to be 'one of the guys' " (Fine and Mcpherson 1993, 127).[16] It is also predictable that they are conflicted regarding the expression of sexuality that is not exclusively dependent on men's and society's notion of the good woman. Yet, as Audre Lorde explains, "The erotic is a measure of our sense of self and the chaos of our strongest feelings" (1997, 280). Where the erotic may represent power and joy, it can also be objectified and represented as a loss of power through voyeuristic fantastic reinterpretations. It is precisely the tension created by unbridled male sexual exploration and the desire of young women to represent themselves honestly and unashamedly that creates an energizing space for young women. This space is one where all hiphop artists gain membership through artistic skills and where audiences and crews insist that their lives—including contradictions—be represented.

Hiphop is a vehicle through which to gain insight into how young African American women offer resistant voices. In fact Tricia Rose argues that hiphop women provide for themselves in a relatively safe free-play zone where they creatively address questions of sexual power, the reality of truncated economic opportunity, and the pain of racism and sexism (1994, 146). As Gwendolyn Pough explains: "When you call someone your sister or brother, or comrade in the struggle against racism, a bond is created. In that bond there is love. Rap music therefore offers space for public dialogues about love, romance, and struggle in a variety of combinations"

(2004, 86). Yet both freedom and play are complex notions in this zone since women are held to standards regarding notions of righteous and good that are related to subservience, motherhood, and silence. It is, therefore, a zone where they can play if they enter it armed with knowledge, skills, and a strong sense of women's history in general and black women's in particular. The pheminists of hiphop represent the science of how to incorporate emotion and desire and stand up for oneself, and protect, represent, and be oneself.

The women in Project Blowed are as much concerned with the development of artistic skills as is any other member. What distinguishes them from the men is that they build additional spaces for women to perform, and they are committed to building the cultural aspects of hiphop. For example, Medusa organized Feline Science, a performance venue that "is centered around the idea of the womb being your first universe, your first place of feeding, healing, and nurturing—it represents everything in its working order to give birth to the new."

Tasha Wiggins, a long-term participant in Project Blowed, explains how she organized Brave New Voices as part of the National Youth Poetry Slam, and how earlier she developed an arena for women to perform and thus increase their participation at Project Blowed: "Well, you know, I ran something for a little while called The Womb. And it was like a poetry circle, where we had female DJs, female hosts, and it was a poetry night at KAOS, and it brought out a lot more women . . . I think it might have been like a Wednesday evening. And . . . I think that had a lot of influence on the Blowed. Not only did it bring out women of poetry, but it brought men as well that were interested in poetry and it also brought the men to the Blowed. So, it helped increase the female population as well as, you know, more poetry based men into the Blowed as well."

Though there are many examples of women challenging misogyny and developing strategies to increase women's participation in hiphop, dominant society is not particularly interested in this form of womanhood and feminism. While hiphop women are committed to representing their lives and compete equally with men, their quest is not without peril and retaliation.[17] As the excerpt from Medusa's "Nothing Beats a Failure but a Try" suggests, it is common for hiphop women to support men and at the same time want to be respected and in control of their bodies. Women's representation of sex and sexuality is often within a set of principles that in-

Tasha Wiggins, long-term participant and member of Project Blowed. Photo courtesy of Tasha Wiggins.

cludes respecting one's body, making an effort to present the lives of women with complexity and to discuss sex with honesty, and ensuring that one never disrespects oneself. Supporting a man recognizes race and class hypocrisy in society and does not mean that the men make decisions for women. Rather, irrespective of who is leading, women hiphop artists argue that black men and women in particular are tied to each other through history and in the public imagination. That relationship should be addressed at all costs. Thus Medusa's argument concerns hiphop women who accept responsibility for their actions. She addresses some women who only present themselves as "Sweet Thing" while acknowledging that many men are looking for that. The challenge of the new pheminist is more difficult because the next level has to do with the "real self."

Females in the House
Pheminist Ethnography at Project Blowed

The importance of the symbols that young women learn through socialization about blues and jazz singers and the social and cultural contexts that they index was made clear one Thursday night when Venus, a female MC, decided to participate in the Project Blowed workshop. Chu, the Project Blowed MC, was once again in search of female MCs when Venus answered his call. She was there with some male friends or crew members, who I will refer to here as Friends of Venus (FOV).[18]

1	CHU:	Any females in the house tonight?
2	VENUS:	Yo, hey, right here right here!
3	SOMEONE:	Back up, back up, back up
4	CHU:	Females? Any females? Come on baby, alright, alright *(hands Venus the mic)*
5	VENUS:	Yo, yo, yo, yo, huh
6		Let me freak the mic
7		Like I'ma freak you,
8		Last night,
9		Nah, matter of fact,
10		That was tomorrow,
11		What the fuck, nigga
12		I'm Miss Motherfuckin' thorough
13		Nigga it's like your motherfuckin' pain,
14		'Cause I'm about to bring it on ya
15		Like a motherfuckin' Donna,[19]
16		What you wanna do, nigga? *((to Chu))*
17		Run up on ya,
18		You and your crew,
19		Get run thru like the Venus Poet
20		Gon' be all in you
21		Yo, Don can't battle me,
22		Or the crew,
23		Please grab the mic nigga
24		Bump that shit,
25		Coming through nigga
26		Nigga, nigga fuck that shit,
27		You wanna battle Venus,
28		She comes down here and slice you up,
29		Nigga coming thru,
30		What you, nigga
31		Fake ass 'fro
32		What you wanna do nigga
33		Fuck you coming through
34	CROWD:	*((laughing, booing, pass the mic))*
35	CHU:	*((talking))* Ahh boy, I tell you boy. You got sass like a mothafucka.
36		*((looking at the crowd))* That's Bessie Smith. That's some

37		Bessie Smith right there. *((Speaking to the crowd but looking at Venus))*
38		Y'all better learn 'bout y'all history. I know my jazz shit.
39		I'm . . . bump that shit. I'm on . . . that's cause they shook girl . . .
40		Alright, Yo, for sure
41	SOMEONE:	*((To* FOV*))* You gotta come on down
42	CHU:	*((To* FOV *who is shaking his head))* No disrespect, no dis-
43		respect homie. The crowd, disrespected her homie
44	FOV MAN:	Then I must apologize on the mic
45	CHU:	Na I'm sayin, I gave her the mic homie
46	FOV MAN:	I hope so
47	CHU:	*((begins rhymes))* Niggas wanna hope so,
48		I tell ya how to keep a dope flow -
49		nigga, I don't give a fuck about a nigga or a ho,
50		keep it low nigga
51		keep your punk ass on the floor . . .
52		you don't test my mic,
53		you the same nigga popping that woo woo woo, wooo wooo,
54		I give you the mic . . .
55		you ready to fight,
56		you better take the shit right, nigga
57		before you get the Kleenex,
58		there's tissue in the issue,
59		'cause I wouldn't wanna miss you . . .
60		I wanna pardon nigga,
61		startin nigga . . .
62		throw my hand on the trigger . . .

By line 34, the crowd is overcome with laughter and some are covering their faces with their hands as Venus and her friends turn angrily toward the critical audience. "Pass the mic" was heard several times during the performance. Clearly those present did not think Venus had lyrical skills. While her rhyming flow may not have been up to par, she also made several mistakes as an underground woman performer. The most egregious occurred the moment Venus mentioned freaking (or performing wild sex with) the men in attendance (line 7). The majority male crowd smiled, looked at her body, and began commenting on whether they wanted her. It is not unusual for a woman to use direct sexual references and still receive respect from the crowd. However, it is unusual for an MC to participate in her own sexual objectification. Unfortunately for Venus, she constructed an identity that suggested that she was unaware of the pheminist symbols. For example, she repeatedly used the offensive words *fuck* and *nigga* in ways that provoked the crowd as she framed her lyrical flow. As mentioned in chapter 2, the excessive use of these words may signal that an MC is not skilled enough to develop a lyrical argument. In line 16, when she asks what Chu wants to do, she answers in lines 17, 20, and 22 that she will run through and bombard everyone. Though she may have intended to speak metaphorically, what she said was interpreted as sexual. The crowd laughed and shook their heads, saying pass the mic, and her crew became more agitated.

Not only had the crowd called for Venus to leave the stage because she lacked skills, but also because she rhymed about only valuing herself as a source of pleasure and exploitation for men. Chu offered the most deafening rejection when he pretended to compliment her skills in lines 35–40. We know he's indirectly insulting her because he's not looking at Venus as he talks to her. We also know he is insulting her because we know that Chu knows that the blues legend Bessie Smith, much like Medusa, mixed her sex talk with irony and critique. He explicitly states his knowledge in line 38 when he says: "Y'all better learn 'bout y'all history. I know my jazz shit." He also suggests that he will take her up on having sex (lines 39–40) when he says, "I'm bump that shit, I'm on it." It becomes even clearer that disrespect is an issue when a FOV tries to take the stage and is asked to leave (line 41). Chu states that it was the crowd that disrespected her after he gave her the mic according to the rules.

Venus's time is over and her crew is supposed to accept that the crowd made its decision. Because a FOV did not want to respect the rules, Chu launches into a direct lyrical attack on Venus and the FOVs. In lines 47–62 he refers to Venus as a ho and calls her friends niggas ("*and not in no good way*"). The people around the stage get more agitated as the FOVS (and Venus herself) seem to want to physically fight for her honor. More insults fly as cooler heads jump onto the stage and agree that the main male FOV can participate in a battle. Though he takes the mic, he only looks at the crowd as they yell and laugh. Venus screams more obscenities and yells that she supports her man. Everyone calms down and gets back to business.

In contrast to Venus, Medusa is an MC who uses sexual references that maintain focus on herself as a lyricist rather than a sexual object.[20] In "Neck Lock," Medusa uses references to sex as a metaphor for her lyrical skills:

1	MEDUSA:	*((talking))* They tell me if I want some, get some.
2		I told them I'm here to make your neck lock
3		What you wanna do? What you gonna do with it?
4		Check it
5		*((begins rhymes))* I'm having this love affair with the saucy
6		rhymes, and I been kicking 'em
7		Soon as they leave my mouth, I be missing 'em
8		Bump the track ever quicker than any pimp can
9		Imagine taxing every beat that sets off heat
10		I'm beginning to feel like I'm some kind of hiphop freak
11		Leading you freaks to this freaky situation
12		Medusa style what?
13		Who you think you spacing?
14		You telling me you didn't see the hidden track when you came
15		around back?
16		Imagine that
17		They looking for they momma
18		And I'm the only one fitting a description like that
19		So drop the drama
20		I come with caution, the original tough skin
21		Like your momma, auntie, and they friends
22		See I'm the one who cares about where you're goin' and where you been
23		I'm not just flexing
24		I do it for the love of shocking your mind, body, and soul
25		When felines on the market
26		You would want to take hold and buy some stock
27		'Cause the buzz from the under is we bound to make some
28		necks lock
29	CHORUS:	Other MCs may make your head rock, but I'm gon make your neck lock

30 Other MCs, they may do it non-stop, but I'm gon make your
neck lock

In "Neck Lock" (an expression that references a physical reaction to orgasm) Medusa uses numerous sexual references to describe the intensity and significance of her lyrical skills. She begins by using the expression "want some," which is also used in reference to sexual desire. She describes her rhymes as saucy (line 5–6) and mentions pimps and freaks as well as alluding to anal sex (line 14–15). She then asserts that her point is to shock the listener (line 24) into focusing on her lyrical skills.

In "Pimps Down, Flows Up!" Medusa continues her critique of the current state of affairs in hiphop where the pimp and whore personas overwhelm the characterization of hiphop artists and female fans.[21] She first introduces her motivation for writing the lyrics as she talks to her audience.

> So that you get the poetic sense of hiphop,
> I have paragraphs so mad-
> I said I bring tension
> Worth mentioning like a good workout
> This ain't no floor show
> But we can flow sure
> This is for my peeps!
> Cause we about to get this clear, right
> This is my pimp

Medusa then launches into her performance and her attack is on how the pimp-whore stereotype undermines hiphop, black people, and women in particular.

> Now it's pimps down. Flows up
> Medusa's on the set
> Hurry up, run, duck
> When I reach for the mic it's like
> Wait a minute girl, wait hold up, girl hold up
>
> Now it's pimps down. Flows up
> Medusa's on the set
> Hurry up, run, duck
> When I reach for the mic it's like
> Wait a minute girl, wait hold up, girl hold up

I got paragraphs for mad they correcting Hitler's diagram of man
He was like MCs now what they talking—the wrong shit and still
    got a gang of fans
Well here I am up and jumping the *boogie-to-the-rhythm-to-the-*
    boogie-to-be

Mine to ride till I finish the *oops upside your head*
With this underground style
I teach your sister with the first verse
And the beat goes on cause y'all in denial
I heard you call *Tyrone* for help but you couldn't get no dial tone
I'm like *shake them shake those balls*
So I can lay my thang
And don't worry I'll let you get some licks in before my Domino
    will lock up a gang
I'm gonna lyrical spit in any category
See the cats coming y'all know my story
Don't have to shade me cause I be fucking with the tramp story
With the old
Medusa will get your backpack
C9 and 45
Pay attention
Tell you a little something about you
A pimp ass show
I'm tryin to see how she's going to rhyme
Pimps down and flows up

Call that rappin'? I'm instigatin' the rappin'
With that want some, get some
I'm instigatin' the rappin'
With the flows up
Medusa's on the set hurry up
Wait a minute girlfriend hurry up

    "Pimps Down, Flows Up!" is in reference to a unexpectedly popular
HBO documentary from 1999, *Pimps Up, Ho's Down*, which examines the
life and perspectives of pimps. Medusa's argument is against what has
become a relentless parade of artists who command the attention and

Women in the crowd at Project Blowed. Photo by Tony B, courtesy of Project Blowed.

devotion of young, beautiful women who in turn are mistreated as sexual objects. She defends hiphop by claiming the underground as the place where hiphop lives. She indirectly speaks to the men who support sexism and misogyny as she states: "With this underground style / I teach your sister with the first verse." She also compares the support of hiphop MCs who use these styles as being like following Hitler and his notion of race and man, and she rhymes and argues: "He was like MCs now what they talking—the wrong shit and still got a gang of fans." She boasts that she can lyrically spit in any category and on occasion reels off old-school flows from the Sugarhill Gang like, "Well here I am, up jump the boogie to the rhythm of the boogie, the beat."[22] Instead of directly criticizing the misogyny and sexism, she references it by using lyrics produced by MCs known for producing misogynistic lyrics like Mystical, Beanie Sigel, and Jay-Z. She also references songs popular in African American communities like "Oops Upside Your Head" (Gap Band, 1995) and "Tyrone" (Eryka Badu, 1997).[23]

Medusa further exposes sexual ideologies when she sings her crowd-pleasing anthem "My Pussy Is a Gangsta." This song is particularly striking because she uses gangsta, a hiphop term associated with misogynistic, predatory, and sadistic men, with a woman's sexual and reproductive or-

CHAPTER FOUR

Medusa's "W" sign. Photo by Badru, courtesy of Project Blowed.

gan. She skillfully unfolds a story of a woman who is powerful in bed but does not realize her full potential until she looks beyond pleasing others. The story is, in fact, one of the uncaring gangsta who doesn't really care about and respect herself. As she sings, women smile broadly and yell and nod their heads in affirmation while men stare, smile wryly, and often lower their heads as though they are a bit guilty of something. In an interview Medusa explains why she wrote the song and developed the rhymes: "Some women abuse . . . using femininity to their extreme advantage. In that song I'm saying 'This pussy is a gangster, but I don't want her to be,' . . . because if I'm not using the pussy to get to you, then you're not going to be chasing me just for the pussy. In other words, we'll have to deal with each other on a whole other level, a mental and spiritual level, and that song is about how it's hard to really get to know someone on that other level. When you cut that G out of the game, you kind of have to deal with your real self for a minute" (Hassey 2005).

The manner in which Medusa and other artists represent sexuality, sex, oppression, and so on to highlight rather than supplant their lyrical skills is at the heart of the underground. Overwhelmingly, underground women artists argue that feminism and sexuality do not determine their skill as an artist, and they are determined to say it the way they see it. Women MCS reflect a multiplicity of perspectives and discourses about relationships, sex, desire, friendship, and issues facing young women.[24] They do not submerge their sexuality but rather want to be judged with it intact as a way to highlight their skills. They are pheminists, and irrespective of and because of their sexuality they are focused on their community and their right to be heard and represented.

You Asked, I Came—Now Listen

The females of the underground who practice their skills at Project Blowed do so with determination, skill, and a great sense of self-worth. Their discourse represents their knowledge as women who desire to thrive in a society that is sexist, racist, and biased against the working class. They recognize that participation in hiphop as equals is also a political act that highlights the life of women throughout society in both direct and indirect ways.

Tasha of Project Blowed recognizes that the situation for young women is difficult. She also realizes that because of her activism things may get better. She describes her experience with Brave New Voices and the National Youth Poetry Slam (two events for young people engaged in hiphop culture that included girls who were full of hope and purpose):

I'm ready for female MCS to come out with lyrical content and be female MCS. I lost full faith in that, until last month. . . . [They were] ages thirteen to nineteen. It was Hiphop. And it gave me faith in Hiphop again, even though they put it under the word poetry. I mean, poetry is Hiphop and Hiphop is poetry. But it made me see girls being girls, and women being women. The big difference was that they had a lot of knowledge, a lot of information. They were being politically influenced. These were conscious kids saying something.

Yeah, and this made me realize that this next generation can definitely make the change in this musical content. And it's going to have to come from a knowledge base because just shaking it, and juggling it, and talking about the same thing that the people in the mainstream are talking about isn't going to work.

But, I didn't have faith until this event took place. April fifteenth, it took place. And it made me realize there was hope for the women in the game.

Female MCS use hiphop to develop and display their lyrical skills as well as to present and challenge what it means to be a young black woman in America and elsewhere in the world. They are aware that the same system that stereotypes them as promiscuous, culpable, and irresponsible actually exploits their lives and bodies to promote sexism, racism, and class privilege. Women in the underground do not assert that their aim is to use their musical and verbal skills to destroy racial, gender, and class discrimination. Instead they prefer to expose the bigotry so that it can be seen and critiqued and manipulated as a symbol, warning, and memory of what it has meant to live under both its legal and de facto reign. They speak of their part in a tradition of mothers, women singers, activists, and organizers who have worked to place the lives and values of black working-class women within general American and African American culture. They believe that the torch was passed to their generation, and they plan both to run with it and to use it to incinerate female stereotypes—if necessary.

The passion in hiphop for a "fresh" representation of womanhood is not focused exclusively on the inclusion of young African American women. It is part of the "world economy of passion" (Savigliano 1995) and proposes to reframe feminism to acknowledge and incorporate aspects of all women's lives. Yet this passion is not only about emotion, and desire, but about the emotional connection that one has to aesthetics, culture, memory, and so on. Hiphop women argue that the desire to be included as women in society is the passion to be accepted as a product of all of women's experiences. Furthermore, as Dionne Bennett argues, this desire and passion has political implications in that it makes "the most private of interactions culturally and socially meaningful" (2003, 14).

Most successful female MCs recognize that for them the only place where they can negotiate race, class, gender, and sexuality with relative freedom is the hiphop world. It is not an ideal space but rather one populated by those searching for discourse that confronts power. Everyone in that world expects to be respected. Young feminists are watching as hiphop women develop their skills, represent their communities, and demand respect from and for their brothers who along with the rest of society are slowly and reluctantly losing their hostility and ambivalence about showing solid respect for them. They accept their turn at being "the problem" with a refreshing kick-ass fierceness that encourages women everywhere to discuss their lives openly. As Medusa explains: "I ride to the rhythm that is given to me and I travel to where the spirits take me through and you know what I'm sayin? 'Cause this is what Medusa is all about— bringing the generations together, giving you all the facts of music from the past. I'm showing you that there is something to look forward to."

Politics, Discourse, and Drama

"RESPECT DUE"

Life as we know it is about to change
I smell it within the air the weather is
  getting strange
Drugged up sedated and numb from the
  pain
The sickness in Amerikkka has spread to
  her brain
She is no longer fit to make good
  decisions
She is completely blind and void of any
  vision
She parties hard and she keeps her
  conscious mind in prison
Therefore she's heading for the ultimate
  collision
She can no longer hide the scars on her
  face
The innocence now gone is hard to replace
She has no shame no remorse or any grace
She embraces the devil and she hates
  over race
Ms. Amerikkka the beautiful the free
Fallin' within the cracks I wish that you
  could see
She buried a misery within society
It's obvious you have no regard for me

Chorus:
We caught up—in the belly of Amerikkka
Lost—in the stomach of Amerikkka
Broken down—in the bowels of
  Amerikkka
Sinking—in the garbage of Amerikkka
Stuck—in the brain of Amerikkka
Suffering—in the body of Amerikkka
Lying—in the wicked spirit of Amerikkka
Dying—in the old soul of Amerikkka
Trying—in the good ole spirit of
  Amerikkka

ACEYALONE, "Ms. Amerikkka"

ON THE FATEFUL NIGHT of January 4, 1996, Leimert Park Village turned on Project Blowed, which by this time was one of the premiere underground hiphop scenes in the United States and the hippest corner in LA. Just before the LAPD launched their offensive, the Project Blowed MCs were involved in their workshop: caught in the rhythmic and intoxicating flow of competition and representation, the crowd was judging the lyrical battles with their hands waving Ws in honor of the victor. But then the riot squad burst in with guns drawn. By all accounts, before that moment it had been a creative and exciting night. Ben Caldwell recalls the scene as follows:

CHAPTER FIVE

I was like standing up here, videotaping, and it was one of the better nights. It was the best night that I felt that we had, it was just really, really sweet. It was really kicking and, it was like a posse of guys who were a part of the Good Life that were there. They were just like having fun and so it was really, good. And they were just passing the baton on; and each one of them had, you know, really some serious stuff to say. And I was like saying, "Wow, now this is really good." And I was really impressed!

So in the middle of all of this, someone's like "Ben," and this guy is showing me his shield and said, "Come outside!" He was, one of the undercover guys.

According to those present, the LAPD then entered the main room. The DJ froze the turntables, as all of the people inside were ordered to lie on the floor, face down, and spread their arms and legs. Some individuals were screaming, others were swearing and talking in loud tones. As the undercover cop escorted Ben outside, one very pregnant woman with dreadlocks was explaining to an officer that she could not lie on the floor. She was grabbed by her hair and pulled back. Some yelled that they had rights; and the authorities explained that they had none. Outside, the police told Ben that they had come in response to complaints of overcrowding. In fact, the fire marshal had visited weeks earlier and set the limit at one hundred; given that limit, Project Blowed was not overcrowded. Then the police argued that there were fire hazards (there were none), and that the merchants had complained of noise. Then they said there were reports of gang activity. Everyone inside was ordered to disperse.

In an article titled "Clubbed at KAOS," the *LA Weekly* reporter Donnell Alexander offered a report of what happened: "The trouble began when LAPD vice cops raided KAOS Network at about 11:30 PM. Police demanded the workshop be closed because the crowd size exceeded the fire-code limit. Within a half-hour, artists were confronting police, who had grown to a large throng of officers from the Wilshire, Southwest and 77th stations." What really happened? Alexander reports that vice officers said they received complaints from the community and from Leimert Village merchants. They said a female inside Project Blowed pushed a female officer. Once outside, the crowd defied the police incursion, threw bottles, and refused to leave the area.

According to bystanders, a somewhat different set of events occurred. They recounted that the police forced to the floor a Project Blowed participant who was very pregnant and demanded she lie face down. Those present said the police soon ordered the Project Blowed participants to disperse, but then they would not allow them to go to their cars to do so. The youths refused, however, to walk out of the neighborhood after midnight and leave their means of transportation behind.[1] Meanwhile, the police continued their interrogation of Ben, who recalls: "So I was out there. And we went. And then I showed them that I had my business thing [license] that I had to get with the city. It had me as a school and also as a professor, professional filmmaker and, and professor, you know. That was a part of what my job was, and it is a part of my class. And they said 'OK that's not going to work. You're gonna have to tell everybody to get out.' "

When Ben reentered his establishment, he was not aware of the activities that had developed inside while he was being questioned outside. He reports that he went to the stage and stated to those gathered there: "We're surrounded, so just chill out and just disperse and go home and we'll come back next Thursday. And we will deal with these guys. And so, they went out. And they were surrounded! It frightened everybody! And they said, 'Ben, I can't get to my car you know 'cause the cops have our cars in' and I'm like so I'm like, 'What's up with this? You know, they can't leave. You're telling them to leave and they can't leave!' And they were like 'Oh, yeah.' As they [the police] were doing it, they came closer and closer to my front door. Then they were going into my building! And that was at the point that I came from outside to in. When I came in, then there were some real interesting dramas."

The police attack on Project Blowed may have been the result of politics, racism, corruption, jealousy, and so on, but it was also framed within African American discourse styles. Discursive practices can function as symbols of political ideology. This is especially true in hiphop. African American speech communities have a highly developed system of discourse that arose during slavery and continued to develop until the end of the civil rights and Black Power movements. This system of discourse ensures that even when communication is suppressed and monitored, it is possible to convey ideas that contradict dominant ideology (Morgan 2002; Smitherman 1999, 2000; Labov 1972; Baugh 1999; Gates 1988). It is in this sense that the analysis of the relations and interactions that were the catalyst(s) that motivated the police attack on Project Blowed, as well as Project Blowed's response, provides a treatise on the discourse of contestations based on race, class, gender, ethnicity, sexuality, and power. The untangling includes a cast of players who enact multiple and often con-

flicting identities through language that reflects knowledge of both African American and dominant culture. Just as hiphop battles are constructed through lyrics, words, and verbal genres, political and community
acts involve actors who construct their positions and battles through the
power of the Word.

The Leimert Park cast includes community residents, merchants, politicians, police undercover agents, cultural outsiders, parents, supporters,
and more. As might be expected, these participants represent contested
ideologies on the role of youth, the Leimert Park Village, and African
American adults—that is, the entire African American community. Their
discursive practices include verbal genres, symbols, and interaction rituals
that intentionally create complex contestations. This chapter focuses on
these practices as well as on the ideological growth of the counterpublic as
part of the regeneration of public icons and spiritual and religious symbols. Discourse in African American speech communities is not only
significant as a means of communication; African American discourse
can be a political and highly symbolic act that must be interpreted. In this
respect, community talk is also a form of action. The police assault on
Project Blowed changed "the village" so that it was not only not "a good
day" but also impossible to re-create a "beautiful day in the neighborhood."[2] The event revealed that the "hippest place in LA" could simultaneously turn on itself, devour its young, and deliver a cruel political lesson
in return.

The Revenge of the Village
"You Had the Right to Remain Silent"

Many of the youths who frequent Leimert Park and Project Blowed are the
offspring of a community that has nurtured them. Though relationships
and interactions have been strained at times, the youths did not suspect
that the adults could be a threat to their project. Yet by all accounts the
concentration of proud youth, full of hard-won self-taught knowledge, in
conflict with authority and respect norms, was a potentially incendiary
situation. To make matters worse, the number of artists and entrepreneurs
who routinely worked with youth was limited (see chapter 1), and many of
the shop owners thought their own economic problems were somehow
caused by the youth.

The unraveling of the carefully crafted peaceful existence between Project Blowed and the Leimert Park merchants occurred through a series of complaints and rumors that had predictable implications. The complaints were shared, both publicly and informally, among the merchants, and in some cases also with the police. They are part of a system of indirectness that relies on hearers and overhearers (Morgan 1993; 2002) to use their local knowledge about the history of African Americans in the United States, especially regarding prejudice and racism. This system results in a counterlanguage—an independent method of discourse and interpretation that is known to a group whose interactions are constantly monitored and regulated (Morgan 1996, 2002). This system also includes knowledge of the local community and discursive practices that recognize the power of talk. Knowledge of this system reveals how a complaint, within African American speech community norms, can be interpreted as a demand to attack Project Blowed.

Within the African American community, verbal acts may function to save social face as they address multiple audiences, some aware and some unaware, through ambiguity and camouflaging (Morgan 2002; Rickford 1999; Fisher 1976). Participation in social acts, including political organizing, is influenced by how members of the speech community determine what someone actually means and intends. Intentionality and responsibility are viewed as both socially situated and constituted so that speakers and audience collaborate in determining what is meant by what is said (Duranti 1993; Irvine 1993). Thus speakers who are indirect actually mean to target certain individuals and they mean to do so indirectly. Of course, indirection, with its nuanced use of local knowledge and symbols, is learned through practice, and individuals are socialized as to the rules of usage. This is why a phrase like "you people" is considered an extreme insult when spoken by non-African Americans and those of social privilege. One learns early and quickly that *you* is an exclusive reference and does not include the speaker, thus automatically signaling that the speaker believes that he or she does not share the same characteristics of *people* as the target of the utterance. This in turn establishes a dichotomy and a hierarchal system, thereby establishing the separation of *us* versus *them* (Morgan 2002). Because indirection is so prevalent, much is at stake and much must be known in order to determine a speaker's intention and also to make one's intentions clear (see the introduction).

Adolescents play games of indirection as part of social, cultural, and language socialization (cf. Morgan 2002; Goodwin 1990, 2006; Schieffelin and Ochs 1986). Both males and females participate in ritualized and episodic verbal disputes that focus on the tension between *play* and *getting played*. To play is to participate in activities that result in pleasurable feelings. To *get played* is to be made a fool because one did not realize that he or she was simply an object of playful pleasure. African American culture employs numerous expressions to refer to this notion. A related word of significance to play is *game* and the expression *"game recognize game."* One is said to *"have game"* when they have the ability to persuade and at times mislead others to do what they want.

Childhood verbal games of indirection like signifying and sounding (e.g., "yo mama" jokes) are concerned with learning the difference between play and being played (Morgan 2002). These are games of possible and probable social contexts. Whether a context is plausible or implausible is based on both political stance and local knowledge. Consider, for example, the following popular joke: "If a black and a Mexican are in the back of a car, who's driving? The police!" The irony of the joke, at least according to the numerous adults and several young people I spoke to, is that it is a critique of the reality show *Cops*. In this show, whenever there is a black or Latino male suspect, he is being placed into the back of a police car. So it is a comment on racist representations as well as surveillance and the way in which the communities share the problem of racist treatment and representation.

The notion that indirection may be used to represent political and ideological positions also seeps into debates surrounding how African Americans should be referred to in legal writings. In May 2005, the Federal Court of Appeals, Seventh Circuit, heard a case concerning an informant who supplied testimony at an earlier trial in order to determine whether any legal procedures had been violated. A footnote in the opinion of the case referred back to the original trial and raised the question of whether there had been an indirect racial insult: "The trial transcript quotes Ms. Hayden as saying Murphy called her a snitch bitch 'hoe' . . . We think the court reporter, unfamiliar with rap music (perhaps thankfully so), misunderstood Hayden's response. We have taken the liberty of changing 'hoe' to 'ho,' a staple of rap music vernacular as, for example, when Ludacris raps 'You doin' ho activities with ho tendencies.' "[3]

What was the intentionality of the footnote reference? Was it intended as a racial insult? Was the clerk who wrote this "clarification" a misguided fan of hiphop? Was it an attempt to bring humor to a reference that will appear in law books for decades? Are sex, race, and class-based humor appropriate in formal legal writing? How did the clerk or judge come by the reference to Ludacris, and did they intend to insult women, and black women in particular, with the quote?

What has this to do with the notion of complaint? Everything. Adult indirect interactions both expose and hide the intention of the speaker in order to unravel who got played and how and why they are being played. The distinction between adult and teenage signifying is that adults "don't play." Thus signifying complaints from adults always index both the speech community and the fact that a serious point is being made. It is yet another way to talk about someone negatively and indirectly. It is not necessary that complaints be based on truth, evidence, or specific instances. Rather, complaints in the African American speech community represent the speaker's attitude and how the speaker feels about the particular target in general. Consequently, we must consider whether a complaint to or in the hearing of the Los Angeles police about the perceived negative behavior of black youth can ever simply be a discursive exercise.

Said It, Meant It

The complaints attributed to Project Blowed that emerged through my interviews and basic interactions with those involved were as follows:

1   Merchants lost business because the presence of the youths
     kept adults away.
2   Youths littered and threw trash on the street.
3   Ben Caldwell was operating a club without a license.
4   The youths used and sold drugs.
5   The youths marked graffiti on private property.

As I described in chapter 1, many of the Leimert Park proprietors represent traditional middle-class African American values of respect of elders and property as well as the black nationalist beliefs that lack of respect is an indication of the absence of African American culture—and good home training. Consequently, their identity as black nationalists or community proprietors did not necessarily include advocating for the youth. Thus they felt it was appropriate to complain.

The structure of complaints as a discourse genre in African American speech communities is particularly significant. For example, a direct complaint like "You play your music too loud" is regularly interpreted as an accusation and a command to turn down the music. That is, it is interpreted and the reaction or lack thereof is considered an acknowledgment of the discourse ideology (Althusser 1971). The listener, target, and speech community member each has the responsibility to interpret the meaning and potential meaning of what is being said (Morgan 1993, 2002; Duranti 1993). Thus while it is a direct statement it is also one that embeds a request or demand for action, but not necessarily a verbal response. One cannot respond with "Thank you," but one can discursively act by saying "Too bad. So what." This particular style is in contrast to complaint signifying where upon hearing the intrusive music an individual will say, sarcastically, "I love to hear my favorite song." Or even "I've heard that song ten thousand times already!" or "So all you know is Jay-Z?" All questions and statements recognize that the playing is loud enough to hear, but neither requires an immediate and direct response. It is the speaker that generates the implication (Grice 1975; Levinson 1983), and by commenting on something not inherent in the logic of the social context the speaker has introduced the complaint discourse. Consequently, the target or offender appears guilty if he or she argues with the implication, since the music is too loud!

Because one must be aware of speech community norms, it is possible to provide a signifying complaint where others do not understand it as such, as well as to provide a regular directed one. As described above, complaints often mask the social and cultural basis of the conflict; though within the speech community the masking is highly marked. The question arises when the complaint is directed to an unambiguous symbol of state power like the police. At issue is not whether one intends for the police to interpret the complaint as a request to act; it is well within the realm of possibility. Rather, the issue is whether a member of a speech community can reasonably defend making an indirect complaint to the police about young black men in America. Can a person reasonably argue that they were using a discursive strategy (just talking) rather than an indirect request for action? This question is relevant even if the police are members of the African American community since they must choose the speech community ideology that will direct their action. Considering that Leimert Park's signifying complaints occurred during the height of the criminalization of the urban black male described earlier, the act of complaining was a reckless one that symbolized the merchants' distance from the youth of Project Blowed.

Ben Caldwell and Project Blowed worked to address the merchants' accusations, many of which were not true. Because the complaints actually masked the general grievance among the merchants that the youths did not show them their proper respect, and since the youths largely ignored the grievances from the merchants, the problem could not be mediated. The youths used mainly respectful language toward the merchants, but they did not consider them figures to emulate. They reasoned that the merchants had made too many compromises to the system and did not deserve more than a polite greeting—and they made that position clear. In particular, the youths did not make an effort to listen to the merchant's talk about what they had accomplished in life, and they did not insist that visitors to the community show them respect as well.

The youths felt that the energy and future of Leimert Park rested with them, and the merchants strongly disagreed. According to Ben Caldwell, the simmering animosity between the members of Project Blowed and the Leimert Park Village merchants was palpable:

It was bad. It was bad. It was bad. It was too bad! One of the things that was happening was Blowed was starting to rise up on one level. And the kids were getting cocky—and, they were kids! Still, um, it was a lot of energy; the mental energy was real tight in here.

Another thing that was happening—I was going to sell my building. . . . The guy who was really interested in buying this facility was starting to work the community . . . and they didn't want hiphop in the mix you know. So, I was being talked about very badly. They were really kind of, dissing me, a lot, mainly because of the youth. It was a rough and ready element and they were a little bit frightened by the kids, even though they had never really done anything. It was nothing really tangible. It was just their own fear.

In fact, the police defended the raid by alleging that they had complaints regarding gang activity and overcrowding—complaints that were never mentioned in discussions with merchants or residents. The police did not interpret complaints about loss of business, increased trash, and graffiti as a manipulation of and reference to public, negative, and stereotypical symbols of black urban youth. There was no indication that the LAPD considered that the merchants might have used those symbols as signifying weapons with which to chide the youth. Instead, they referred to the complaints as indicative of gang activity. Likewise, the accusation that Ben was operating a club without a license suggested overcrowding to the LAPD rather than potential jealousy or competitiveness from merchants.

The merchants, the older generation, spoke negatively about the youth in the presence of the police and their agents, though not necessarily directly to them. Yet they were very aware of the stereotyping of youths and the regular attacks on them. The merchants who participated in this type of complaint knew that when Emmett Till was lynched in Mississippi in 1955, it was after white supremacists "overheard" black men saying he whistled at a white woman while at the local grocery store. They talked about this in a situation where they knew they could be overheard and that Emmett Till could be severely attacked for the accusation. The white supremacists that heard that story lynched Emmett Till in a fashion that was savage even for the time. The Leimert Park merchants may have wanted something to happen, but they had no control over what would actually happen. And they knew it. The youths could not prove that the older generation set them up through their complaints. Most of the older merchants claimed that they did nothing wrong and were not responsible.[4]

Flipping the Script
By Any Means Necessary

As the attack on Project Blowed reveals, profound misunderstandings resulted from the impasse created by an older generation, whose mode was to organize politically around shared circumstances and uniform methods of recognition and representation, and the hiphop generation, whose aim was to celebrate diversity and engage in contest and debate. Yet black political thought has historically reflected lively critique and debate regarding the nature of political power and representation. According to Michael Dawson (2001), it is traditionally framed around contrasting visions of freedom and how to achieve these visions. Past political leaders and iconic figures like Jesse Jackson, Fannie Lou Hamer, Marcus Garvey, Malcolm X, and Martin Luther King Jr. each embody ideologies regarding the concept of just societies, citizenship rights, representation, and power.

There is clear evidence that the hiphop generation "flipped the script" and thus effectively destroyed an idealistic representation of black leadership. This representation was then replaced with one that thwarts the mischief of "politics as usual." The question for many is how to create unity and develop political leadership and effective representation based on a hiphop discourse style that, while acknowledging indirection, is actually based on directed critique, contestation, and fragmentation. While the result may appear to some to be the dissolution of a political movement, it is also an act that reclaims and recuperates the political movement. The hiphop political movement is in the form of the fracture discussed earlier (Turner 1974, 1982), where the contestation itself becomes the positive force that increases activity and creates a new or at least renovated arena for activity.

In the 1990s it was essential for youths to create a support system of their own since they lived through many political attacks from those in power, which were met with muted responses from their communities (see chapter 1). These young people were under constant attack, and they were even named superpredators (DiIulio 1995). The press then created a situation of anxiety based on the juvenile superpredator about to unleash a reign of violence and terror on American society (Males 1996, 1999). The attacks on youth included brutal sentencing laws that treated crack cocaine —used in higher proportions by poor and working-class youth of color— with extremely severe punishment compared to laws relating to the powdered cocaine used mainly by members of the white middle and upper class. With the addition of the three-strike laws where a petty third offense can mean a lifetime in prison, coupled with brutal and relentless gangs that deliver street justice with no protection from law enforcement or parents, young people had no one to represent and no one to protect them. The notion of stable political leadership and symbols all but abandoned the youth's communities.

As Faria Chideya (2004) observes, both the Republican and Democratic parties were hostile to the new critical voices of hiphop youth. In the late 1990s, the people of the United States saw their country invade both Iraq and Grenada. They also witnessed President Bill Clinton attack Sister Souljah, a politically conscious black nationalist rapper, in order to show middle-class communities that he did not favor black youth. In this environment, rather than abandon previous ideological models hiphop youths incorporated them into the fragmented, unstable, hypocritical life that was their reality. They developed a perspective that pitied anyone who argued for participation in what they perceived as a corrupt system. Hiphop was at least one answer to those who wantonly attacked youth, and it expressed that those who represented the other perspective were the problem. It was this situation that led to the conflict that January night in Leimert Park Village.

With the introduction of hiphop lyrics and activities, an enigmatic political ideology spread among youth in black communities that contested both the visions and the strategies to achieve freedom previously developed as a defining force among black political ideology. While hiphop artists argue that America's true religion is money, African American's conviction is the relentless pursuit of true freedom, fairness, and equality. It has included back-to-Africa movements, armed struggle, Christianity, communism, parliamentary politics, the courts, black nationalism, the Nation of Islam, migration, liberalism, conservatism, and pyramids in Egypt and, recently, on Mars. As Dawson explains:

In turn, grassroots African Americans have reinterpreted and applied these ideologies in ways not always anticipated, or approved of by activist and elite ideologues. Throughout black history these different visions of freedom have been influential in shaping black political attitudes and practice. At other times, these ideologies have been quiescent, having a barely noticeable effect on either political practice or debate with black communities.

These ideologies, and the discourses around them, form the core of black political thought, which historically has not only captured the range of political debate within the black community, but has also produced one of the most trenchant critiques of the theory and practice of American "democracy." (2001, 2)

For the hiphop generation, symbolic public and political figures and their respective ideologies and discourses include the deconstruction, reformulation, and critique of power and injustice in general, irrespective of whether an iconic figure is part of the African American freedom and political movement. For hiphop youth, ideological leaders and figures prominent in African American political and social history are commodified, commercialized, and recast within a public, high-tech, global economy. The overall commodification is not regularly viewed as disrespectful but rather the explicit recognition of the market and ideological value associated with the person/icon.

The critique by youth results from noticing the difference between public and private recognition of the contributions of political figures, and realizing that these figures have been appropriated and reconfigured to fit the hegemonic discourse. They live in a world where Martin Luther King

Jr. is a holiday rather than a symbol of freedom, justice, and equality. This holiday is also a time when authority figures, who have introduced and supported laws that target youth of color and poor youth, give speeches about race and class tolerance.[5] Once hiphop youth have critiqued, picked apart, and reassembled iconic figures for themselves, the public person becomes associated with symbolic representations that are highly indexical within the hiphop community and yet paradoxical and sometimes insulting outside of it. Hiphop artists reassemble the ideological positions associated with previous leaders to reflect the major shifts in the life of the young, vibrant, technological African American community. They rebuild and recast leadership as flawed and struggling and focus on the lessons of leadership as they relate directly to their pursuits at every level. Respect is then recast and "flipped" within the reassembled ideological and symbolic figure. At times this recasting can be very painful to watch.

For example, Malcolm X's famous pronouncement "by any means necessary" is made in reference to the measures needed to secure freedom and equality. In contrast, the expression became a symbolic threat in legendary hiphop battles, often without any clear political message. At the same time the symbol of the letter X, once emblematic of black power against white supremacy, became a fashion statement. In fact, the hiphop artist KRS-One created an album cover in homage to a famous photograph where Malcolm X holds a rifle while looking out a window as he protects his home and family. While Malcolm X is fighting at the level of race, class, and ideological betrayal, KRS-One's album cover represents the artist, with a rifle, looking out a window to protect his turf (the Bronx) from rappers in Queens. At the same time, he is focusing on the fact that Malcolm X recognized he was a danger because he sought truth and encouraged others to "fight the power."

Similarly, the group Black Star (Mos Def and Talib Kweli) chose the name of the ship used by Marcus Garvey as the vehicle that would deliver those of African descent, especially the working poor, from the racism of America to the shores of Africa. Yet Garvey was also very much a supporter of capitalism and Christianity. Black Star became the name of a group who, while promoting social consciousness, also promoted no formal participation in the political process. Rosa Parks, who is often considered the mother of the civil rights movement, refused to move from her seat at the front of the bus in order for whites to sit there. The group Outkast released a song, "Rosa Parks," in which they argue for the right to party all over the bus. Their focus on the right to bring hiphop into every corner where youths reside and travel seemed to many to be too trivial a reference considering the icon. Yet, Outkast's song did indeed focus on rights.

It is not just that political figures are re-created but also that they may share the spotlight with the likes of Dolemite, an X-rated comedian and actor who performed in 1970s B movies depicting the glories, trials, and tribulations of pimping. From the perspective of many established leaders and scholars, the act of positioning long-revered figures of African American political and social history alongside those who exploit and promote stereotypes of the community represents an abandonment of many of the gains of the civil rights and Black Power era. Bakari Kitwana (2002) argues that it represents the dismantling of the bridge between the civil rights movement and the hiphop generation and "the bitter generational divide between hip-hop generationers and our civil rights/Black power parents" (2002, 203).

Just God and I and I

Just as fragmented symbols of political and ideological leaders and leadership are reconfigured and "flipped" in hiphop culture, religious beliefs and practices are also formed around complex and innovative interpretations. Moreover, because Christianity shapes African American political thought (Dawson 2001), interpretations of spirituality influence the understanding of politics and power (cf. Decker 1993, 59). Political thought often results from the melding of black nationalism, traditional black political ideologies, religion, and the right to represent individual experience. In hiphop, however, it is the versions of Islam and Rastafarianism that symbolize independent political thought and that critique racism and class privilege. In hiphop, therefore, religion and spirituality are not just doctrine but also signify the melding of fractured leadership and ideologies. As a result, hiphop does not simply reflect and represent spiritual ideologies and employ iconic symbols; instead, spirituality itself plays a role in hiphop battles.

The symbols of Islam and Rastafarianism are consistently woven into hiphop lyrics, especially freestyle, as a sign of skill as well as inclusive ideology. The representation of spiritual belief is not based on orthodoxy but instead is in the form of contestation and fragmentation. As a result, a space is created where aspects of any religion that supports hiphop norms and artistic practices are woven into hiphop ideology. For example, one of the many variations of Islamic interpretation that arose from the Nation of Islam in the United States is the organization called the Five Percent Nation. Its founder, Clarence 13X (also known as Father Allah), claimed in the 1960s that God was not a deity or external force but rather was to be found within the Asiatic black man.[6] Members of Five Percent believe themselves to be "poor righteous teachers" or those who know that the original black man is God. In Five Percent, knowledge is often called "ledge" and "no ledge," and members imagine every letter of the word "Allah" to be part of the acronym for "arm, leg, leg, and head." The number seven is important for the gods since g is the seventh number of the alphabet. Members of Five Percent also believe that any corrupt person, irrespective of race, is the "devil."

Five Percent also developed a system of teachings known as the Supreme Mathematics and the Supreme Alphabet. According to Juan Floyd-Thomas, "The 'divine sciences' are a set of principles and an evolving system of analysis, attached to numerals as well as letters of the alphabet, which serves as keys to divine knowledge" (2003, 56). In the philosophy of Five Percent, the ability to separate words and divide numbers into meaningful segments often signals political thinking.[7] According to Felicia Miyakawa (2005, 24–30), the mention of the word science and the notion of science suggests that facts and ideas will be presented that can be logically argued.[8] While these beliefs are not typical of Islamic teachings, Floyd-Thomas argues that they advance "a more personal and empowering theology that places black people as well as the desire for human dignity and self-governance squarely at its center" (2003, 57).

Though the origin of Rastafarianism is vastly different from that of the Five Percent Nation, a number of principles are common to both groups. Rastafarianism has its roots in the teachings of the Jamaican black nationalist Marcus Garvey. In the 1930s, Garvey preached a message of black self-empowerment, and he called for all blacks to return to their ancestral home of Africa, more specifically Ethiopia. He taught self-reliance and denounced the Eurocentric worldview and the colonial indoctrination that caused blacks to feel shame for their African heritage. In 1920 he prophesied the coming of an African leader when he said: "Look to Africa, when a black king shall be crowned, for the day of deliverance is at hand."

Some considered the prophecy fulfilled in 1930 when Ras Tafari was crowned Emperor Haile Selassie I of Ethiopia and proclaimed "King of Kings, Lord of Lords, and the conquering lion of the Tribe of Judah." Haile

Selassie claimed to be a direct descendant of King David, the 225th ruler in an unbroken line of Ethiopian kings from the time of Solomon and Sheba. Garvey and his followers took great pride in being of African descent and wanted to regain the black heritage that was lost in the Americas. Rasta doctrine declared that Haile Selassie is God and that Rastafarians (and all men of pure heart) are divine (Nettleford 1978, 187).

The use of a particular word formation system to signal a spiritual philosophy is also present in Rastafarianism, where "Dread Talk" represents spiritual redemption and an ideology that challenges power and perceived racial and colonial oppression. Velma Pollard (1994) identifies three types of Dread Talk: Category I where items bear new meanings; Category II where words "bear the weight of their phonological implications, e.g. 'downpress for oppress'; and Category III /ai/ words that have a pronominal function" (1994, 8–14, 24).

In Dread talk, "I and I" is a complex reference term for the oneness of Jah (God) and every human. The Rastafarian scholar E. E. Cashmore (1984) further argues that "I and I is an expression to totalize the concept of oneness, the oneness of two persons. So God is within all of us and we're one people. In fact, I and I means that God is in all men. The bond of Ras Tafari is the bond of God, of man" (1984, 4). The significance of the black man in relation to God is also represented in the number nine, since *I* is the ninth letter of the alphabet. Those who are familiar with the significance of the number nine (e.g., the name Cali 9 given in chapter 3) are also aware of its significance within Mayan culture and in numerology.

Rastafarianism also uses a system of reassignment of phonemes and morphemes to reveal the evil of words already in existence and to show the power of words to represent a new reality. *Downpression* replaces "oppression" because oppression holds man down instead of keeping him up (pronounced *op* in Jamaican patois). *Overstanding* replaces "understanding," referring to the enlightenment that raises one's consciousness. *Irie* refers to positive emotions or feelings, or anything that is good, *livication* replaces "dedication" to rid itself of a connotation of death (because of the pronunciation of the first syllable). Finally, *Zion* refers to either Ethiopia or the whole continent of Africa.

The colors green, gold, and red (from the Ethiopian flag) are a symbol of the Rastafarian religion and are frequently seen on clothing and other decorations. Red stands for the blood of martyrs; green stands for the vegetation of Zion (Ethiopia); and gold stands for the wealth and prosperity that Africa has to offer. The symbol of the lion is also important in Rastafarianism, for which it symbolizes Africa as well as Emperor Haile Selassie, or Jah (God), himself.

Both Rastafarianism and Five Percent enjoy a presence in the underground, and both are represented by counterlanguage systems that support the ideology of the black man as the original man and therefore powerful. The use of these spiritual symbols need not be a rejection of one religion over another; rather, they are signs of the black people who have regained their prominence in the world. Through reformulation in hiphop, their components become a powerful symbol of independence and leadership that does not buckle under pressure from dominant society. Moreover, their language ideology engages the necessity for hiphop to continue its creative exercise. Both Rastafarianism and Five Percent rely on a system of reassigning the morphemic system and the meaning and reference of both grammar and reference. Both consider the presence and use of their linguistic system to be indexical of their spiritual and political ideology and critical thinking and analysis. The placement of Five Percent and Rastafarian words and concepts in a rhyme and argument can signal a political stance. Speech actually represents what is actually believed.

Mic Check One
Is the Bridge Over? Don't Try to Play Me Out

Four years ago I stood in a room at KAOS Network as BJ, a young artist and poet, defended his refusal to vote in an important election. He was speaking to Margo, a young graduate student who was there to work with "troubled" yet creative urban youth. The reasoning expressed by BJ was flawless and based on his nineteen years of experience and guided by his exceptional intelligence. Margo presented her earnest yet patronizing argument on why someone as gifted as BJ should vote. In an agitated yet barely audible voice, BJ told Margo that there was nothing she could say to convince him that he should participate in any organization where there was a leader and a chain of command that had to follow the leader. He said that the only reason he was able to leave his past lifestyle as a violent street gang member, and live with the guilt of the things he had done during that time, was to understand that he'd never again participate in anything based on a single leader—unless it was the Lord and Savior Jesus Christ.

Then BJ revealed that his salvation was tied to being able to accept and understand that there were no leaders "who ever supported me or any young black people that I know." He argued that, based on his gang experience, when individuals agree to support a single leader they are duty bound to follow that person whether they agree with the leader or not. He said that the only thing the leaders ever did was try to destroy him and his friends. He then equated the president of the United States to a gang leader: "Even if you know that what he's saying is a lie and wrong you have to do it because he's the leader." Margo pleaded that he was a "bright shining star" and argued that that sort of thinking was far behind him. But BJ looked at her, shook his head, and said slowly and with considerable vehemence: "I hate to disappoint you, but doing it this way is the only way I can live and look you in the face."

The perspective held by BJ is widely supported in the hiphop community, and it highlights the tension between youth's recognition of unbridled power, betrayal, injustice, and arguments for participation in organized politics. However, penetrating and critical analyses like those put forth by BJ do not always result in abandoning participation in formal and activist politics. Russell Simmons, one of the first major producers of hiphop and a successful businessman, leads voter registration efforts directed at youth and passionately argues that urban youth participate in formal electoral politics. Nevertheless, on February 11, 2004, Simmons was interviewed by Charlie Rose on 60 Minutes II. Rose insisted on referring to all of hiphop as "gangster," much to Simmons's irritation. Then Rose asked Simmons why he thought gangster hiphop should be used to organize youth around political issues. In reponse, Simmons had this to say: "The arrogance of white men is why I'm here today. My independence is because they didn't accept me. So I've made more money every step of the way. The conditions of suffering . . . in our impoverished communities are not acceptable. The reflection of those conditions is less concerning to me and I work every day about changing those conditions. Why aren't we talking about the gangsta' government we have? Gangsta' rappers, they're imitating the gangsta' government." Rose seemed quite bewildered that someone of Simmons's stature would refer to the government and the president as "gangsta." Simmons, in contrast, seemed outraged that Rose saw hiphop artists as exclusively negative and yet he was not able to see the U.S. government as corrupt.

While fans of hiphop may be critical of politics and resist participation, that critique does not mean that their overall beliefs are different from those of others in their community. Rather, it may be that their form of critique of the political process and their sense of the power of words is different. Their ability to experience stability within change produces confusing and complex interpretations of what they say, mean, and want. As Peter Christenson and Donald Roberts note: "The dominant characteristic of adolescence is *change*—change in physical, emotional, intellectual, and social functioning. During adolescence, the 'still-nearly-a-child' leaving grade school evolves into an 'almost-adult.' Over the course of a fleeting 6- to 12-year span, youth develop an image of themselves, of others, of society, and the relationships among these concepts, and they come to grips with a myriad of social and cognitive issues that must be resolved before achieving fully functioning adulthood" (1998, 18).

Unfortunately, adolescence in Western societies is regularly described as a time of challenge to parental and adult influence. Yet it is also a time of emotional, biological, and social change and fluctuation (cf. Steinberg 1990). Young people often reflect views both counter to the status quo and in support of it. As Christenson and Roberts observe, "Young people think about politics in ways that the traditional political science continuum of 'liberal' and 'conservative' does not fully account for. . . . Young people are 'pre-socialized' before they are influenced by popular culture. . . . Thus, the popular culture either contradicts or reinforces existing political values more than instills new ones" (1998, 123). They go on to argue that hiphop fans, along with fans of country music, show a much higher correlation with their parents' opinions than do fans of alternative music (130). In addition, though they may see their musical tastes as different from those of their parents, "they are a little less likely to believe that their tastes and newer lifestyles contribute to the breakdown of society" (131).

These findings for the hiphop community are not surprising since they grew up with their parents' soundtrack of jazz, blues, and soul as well as their views of comedy and social values. As Aceyalone explains:

I grew up in the 70s, and so [we had] a lot of just soul and funk, and, pre-hip hop, you know. That stuff like where you just getting into George Clinton, you know. Psycho alpha disco fada, you know . . . out the blue, that to me, that was different music then. I took to it more vocally than I did musically. I just dug what they were saying, you know, along with the whole funk era. Then later on, I discovered jazz and stuff like that. And then Hiphop, sort of, weaved its way in there.

So I grew up listening to a lot of funk. So just, basic black music, blues, here and there. We'd have radio stations on around the house, you know, music has always been a part of me.

Though hiphop youths heard their parents' music during childhood, their interest is in music as an artistic, political, and social cultural product. These youths immediately learn from their parents about the musical tastes of others and the fact that black musical preferences are often different. They then learn about the segregation of music on the radio. Thus their training is that those in power regulate their musical pleasure, yet the music prevails and continues to be evaluated by its knowledgeable and intended audience. They learn that their pleasure is political and their parents' music is the music of African America as well. Consequently, it is not surprising that while participants in rap and hiphop music have various meanings within the community of fans, there are some aspects that suggest that they, especially African Americans, engage in critical analyses not shared by others (Jackson 2003).

Mic Check Two
Politics Reloaded

The reconstructed vestiges of religious rhetoric are embedded in hiphop discourse that depicts political leaders who have had consistent ties to religious institutions. While in African American culture historical figures like Malcolm X, Martin Luther King Jr., and Marcus Garvey may be discussed as indistinguishable from and representative of their respective religious faith (e.g., Gregory 1998, 163), this is not the case in hiphop. Rather, the notion of the ideological leader of the people is deconstructed in relation to contestation and conflict over ideal and pure notions of tests of power and temptation. That is, the real or reality of power in leadership devastates the notion itself, thus reducing the possibility of honest, individual leadership to the status of a joke.

While the notions of contestation and fragmentation of public icons, historical and political figures, and spiritual beliefs are the foundation of political belief, rather than signaling the death of political participation, these notions provide new strategies for it and introduce others. The potential for political activity within hiphop's system of contestation and fragmentation is evident in Ben Caldwell's report of the response by the Los Angeles art community after the police attack on Project Blowed:

Well to me, what happened was, it wasn't really as much of a fallout as more of a unity. After that, people started seeing what we were doing as being more real or something. I couldn't understand, but it seemed like since the crows came to you, almost killing you and stuff, then people started noticing. "Wow! He's working over there with you people. They didn't do anything. Why are they messing with them?"

So that kind of whisper was going around and around. And then we were organized really pretty well. I was like OK, this will be a good thing to teach the youth about how to fight back with media. So we organized a press conference, a press release, and sent it out and got it out there.

Then some of my friends in the art world started organizing the Internet and started sending out letters to all, to organizations, Ridley Thomas, the police chief. And so they organized that, set it out through the cultural net which was the Getty. . . . It was just a real interesting thing how major kingpins of the art community really got involved in helping us because of the networking that I had done with them before. So it was really kind of, very interesting. It was good to see that. I mean, I didn't even know that power was there in myself you know. . . . I thought, we came across on our press conferences really secure, professional, and focused. So that really amazed them—and that for our presentation we had our own video. We made it in front of the TV cameras and the news media, and it came across as a kind of a focus thing.

And then that following week . . . we called the Republic Defenders. They brought a whole contingent of public defenders . . . and they did a workshop with the guys, telling them their rights and what they could do. So it was just like, a first trial. I hadn't really seen how if we get into tight spots how we could really muster a lot of support. And the support wasn't lightweight. I think that that was a very interesting thing. And I think on the youth side, for a lack of a better way to say it. I think that they ended up respecting me more. They saw what was out there, and they saw how I dealt with it. And they saw how calm and focused I was about doing it. And I think that came across all right to them. And it really helped in the sense of our own camaraderie. I mean maybe, maybe it's, because it's one of those watershed moments and it shows you know on which side, where, which side are you on. And I think that that showed on all of us. And it really helped crystallize our togetherness as a group of people.

Though Ben and Project Blowed had the support of various organizations and communities, that support did not mean that the problem initiated by the raid was over. In light of the attention of the Los Angeles arts community and other professional groups, the police did not want to lose face. They wanted to assert that they were right and that there was gang presence. But they were dealing with Ben Caldwell, who knew that the young people were watching.

Then what we did with Blowed, I just ended up still going. I didn't need to stop. We went the following week and the following week they brought more police. And then the following week we had it; they brought more police. So for three weeks in row they, they kept hassling us. But each week I tried to make sure that we had a reason or had paperwork and were able to back it up, to where they could leave and stuff. And then following that, the justice department gave me a call. They sent a representative to start helping us and that was very helpful. Then I had some of my friends on the West Side and they hooked me up with a group of advocates for the law—when there's been real injustice is done.

The art world as an evolving political community that emerged from the attacks on Project Blowed became a stable force to promote the underground and its activities and to protect it from political forces. These activities resulted in coalitions and renewed the building of the community of activists who work with youth of color in Los Angeles.

Mic Check Three
Fear of a (Hiphop) Black Planet?

In spite of the flurry of political awakening and activity around Project Blowed, consciousness-raising and overall political analysis are the practice of hiphop. Political action is viewed as an uncomfortable strategy because it requires that youth rely on those in positions of power. They participate when they integrate hiphop's values into society in general and political situations in particular. This is true of Tasha, one of the active participants in Project Blowed.

I work with this group called the Hiphop Coalition, which is an organization that is actually helping to register people as voters. . . . Something that they had mentioned in the last meeting was that if all these people, all these youths that are coming of age at this point, turning eighteen, will be first-time voters. This group of youths alone . . . could determine who the president is. So that's huge! So, what we're trying to do is educate seniors in high school—these people coming of age, these people that are interested in hiphop—to say okay. These are the politicians that have your interests at stake. These are the people that don't care anything about you. This proposition means this, this, this, and this, you know. So we're trying to educate them through that music . . . taking this hiphop. Because so many people, you know aren't caring enough, and next thing you know the education budget is being cut!

And you know, people constantly complain about it. And I was the same way! I would constantly complain "Aww, these laws, these are horrible." And I didn't vote, until maybe about four years ago—a little too long for me to go without voting—but I had to say I spent this long without voting. Maybe if I do vote, it'll make some changes.

Aceyalone explains the incorporation of hiphop and its importance in awakening and developing political participation, as follows:

Well, I think that hiphop is a popular culture, so that involves politics in everything. It's in advertisements. It's in everything. The next, future generation of politicians will know rap songs. Even up to the senate, I meet different people from all aspects of life that tell me about my music or the music I represent with all of us as a collective.

Everybody that listens to hiphop is not just urban and not political. I am sure there are some lawmakers, doctors, and different people in there (besides the ones that I know specifically that told me that). I think it's growing; just like any other music, it's found its way into popular culture. I think that involves politics. I don't know how politics is going to change it. The politics is between hiphop and the people that are trying control it—and they have good control. But you still have the underground that keeps developing. . . . You still have the underground people developing and keep redeveloping. . . . Political, political, politics, like lawmakers and stuff like that, I think the influence is that you are going to have someone who is much more in tune with who people are, and what people are doing.

Rappers have had a lot of time to speak their mind. This is my prediction. I can see ten or fifteen years from now, someone in office. They really were hiphop fans. They weren't out of touch and there was no generation gap.

Within the discourse and symbols of spirituality and politics there is a growing hiphop ideology that one should not simply participate in politics, but instead should take it over and make it hiphop. The indirect discourse styles of the older generation of community artists, builders, and orga-nizers are seen as problematic. Political collaboration with the younger generation includes a notion of leadership and spirituality that is open to change at all levels of diversity and complexity. Hiphop's reality thus requires the representation of everybody all the time—sometimes local, sometimes national, sometimes international, but never ignored. It is not about narrow interests but rather about the people—who are diverse, who represent social class, and who believe that everyone should participate. The notion of one leader is dismantled, and the model of collaborative leadership where one may represent for the group is hiphop youths' view of political organization, and I suspect it is their future. Yes, the bridge is over, but they have united the landscape through widespread inclusion and critique.

It's Hiphop Nation Time

ENTER THE KAOS

HOLLYWOOD, CALIFORNIA, December 2004. It's nearly 10 PM and hundreds wait in a steady drizzle as the doors slowly open at the Hollywood club Qtopia for one of the most anticipated underground celebrations ever held. All of LA is in the house. Outside the b-boys and b-girls are hanging around and trying to stay loose and limber. The DJs are talking in groups, the graffiti artists are writing in their piece books, and the young MCs are in small ciphers as they whisper their flows—tonight is not for them but to show respect to those who have come before. The young bodies move slowly and collectively, as though they are taking the same breath and beating with the same heart. People laugh, sing, talk, and dance, all the while keeping their eyes glued to the door. It looks and feels as though the entire world is represented tonight. Asia and the Pacific Islands are in the house. South America and the Caribbean weigh in, as well as Africa, parts of Europe, African America, Azatlan, Little Tokyo, Chinatown, and even the Bu (Malibu, that is).

Project Blowed is celebrating its tenth anniversary and everyone is ready for the lyrical festivity. The group has not only survived through the Good Life and on to Project Blowed, they have erected the underground and built it into a powerful force, and it is obviously growing strong.

Inside, the entire venue continues to bustle with thousands of fans and members of Project Blowed. Backstage, onstage, around the stage, and in the VIP section, the men greet with smiles and handshakes and shoulder hugs. The women greet with smiles, full hugs, cheek kisses, and touches to the arm and back. Those present include Aceyalone, Busdriver, Abstract Rude, Myka 9, Abstract Tribe Unique, Power Tung, Otherwize, Medusa, Longevity, NGAPhish, Riddlore, Rifleman a.k.a. Ellaykhule, Hip Hop Clan, Acid Reign, Nocando, Subtitle, Xholo Lanxinxo, Toca, Cypher 7, Mr. Perkins, Black Silver, Volume 10, Phoenix Orion, Terradacto, Jah Orah, NoNsTop, Power Tung, Wreck One, Longevity, Badru, Tasha, Dara, and more. Ben Caldwell is smiling. Everyone is there to represent. Some are overwhelmed. All are home. Westsiiiiide!

You Left Out LA

Hiphop was developed in the 1970s on the East Coast by teenagers and those in high school and their early twenties. The founding generation developed a culture that had the youth as its core and identified the transition into adulthood as one filled with responsibility, expertise, self-criticism, and the power of hiphop. As hiphop's audience and legions of fans increased, its mass appeal and commercial potential became evident. In order to be in the game, one needed an identity that even if it did not rival New York and the East Coast it could stand up to New York's claim to be the only source of the real hiphop. In a city where cultural variation and bilingualism are mainstays of working-class communities, the construction and foregrounding of the symbols and metaphors of LA guaranteed an ebullient, and sometimes menacing, youthful African American presence. It was not surprising, therefore, that the ultimate emergence of the West Coast as more than just mere imitators and students of East Coast hiphop introduced a new development in hiphop culture. Los Angeles delivered, and for the first time the hiphop community had to question its aesthetics, norms, and standards of representation.

As practitioners on both coasts asserted the right to define hiphop, distinct identities and performance style shifts began to emerge that further instantiated regional differences as well as national identities. The drive to distinguish and articulate the linguistic and geographical characteristics that identify each coast's major cities and neighborhoods initially resulted in the marginalization of the South and the Midwest (e.g., Chicago and Detroit). Soon, however, the South emerged as a major force, and the Third Coast (the southern U.S.) and the Dirty South began to forge a distinctive place in hiphop culture. The emergence of hiphop local identities altered the urban African American landscape and included music sampling (cf. Rose 1994; Keyes 2002), conscious language-style choices (Morgan 2002), and local music and arts culture, and it highlighted national and local politics, social class, and racial and educational issues. Artists appeared who put fame and financial rewards before the development of the artistic skills and knowledge of hiphop values and practices. It was during this period that the underground emerged as the most significant source of MC skill and knowledge. It stood in contrast to what would develop into a commercial onslaught to harness hiphop's creativity and energy and market it to the masses. Suddenly, time spent in the underground and reports on MC skills and participation in verbal battles became the passport to hiphop acceptance and respect. What's more, the emergence of regional undergrounds that practiced hiphop skill values set the stage for hiphop to represent locally and as a nation simultaneously. The bigger hiphop got, the harder the underground worked.

In this book I have explored underground hiphop in LA as a physical and expressive location where black youths and progressive youths develop lyrical skills, identities, social relationships, and theories about society and culture. The MCs of underground hiphop have been the focus of this study because through their words and the ideology of the Word, they simultaneously construct and represent the complex states of mind of the hiphop nation. In particular, in these pages I have explored the importance of the long-term (LT) members' involvement in and use of language ideology in constructing, developing, and sustaining hiphop culture. The development of the underground by LTS and their commitment to it continues to affect the future and power of hiphop worldwide. Though the underground developed nearly fifteen years after the introduction of hip-hop, it came about in discourse with, and as a shout-out to, many of the original aspects of hiphop. It resurrected the art of the four elements (MC, DJ, b-boy and b-girl, and graffiti artist) and demanded creativity and skill evaluated by those true to hiphop. In its early years these elements signified hiphop's presence and essence. Just as the earth and human beings are comprised of elements that bind them and make them whole, so is hiphop. The underground also focused on the cipher and the performance venue as places ruled by the audience and LT fans of hiphop who believe in skill. Members of the underground supported hiphop as a political act in the form of art, culture, and society. They focused on hiphop's origins to bring in a new way of building hiphop culture.

There are at least three forces behind the early development of the social, cultural, and political power of hiphop. The first force is the originators of the genre: hiphop was founded by black and brown youths who typically received limited formal education, enjoyed few social class privileges, and routinely were demonized and dismissed by society. The second force is related to location: the South Bronx had long been declared a war zone that was uninhabitable and without resources, and thus suffocating from a culture of poverty and hopelessness. In contrast, young people treated the Bronx as a resource and the center of energy and American culture. The third force is what the originators of the genre did with it. Without formal training, urban youth influenced society and the world at the highest level of thinking and artistic creativity. Hiphop created a new visual, poetic, and dance aesthetic, raised philosophical questions, introduced new technologies, and reinterpreted old ones. Hiphop decisively united into a powerful "workforce" of art the artistic traditions of dance, verbal art, visual art, musical and sound production, and traditions and cultural practices that previously coexisted yet only occasionally bonded together in African American culture.

I have focused on African American culture in my discussion, and I argue that hiphop's development and how and why it grew beyond the confines of its musical genius cannot fully be captured without understanding that it fit into an already established protest/art format that is identifiable worldwide. Of course, many of hiphop's participants and innovators are not of African descent and are fully invested and accepted in the hiphop culture and evaluated within the same standards as everyone else. This is true even though hiphop's beginnings, and those of Project Blowed, include participants who were born outside of the United States or raised by first-generation immigrant parents. I argue that in order to understand the language, discourse, and power of hiphop, we must understand the influence of African American culture, art, and politics. That is, the African American experience throughout the world is understood as one that has resisted and fought bigotry, stereotypes, and injustices of many kinds. It is a culture with a history that symbolizes "Fight the powers that be" while also representing and protecting others. This is not to diminish other cultural contributions but instead to acknowledge that it is the struggles and sacrifices of the African American community, especially as a symbol of marginalized communities and cultures, that informs hiphop's sense of fairness and call for "keeping it real." In spite of this, hiphop remains in a discursive battle with and within African American culture. African American culture celebrates art and politics and it has persistently addressed issues of inclusion, citizenship, and difference, and it stubbornly insists on fairness. It is not based on a remembered and sometimes competing nation-state model of cultural production. Instead, it developed within the confines of a U.S. system of injustice (just us), manipulation, and complete control. Yet hiphop, with its devotion to critique, challenges intergenerational unity. Still, African American culture incorporates hiphop while recognizing that its very existence challenges dominant society and African American norms.

The underground began in earnest when hiphop was on the verge of losing its place as a socially relevant arts movement. It did not resurrect itself outside of other styles of hiphop but rather in discourse with them. As such, it added to and created hiphop's counterpublic representations through unauthorized biography, critical artistic and linguistic expression, and think-tank ciphers. Through its presence in the counterpublic, the underground re-created the political and social critique of early hiphop while developing new lyrical styles and standards to critique political and social symbols and promote artistic expression. Hiphop introduced reformulated religious and political symbols and icons so that they represented the ideology of people of color at the foundation of both life and human thought. These symbols remain at the center of hiphop's foundation narrative and are of crucial importance to its political presence and its reformulation of the American nation myth.

Hiphop narratives and biographies are set against dominant culture's powerful discourses that represent black youth as valueless. In contrast, hiphop casts black youth as indispensable to the nation and redefines the ideal city landscape and reshapes the national and world imagination. The underground brings texture to these places and their reality by providing layered local political and social knowledge about places and lives. It introduced a public discussion of women's issues as well as social class, racism, and other forms of injustice. Suddenly a space existed where serious youth were taken seriously. The underground, in discourse with commercial hiphop, developed rhymes and reasons to respond to issues of misogyny and sexism, racism, class elitism, economic disparity, and educational failure, and to celebrate all of aspects of hiphop culture.

Do Unto Others

The power of hiphop's social organization results in collaboration as well as situations where there is education, discussion, and critical evaluation. Membership in a crew enables audiences to quickly understand the artist's role and status within hiphop culture. Youths work together on ideas, strategies, messages, styles, art, and so forth. Both nationally and internationally, the crew system allows people to change roles and relationships while maintaining responsibility for the social organization. Crews and posses work to change the prevailing standards and status quo.

Perhaps the most wide-ranging outcome of underground hiphop is its attention to the art and role of practice, critical evaluation, and performance in order to develop artistic and technical skills. Evaluation in the underground is a thing of great value. It has helped young people learn responsible criticism, how to handle criticism and disappointment, and how to make the entire process gratifying. It also encourages the discourse between hiphop and other forms of art such that it has invigorated spoken word, public art, and interactions with other musical genres. Hiphop norms of linguistic formulation have had widespread influence on popular culture and on the daily lives of many individuals. Besides the use of new and changing vocabulary and expressions, hiphop's system of word formation is regularly applied in popular culture. The emergence of think-tank ciphers is the result of members of the older generation of hiphop taking their practice of battling and serving as critics and then using it to develop careers, professional lives, and activities that challenge power and redefine their relationship to it.

One of hiphop's lasting contributions may be that it has made linguistics and the power of discourse visible and exciting. Hiphop is not only concerned with the manifestation of words, discourse, and grammar but also the significance of those elements when used by particular people, at particular times, in reference to particular events, and for particular audiences. It is concerned with power and the contradictions inherent in the desire to be heard on one's own terms. Hiphop culture comes into existence when, from a philosophy of language perspective, participants are preoccupied with discovering the speaker's intentions and then evaluating those intentions. Hiphop culture does this by first critiquing power relationships and researching and interrogating multiple aspects of the material world. It then evaluates the speaker's ability to critique that objective reality in artistic and skillful ways. The speaker and artist must represent their knowledge as well as the power relationships that it reveals and creates. So in hiphop when the MC commands the mic, the direct consequence of his or her talk is power in hiphop.

By demanding the right to judge the authenticity of the referents and symbols of its members, the hiphop speech community creates an environment where membership must always be tested, proved, or defended. Consequently, authenticity or what is "real" has market value both within and outside the hiphop community. It is therefore not surprising that success or failure in hiphop is determined by how an artist privately lives and publicly constructs his or her lifestyle, chances, and choices, along with speaking and linguistic skill and the ability to represent cultural and local knowledge. What is real is the ideology of the hiphop Word. One must constantly represent, question, practice, learn, challenge, and check with the audience that they continue to represent hiphop.

Doing What We Love
The First Time

Finally, we must not forget about satisfaction and enjoyment, especially when the subject is youth and young adults. Whether in the form of ethnography or hiphop critique, it is gratifying for individuals to explore the narratives, language, flow, battles, and battle scars experienced in the hiphop underground. This ethnography has shown that because of its principles and practices underground hiphop is empowering and life saving. I raise questions about why youths need to build a culture that offers them what society claims to provide because society, and academic institutions in particular, must be more accountable to young people. I remain haunted by the young men and women who, when answering my questions about why they participate in hiphop, recite the N.W.A's refrain:

> A young nigga got it bad 'cause I'm brown
> And not the other color
> So police think they have the authority
> To kill a minority

At least twenty times during this study I've had these lines repeated to me by young people across social classes. There are also countless times where they quote Notorious B.I.G.'s line, "Stereotypes of a black man misunderstood—but it's all good." Afterward, they tell their story of being stopped and harassed by the police, treated suspiciously by their bosses, and so on. As one young man said to me, "I know they were trying to break me so I won't be somebody. Hiphop gave me a reason to make them wrong."

Women know the same lines as the men, and they often talk about learning and hearing things that helped them and other women. They also recognize the contradictions inherent in supporting hiphop as they mention that they are weary from defending themselves from misogyny and sexism. At the same time, they appreciate the lessons they learned from performers including Salt-n-Pepa, Queen Latifah, MC Lyte, Lauren Hill, Eve, Mia X, Lil' Kim, Foxy Brown, Missy Elliott, and more, including: Don't let a man get away with hitting you. Don't stay in an abusive relationship. Don't have sex if you don't want it. Don't have sex if it's not good. Don't let anyone call you a whore; and don't give them a reason to. Stay a strong black woman. There is also special mention of Tupac, who wrote lines in support of women, mothers, sisters, and friends and told men to "respect our women."

On its tenth anniversary album cover Project Blowed is represented by a light bulb burning brightly against a blank background. Do the members of Project Blowed ask us to wake up? To think? Do they want to know what are we doing? Are they asking "Do we dare try freedom?"

The real hiphop is a battle. It is about art and real lives and real issues. In hiphop, there is no such thing as a battle lost—just one that is not over

Album cover for Project
Blowed, 10th Anniversary.
Courtesy of Project Blowed.

until we pay our dues to hiphop. This is not an idealistic conclusion, though it is a hopeful one. This is not a test. Hiphop is not naive and afraid of irony or the truth. It builds youth into adults with steely resolve—adults who won't walk with their predecessors unless they also recognize, represent, and come correct. It is a long battle and they have the rhymes to accompany and lead it. In the midst of the questions that swirl around whether hiphop will last, there is the underground and there is still the Word—and there are those who want to take it to the next level. As hiphop youths grow older, they don't want to be like their previous generation or anybody else. They want to be much, much better. They want the world to be the real hiphop.

Transcription
Conventions

CAPITAL LETTERS indicate some form of emphasis that may be signaled by changes in pitch or amplitude.

BOLD CAPITAL LETTERS indicate loud speech.

Italics indicate a change in the quality of speech.

.   A period indicates a stopping fall in tone, not necessarily the end of a sentence.

,   A comma indicates a continuing intonation, not necessarily between clauses of sentences.

: :   Colons indicate that the sound just before the colon has been lengthened.

?   A question mark indicates a rising inflection, not necessarily a question.

!   An exclamation point indicates an animated tone, not necessarily an exclamation.

-     A single dash can indicate a short untimed pause; halting, abrupt cutoff; or, when multiple dashes hyphenate the syllables of a word or connect strings of words, the stream of talk so marked has a stammering quality.

[All overlapping utterances, including those that start simultaneously, are marked with a single left bracket.

]   The point where overlap stops is marked with a single right bracket.

=   When there is no interval between adjacent utterances, the second being latched immediately to the first, the utterances are linked together with equal signs. Equal signs are also used to link different parts of a single speaker's utterance when those parts constitute a continuous flow of speech that has been carried over to another line to accommodate an intervening interruption.

(.) A period within parenthesis indicates a one-second pause.

( ) When intervals in the stream of talk occur, they are timed in tenths of a second and inserted within parentheses either within an utterance or between one.

(( )) Double parentheses in italics provide the transcriber's description of the quality of talk and the activity related to talk.

Introduction
I Am Hiphop

1 Throughout the text I write the term "hiphop" without a space or hyphen. I do this for two reasons: first, the meanings of the words hip and hop are not related to the meaning of hiphop culture; second, I use the term to refer to both an art form and a cultural practice.

2 The Good Life is described in detail in chapter 1. It was a health food restaurant in the Crenshaw area by day, but on Thursday nights it became an underground hiphop venue.

3 In his book on LA hiphop, Brian Cross (1993) provides an extensive report on police abuse in LA from 1965 to 1991. The group N.W.A was active from 1986 to 1991. As illustrated here, the group was known for its explicit lyrics and was banned from radio, which by all accounts made it more popular. Though group members referred to their style as reality rap, they are known for popularizing gangsta' rap in hiphop. Many police departments attempted to ban all play of their records, and the assistant director to the FBI (Mitt Ahlerich) sent a letter of protest to their record companies: Ruthless Records and Priority Records.

4 In 1990, the American Family Association (AFA) had 2 Live Crew's (1989) album *As Nasty as They Wanna Be* classified as obscene in Florida's Broward County. Record storeowners who sold the record after the ruling and members of 2 Live Crew who performed it were arrested. In 1992 a Court of Appeals overturned the ruling. Henry Louis Gates Jr. was an expert witness in the case and defended his testimony in a *New York Times* op-ed essay (1990). Baker (1993) also reviews the case within cultural and political arguments.

5 For examples of this type of narrative, see Chang 2005; Adler 1991; Spady, Lee, and Alim 1999; Toop 1999; and Jenkins et al. 1999.

6 The racial conflict surrounding these matches was brilliantly represented in Ralph Ellison's novel *The Invisible Man* (1947).

7 DJ Jazzy Jeff (Jeff Townes) and the Fresh Prince (Will Smith) both went on to have very successful careers in hiphop and in television and film. Will Smith became a major actor and Jeff Townes became a major producer of soul and neosoul music.

8 A drunk driver took Tarek's life on April 29, 2006, as he walked a friend to her car.

9 In fact, according to the Hiphop Archive, there have been more than twenty student-run conferences on college campuses throughout the United States since the 1990s.

10 At a 2002 conference at Harvard University, titled Roundtable on Education and Community Activism, and a 2006 conference at Stanford University, Know the Ledge: Hiphop Scholarship Meets Hiphop Journalist, several leading artists, organizers, and journalists argued that hiphop does not belong in academic settings. I do not mention names here because some of the participants now consider their original position to be stereotypical and not a representation of what they actually consider to be complex arguments about power and control.

11 There are now a number of works on hiphop that explore these topics; see, among others, Perry 2004; Stokes 2007; Pough 2004; Richardson 2006; Quinn 2004; Osumare 2007; Darby and Shelby 2005; Miyakawa 2005; Krims 2000; Forman 2002; Forman and Neal 2004; Fischer 2007; Alim 2007; Boyd 2002; Condry 2006; and Dimitriadis 2001.

12 Of course, this does not mean that the transcripts are perfect. Because most of the lyrical competitions occurred in environments where there were often technical difficulties and interruptions, I checked and rechecked several segments until there was a general agreement over what was said. Accordingly, all analyses and theories presented in this manuscript are based on undisputed transcripts.

13 National Geographic Online, http://www.nationalgeographic.com (site visited 2006).

14 Project Blowed, http://www.projectblowed.com (site visited 2006).

15 Abstract Rude, http://AbstractRude.net (site visited 2003).

Chapter One
The Hippest Corner in LA

1 See Allen and Turner 1997; and Bobo et al. 2000. Before this law, immigration to the United States largely depended upon an immigrant's country of birth. Seventy percent of all immigrant slots were allotted to the United Kingdom, Ireland, and Germany. The new legislation (P.L. 89 236; 79 Stat. 911; amended the Immigration and Nationality Act of 1952) eliminated the various nationality criteria and was based primarily on family reunification and needed skills.

2 This report was sponsored by the United Way of greater Los Angeles in 2003.

3 I use the terminology of the community residents I interviewed to refer to the various acts of civil unrest.

4 The report was named for John McCone, a former director of central intelligence who had led the inquiry into the Watts riots.

5 This is a description of the area as it was until 1998. Some of the merchants have relocated due to disputes with realtors and with the area's council representatives. The Museum in Black closed in late 2001. In addition, several of the major forces of Leimert Park have since passed away; in particular, the deaths of the great jazz drummer Billy Higgins of the World Stage and Richard Fulton of 5th Street Dicks are major losses to the community. They were great supporters of the youth involved in Project Blowed.

6 The other businesses that work with youth are the Dance Studio and the World Stage. At the World Stage, the jazz drummer Billy Higgins, the poet Kamau Daaod, and the poet and writer Michael Datcher and others conducted a forum and workshop for artists.

7 For example, in 1997 the merchants of Leimert Park Village waged a public and bitter campaign against then Councilman Mark Ridley-Thomas who introduced more costly parking meters to the area. The merchants' protest included weekly caricatures of Thomas and various accusations that were distributed to merchants and posted. In response, Thomas claimed he felt his life threatened and called the FBI for support (Samad 1997).

8 *Los Angeles Times*, March 23, 1996.

9 *Los Angeles Times*, February 12, 1994, and July 6, 1991.

10 *Los Angeles Times*, March 23, 1996; Totten 2000.

11 Throughout this volume, background information on the individuals discussed will be given only in cases where permission was granted to do so.

12 The acronym OG refers to "original gods," "original gangsters," etc., and it is often used as a term for those who create, or "originate," a particular thing.

13 There are a variety of websites that provide the history of and information on the Good Life, Project Blowed, and the various artists involved in these projects over the years. To some degree, the one missing element from the history of hiphop on the East Coast is who worked on its behalf and helped create space for it to develop.

14 I am deliberately not referring to them as "older" because this adult group recreates itself as youth get older.

15 See the Appendix for transcription conventions. All ethnographic interviews took place during my field research from January 1996 to June 2006.

16 Those who successfully developed their skills there include Medusa, Aceyalone, Abstract, Ahmad, Jurassic 5, Freestyle Fellowship with Peace, Mikah 9 and Self-Jupiter R. Kain Blaze, The Honorable Sis. B. Hall, The Honorable Sis. Efa, The Honorable Bro. Omar, The Honorable Mr. Ben Caldwell, Bro. Robert 5X Muhammad, O-Roc, Freestyle Fellowship, DJ Kiilu, DJ Mark-Luv, Lance (Dada Supreme), Sheena Lester (RapPAges), Bilal Allah, Akwanza, Media Killer Matt, Thayoud, G-Money, Djinji Brown, Ganja-K, Mark the Murderer, Mathmatics, T-Spoon Iodine, Supernatural, Otherwise, O-Roc, NgaFsh, Rhymin' Riddler? Tray-Loc, Big Kev, Jay B. Nice, King Adisa, Born Allah, King Born,

Mannish Flats, Chu Black, Jammin' D, Assassin X, Tomeicko, Sista Ocean, U.N.I.TY Committee, R.K.A., Chali2na, Mark 7even, Cut Chemist, Eatro Teach1, Hymnal, Sunshine, Xololancinco, 2-Mex, AWOL-One, Ghetto Godz, I Smooth 7, DK Toon, Monister 2-Bad, Ulu Butterfly, Ebony Prince, Irie Lion, FatJack, DJ Dr. EZ, 2000 Crows, Badru, Zagu Brown, Nairb, FoeTeen Karat, Gizmoe, Faxx, Furious Styles, Supherb, Superb SK, Bro. Majid, Raphi, Meen Green, Xzibit-A, p.e.a.c.e., Himself, MURS, Abstract Tribe Unique, Underground Railroad, Earth Quake Brothers, Big Al, Chillin Villain Empire, Hip-HopKclan, J-Smoov, St. Mark 9:23, Imperator, Pigeon John, Bus Driver, Funky Tren, Dark Leaf, Allah Culture, Menace Clan, Furious Styles, Jizzm, Urban Props, S.I.N., Figures of Speech, GP HipHop Nation, Mona Lisa, Dangerous Women, Nau. T Von Ife Sade Mother of Creation Yo Sista Mahogany, Cali Uncle Pep Poppin Chuck, Cre-8 Dimmer Enk-One Ern-Ski, Kinkhy Rhed and Kali-9, Slant Eyes, Puzoozoo, Vixen, Onomatopea, East Side BADstads, M.C. Pro, K-Razz, Poet X, Yo Sista, Jungle Jim Jones, Duke of Earl, Click tha Supa Latin, Lou Dog, MC Pro, Juneteenth, Flawliss Victory, Flaco-7, Open Mic Eagle, Phoenix Orion, K-Razz, Iceberg, Funky Dialect, Wascals, Kram Neves, Droop Capone, Oquendo, Rebels of Rhythm, Biz Markie, B+, M.C. Guess, 5% Nation of Gods, Fruit of Islam, Straight Black, Sleeze-One, Faymus Emcey (Loe Lyfes), Fats RIP, Bigga B RIP, Yusef Afloat War Cloud RIP, Big Bimbi RIP, and Bro. Aki Michael 'Mixin' Moore RIP (The Goodlife Foundation 2007).

17 All interviews with Aceyalone took place on July 30, 2004, at KAOS Network. All further quotations are from this interview.

18 All interviews with Ben Caldwell took place on May 15, 2004, at KAOS Network. All further quotations are from this interview.

19 His collaborator was Ulysses. The Olympic Games were held in LA in 1984, and thus funding was available for projects that might connect communities with visitors.

20 Ben Caldwell was an early adopter of internet and media technology.

21 This film collaboration also included Charles Burnett, Julie Dash, and Roger Smith.

22 All interviews with Charletta Johnson took place on June 15, 2004, in her school office. All further quotations are from this interview.

23 These are fictitious names. Minor facts of descriptions have been altered in order to further protect their anonymity.

Chapter Two
Welcome to the Underground

1 For a typical example of demonization, see McWhorter 2003.

2 In fact, rent parties, where electricity was often "appropriated," are mentioned in numerous novels detailing black life in the 1920s. This process expanded to block parties throughout urban areas in the 1960s.

3 James Prigoff and Robin Dunitz's (2000) extensive collection of African American murals chronicles the movement from paintings inside to those on walls outside in public spaces. Michael Harris (2000) credits the revitalization of the mural movement to the artists who erected the Wall of Respect in Chicago (mainly Jeff Donaldson, Wadsworth Jarrell, Barbara Jones, and Carolyn Lawrence) as well as members of the OBASI workshop of poets and writers. The movement produced over fifteen hundred murals.

4 Lyrics created in the early stages of hiphop were largely defined by the beat, sound, and rhythm generated by DJS.

5 For examples of the critical literature on the role of black DJS and the radio on the development of the music industry, see Keyes 2002; Rose 1994; George 1998; and Barlow 1999.

6 According to the obituary in the *New York Times* (June 26, 2006), George Woods of WDAS radio in Philadelphia was known for stopping his broadcast to discuss current events.

7 This is not to suggest that original innovators cannot be identified for some things. Rather, except for a few cases, especially those concerning technology and DJS, it is difficult to claim to be the first and only when so many youths were involved in the same movement.

8 This refers to the placement of three or four felt-tip markers into larger containers (often empty roll-on deodorant cylinders) to produce a thick and "phat" stroke.

9 This interview was conducted in July 1999.

10 These stages include generalizations regarding gender roles. While girls, in particular, may participate in some of the activities described relating to boys, this only happens occasionally in preadolescence and usually involves siblings and other same-age family members.

11 Badru reports that his mother, on the other hand, was not pleased when she was told by another parent that it was her son who was writing all over the neighborhood.

12 Many of these parental battles lead to new discoveries of techniques. For example, Sherry Ayazi-Hashjin (1999) reports that the art of scratching developed as a result of Grand Wizard Theodore's mother shouting at him for playing his music too loud. He stopped the record with his finger while the turntable was still spinning. Badru also reports that he practiced graffiti on his bedroom walls behind the door since his mother never turned around to see what was behind her or shut the door when she came into the room. He had to learn not only different techniques but also how to execute them without discovery. One day, however, his mother did turn around.

13 A hater, also known as player hater, is a jealous person who constantly points out flaws in others.

14 At the time, two groups from Atlanta, the Goodie Mob and Outkast, were growing in popularity.

15 Arrested Development was also one of the first successful groups from the South and thus helped establish the Third Coast.

16 The theory of counterlanguage is an adaptation of the theory of antilanguages of Michael Halliday (1978).

17 These words were commonly used in *The Flintstones* cartoon series, a Hanna-Barbera Production that originally aired on ABC-TV in prime time from 1960 to 1966. It is also in reference to "Jack and the Beanstalk," a classic English fairytale.

18 This is in reference to Erving Goffman's contention that crucial facts exist beyond interactions and are concealed within them: "For example, the 'true' or 'real' attitudes, beliefs, and emotions of the individual can be ascertained only indirectly, through his avowals or through what appears to be involuntary expressive behavior" (1959, 2).

19 For more on this practice and its implications, see Sapir 1955 [1921]; Whorf 1956; and Morgan 2002.

20 In chapter 4 I discuss how this leads to incorporating critiques of the social and political context.

21 A slow jam is a song that is a classic for slow dancing and seduction. Juicy Fruit is a chewing gum, and there is another reference to candy in the phrase "good and plenty."

22 *Word Up* magazine was one of the first to cover hiphop artists. The seminal *Mr. Magic's Rap Attack* radio show aired every Friday and Saturday night on WBLS in New York City from 1982 until 1989. Every week Mr. Magic would debut brand-new songs from such up-and-coming artists of the time as Kurtis Blow, Run DMC, LL Cool J, Whodini, and the Beastie Boys—all mixed live on the air by legendary DJ Marley Marl. For more on the use of signifiers in representing ideology, see Silverstein 1985, 220.

23 The quotes here are taken from Chappelle's HBO special *Killin' Them Softly* (2000), in which he demonstrates the layers of local knowledge and symbols in discourse about racism. In his various venues Chappelle often performs with hiphop artists.

24 For reviews depicting the racial roles in *Mississippi Burning*, see Marquand 1989; Madison 1999; Davis 1988; and Bland, White, and Corliss 1989.

25 In this case, God refers to the Five Percent Nation reference to the black man, which I discuss in detail in chapter 5.

26 Its hiphop meaning has evolved, and it has been inverted as illustrated by Chris Rock's excited promotion of his comedy special *Never Scaared* (HBO 2006), "*It's gon be ill y'all!*" The evolution to predicate adjective occurred with the inverted positive meaning of the word, though in many cases the focus is ambiguous. There are also forms such as *illified* (Stavsky, Mozeson, and Reyes Mozeson 1995) and *Illtown* (which refers to Orange, New Jersey).

27 In fact the difference is in relation to whether the vowel pronunciation is tense (/a/) or lax (/e/).

28 I have consulted several dictionaries for a breakdown of this process. Those referring to AAE include Major 1994 and Smitherman 1977. Those referring to hiphop include Atoon 1992–99 and several earlier sources (e.g., Fab 5 Fred-

dy's *Fresh Fly Flavor* [1992], and the glossary from *The Source* magazine), though the most common method for current usage was to ask LTS and observe usage in context.

29 The first publication devoted to lyrics was by Lawrence Stanley (1992). The online hiphop lyrics source Original Hip Hop Lyrics Archive, ohhla.com, popularized and helped standardize spelling. On that site, fans submit the lyrics of their favorite artist, as well as add updates and corrections.

30 The regularizing of spelling conventions is impressive considering the various literacy histories of some of the writers. There is often a move toward iconicity in spelling, though except in cases like Amerikkka, in-depth local knowledge is necessary to locate the sound, letter, and symbol relationship.

31 Reclaimed words also include archaic racial insults like jigaboo, handkerchief head, and so on.

Chapter Three
Thursday Night at Project Blowed

1 The purpose of the project was to study how the groups interacted with technology. While the economic differences between the two groups were great, their interaction across class was not the main purpose of the project.

2 Capoeira, a martial art that blends music, dance, singing, and acrobatics, was brought to Brazil by captured slaves from Angola. The Angolan people developed capoeira into a method of defending themselves against their violent overlords, but because they were enslaved they had to disguise their training as recreational song and dance.

3 This is not an exhaustive list and I apologize for any omissions. The spellings represent the latest spelling at the time of this book. Some spellings have evolved over time.

4 The films are played as a subject for spontaneous freestyling. Generally, at least two films are shown with the volume turned off.

5 For specific examples, see Morgan 2001, 2002; and Smitherman 2000.

6 The play is between sounds that are meaningful in English (including all dialects) and sounds associated with other languages.

7 Not all freestyle MCs are consistently clear, however. They often mumble and use garbled speech for stylistic reasons.

8 This is not to say that everything makes sense or that things are always clear. The MCs are evaluated for overall performance, and if they show consistent weaknesses in these areas they are reprimanded by the audience and by other MCs.

9 Many MCs also use verbal pauses like "uh" and "ah" as well as punctuated silences.

10 The extended use of profanity is unusual for Blowed artists.

11 From the CBS News Archives, courtesy the WPAA Film Archive.

12 This use of signification and indexicality requires that the listener be knowledgeable of layers of meanings and their opposites. Names as well as historical

and political figures and referents are often presented as dialogic—if one is aware of local knowledge and how power is realized within specific situations. It raises significant questions regarding the construction of a counterpublic as well as sense and reference (Frege, Geach, and Black 1977), conversational implications, felicity conditions, and so on.

13 Many MCs who participate in open-mic sessions for the first time learn this quickly and seem surprised by this position.

14 This is from the Kool Moe Dee battle album *How You Like Me Now* (1990).

15 Both the performance area and the adjoining room were filled to maximum capacity. Those on security worked to keep the crowd moving so as not to exceed capacity.

16 Westwood is a section in Los Angeles that borders Bel Air and Beverly Hills. It is where UCLA is located, and it was once considered a trendy area for LA youth. At the height of its popularity a tourist was shot in the area, so young people began to avoid it. Prefect is a fictitious name, as are the names assigned to all members of his crew.

17 Otherwise was interrupted because someone tripped over a power cord.

18 CVE (Chillin Villain Entertainment) is produced by Project Blowed members.

19 The number nine is significant to many members of Project Blowed because they believe that it has powerful spiritual implications. Though I discuss this notion more fully in chapter 5, here it should be noted that its significance is attached to the fact that there are nine planets and Mayan numerology as well as Rastafarianism consider it divine. Furthermore, it is relatively easy to develop rhymes around it.

20 I later learned that it was a personal conflict where Red thought Prefect had betrayed him in some way.

21 This was later confirmed by others present.

Chapter Four
(Ph)eminists of the New School

1 All interviews with Tasha Wiggins took place on August 15, 2004, at KAOS Network. All further quotations are from this interview.

2 Tricia Rose identifies and describes three themes: "Heterosexual courtship, the importance of the female voice, and mastery in women's rap and black female public displays of physical and sexual freedom" (1994, 147).

3 Medusa was the winner of the *Source* magazine freestyle battle in 2000.

4 While Medusa describes her sexuality as lesbian, she identifies herself as an MC with mad skills. She explains her philosophy to Erin Raber of *Curve* magazine as follows: "You love who you love. . . . I do my thing. I love men. I love women. I'm just 'love.' But, like, gay pride and all of that, it's like, you know, 'I'm a woman first, and I'm Black first,' and those are my issues first. I'm not going to walk around looking for gay rights, when I haven't achieved my true rights as just a human being, as a Black woman. So I think people avoid

speaking on that because they don't want that to be the primary focus of who they are. Because that can dilute everything else" (*Curve* 10, no. 5 [2000]).

5 For additional examples of this view, see Keyes 2002; Pough 2004; Perry 2004; and Morgan 1999.

6 In the 1990s C. Delores Tucker, chair of the National Political Congress of Black Women and chair of the Democratic National Committee Black Caucus, participated in a national campaign against violent lyrics—in particular in rap music. In 1997, she and her husband sued the estate of Tupac Shakur for $10 million over lyrics in which Shakur rhymed her name with an obscenity. Her lawsuit alleged, among other things, that her husband, William Tucker, had suffered loss of "consortium."

7 This is very much aligned with black feminist arguments: see Crenshaw 1991; and Collins 1990.

8 Garth Trinidad, *Chocolate City*, KCRW, Los Angeles, July 26, 2001.

9 They are not taught about sex and desire in these settings. Though I have always thought that this setting would be ideal for discussion of sexually transmitted disease, women's bodies, safe sex, etc., these topics have not been introduced.

10 Until the late 1990s, these programs occurred during the summer and as part of after-school activities. I have never met a young woman involved in hiphop who did not participate in some activity where she was taught about the history of African American women and what they endured.

11 Nina Simone's "Four Women" was the first song mentioned when I asked several women and girls what and who influenced them about the life of black women.

12 Talib Kweli, like many underground and socially conscious artists, mentions his mother's influence on many occasions.

13 This recording was brought to my attention by two twenty-year-old black women who stated, "He got it right!"

14 In fact, the use of "auntie" by a white person for an older black woman is often responded to with anger (for example, see Kweli's "For Women").

15 See Gwaltney 1981 for a discussion of rape by white men who had economic control over families well into the 1960s.

16 For studies of teenage girl identity, see Fine and Mcpherson 1993; Leadbeater and Way 1996; and Tolman 2002.

17 See Morgan 2005; and Morgan and Bennett 2006; as well as the earlier discussions in this chapter.

18 Venus is a fictitious name. The men with her are very defensive, and they do not treat her with the respect of female MCs who usually appear. They speak for her and act as though she would not be recognized without their insistence. One man in particular became very defensive when the audience rejected her.

19 Donna refers to the "shit," or pimpstress. Don refers to a pimp, or man in control, etc.

20 In the underground, sex is often a trope as Hazel Carby (1987) argues.

21 The words and discussion are based on Medusa's performance at Project Blowed's tenth anniversary celebration in December 2004 and at her performance at UCLA in 2005.

22 This is from "Rapper's Delight" (1979) by the Sugarhill Gang. It was also popularized by Missy Elliot when she was featured on "Up Jumps Da Boogie" by Timbaland and Magoo.

23 The Gap Band song is about smacking people who come to a dance and then don't dance. Badu's song is to a worthless boyfriend who is frequently with his nonworking friend Tyrone. A popular line from the song is, "You better call Tyrone and tell him to come and get your shit!"

24 These two approaches parallel the typical discourse styles of teenagers where males often play verbal games focused exclusively on skill and women focus on verbal practices that require both skill and determining the nature of friendship (cf. Morgan 1996; Goodwin 1990).

Chapter Five
Politics, Discourse, and Drama

1 There are gangs in this area, and public transportation is generally sporadic or even nonexistent.

2 These quotations refer to Ice Cube's song from 1992 "It Was a Good Day," and the song sung by Mr. Rogers on the children's program *Mr. Roger's Neighborhood.*

3 See U.S. v. Murphy, 406 F.3d 857 (7th Cir. 2005).

4 The exception was Richard of 5th Street Dicks. He publicly apologized during a news conference.

5 I use this example because it is the most frequent argument for why youths do not support traditional black institutions.

6 Various police websites designate Five Percent Nation as a gang, though the only reason for this seems to be that the leader and the followers are black. Miyakawa (2005, 16–20) presents a fascinating discussion on the FBI's interest in the group and its attempts to present them as a gang.

7 According to Floyd-Thomas, Five Percent operates as a gnostic religion in that it is based on beliefs in abstruse spiritual truths that should free humanity from the world of evil. He argues that the Five Percent "revolves around fundamental principles such as the divine origins of the cosmos; the presence of evil that corrupted humanity; and the recovery of humanity by nurturing the inner life of true believers" (2003, 56). Similarly, Miyakawa describes it as "an idiosyncratic mix of black nationalistic rhetoric, Kemetic (ancient Egypt) symbolism, Gnosticism, Masonic mysticism, and esoteric numerology" (2005, 23).

8 Of course the logic of the argument is based on understanding the principles of the Supreme Mathematics and the Supreme Alphabet.

Back-packers   Originated by graffiti writers who kept all their cans and
nozzles in backpacks. Now used as a derogatory term for nerd rappers,
hippy-hoppers, and other fringe hiphop followers (most of whom are
suburbanites buying into or co-opting a certain style)

battle   To perform and display one of the four hiphop elements (MC, DJ,
b-boys and b-girls, graffiti) in competition or in comparison to other
individuals

Beat Street   A hiphop film from 1984 featuring break dancing on the East
Coast

b-boy and b-girl   Hiphop practitioners who dance to break beats

bite   To steal or use someone's ideas, style, words, and so on

bomb   Repeated writing with ink over an area

break   The part of a song without lyrics and with a beat only

bud   Marijuana

bum-rush   To attack someone without prior notice; to take over from someone
uninvited

cable   Chained necklace (gold and silver)

cipher   Two or more lyricists freestyling together

crew   Originally a group of graffiti writers; now a tight group of friends and
artists who practice, rehearse, and attend activities together

cut   To rhythmically move a record back and forth while turning the sound off
so that the sound only plays when the record is in forward motion

dank   Potent, high-quality marijuana

diss   To disrespect and insult

ducket   A dollar bill

fade   Blends of color

freak   A person who is sexually wild and liberated

freeze   To hold or pose a position, often while suspended

freestyle   To create rap lyrics spontaneously and with minimum practiced lyrics

g   Gangster or god

gang banging   Participating in violence as part of a gang or organized group

graf   Graffiti

hater   A jealous person who constantly points out flaws in others

hits   To tag up any surface with paint or ink

ho   Whore

jacobs   Jewelry

mack   (noun) A person (usually male) who is smooth and slick and uses women; (verb) the act of flirting and using women

mad   A lot, to the extreme, amazing, incredible

MC   Master of ceremonies or microphone controller; a lyricist who is either the host of an event or an individual with enough flow and skill to be considered a master of the art of rap

mic   Microphone

Mickey D's   McDonald's restaurant

phat   [archaic] Cool (pretty, hot, and tempting)

piece   A graffiti mural

piece book   Art notebooks that contain graffiti drawings and tags

pop lock   Many dancers consider the combination of these terms to be the result of media that disrespects the development of hiphop dance movement. The term "lock" can be traced back to The Lockers, a group started by Don Campbell in the 1970s where he would pause at certain moments. Popping emerged in the late 1970s with Boogaloo Sam who introduced abrupt freezes to robot dances. The result is the illusion of a constant waving motion

scratch   The DJ's act of reversing the rotation of a vinyl record with the stylus in play

skeet   Semen; to ejaculate

tag   A personal signature and identity in graffiti writing

throw-up   A name painted quickly with an outline filled in with one layer of paint

Transformers   A robot toy that is often geometrically shaped and disguised to take on many forms. The toys were introduced by Hasbro in 1984, and were based on the Diaclone line that originated in Japan.

uprock   A competitive street dance involving two or more dancers who perform solo or as a team, dancing alternately or simultaneously in synchronization to the rhythms of soul and funk music and certain rock songs. The dance consists of foot shuffles, spins, turns, and freestyle movements, along with sudden body movements called "jerks" and hand gestures called "burns," which are intended to imitate a fight against an opposing dancer.

REFERENCES

Abstract Rude. 1999. "Come On." *Process of Elimination*. Industry Records.

Aceyalone. 2001. "Project Blowed." *Accepted Eclectic*. Project Blowed Recordings.

Adjaye, J. K., and A. R. Andrews, eds. 1997. *Language, Rhythm, and Sound: Black Popular Culture into the Twenty-First Century*. Pittsburgh: University of Pittsburgh Press.

Adler, B., and J. Beckman. 1991. *Rap: Portraits and Lyrics of a Generation of Black Rockers*. New York: St. Martin's.

Alexander, D. 1996. "Clubbed at KAOS." *Los Angeles Weekly*, January 19–25, 13–14.

Alim, H. S. 2007. *Roc the Mic Right: The Language of Hip Hop Culture*. New York: Routledge.

Allen, J. P., and E. Turner. 1997. *The Ethnic Quilt: Population Diversity in Southern California*. Northridge: Center for Geographical Studies, California State University.

Althusser, L. 1971. "Ideology and Ideological State Apparatuses (Notes toward an Investigation)." In *Lenin and Philosophy, and Other Essays*, 85–126. New York: Monthly Review Press.

Anderson, A. 2003. *Word: Rap, Politics and Feminism*. New York: Writers Club.

Apter, A. 1992. *Black Critics and Kings: The Hermeneutics of Power in Yoruba Society*. Chicago: University of Chicago Press.

Ards, A. 2002. "Rhyme and Resist: Organizing the Hip Hop Generation." In *That's the Joint: The Hip Hop Studies Reader*, ed. M. Forman and M. A. Neal, 311–23. New York: Routledge.

Atoon, P. 1992–99. *The Rap Dictionary*. www.rapdict.org.

Austin, J. L. 1962. *How to Do Things with Words*. Oxford: Oxford University Press.

Ayazi-Hashjin, S. 1999. *Rap and Hip Hop: The Voice of a Generation*. New York: Rosen.

Baker, H., Jr. 1993. *Black Studies, Rap, and the Academy.* Chicago: University of Chicago Press.

Barlow, W. 1999. *Voice Over: The Making of Black Radio.* Philadelphia: Temple University Press.

Baugh, J. 1999. *Out of the Mouths of Slaves.* Austin: University of Texas Press.

Bazin, H. 1995. *La Culture Hip-Hop.* Paris: Desclee de Brouwer.

Beiser, V., and K. Solheim. 2000. "Juvenile Injustice: Proposition 21 Aims to Send Thousands of California Teenagers to Adult Prison." *LA Weekly,* February 17.

Bennett, A. 2001. *Cultures of Popular Music.* Buckingham: Open University Press.

Bennett, D. 2003. "The Love Difference Makes: Intersubjectivity and the Emotional Politics of African American Romantic Ritual." PhD diss., University of California, Los Angeles.

Berger, P., and T. Luckman. 1966. *The Social Construction of Reality.* Harmondsworth: Penguin.

Bezilla, R., ed. 1993. *America's Youth in the 1990s.* Princeton: George H. Gallup International Institute.

Big Daddy Kane. 1988. "R.A.W." *Long Live Kane.* Cold Chillin' Records.

Big L. 1998. "Ebonics (Criminal Slang)." Rawkus Records.

Black Sheep. 1991. "The Choice Is Yours." *A Wolf in Sheep's Clothing.* Mercury/Polygram Records.

Bland, E. L., J. E. White, and R. Corliss. 1989. "Fire This Time." *Time,* January 9, 56–62.

Bobo, L., M. L. Oliver, J. H. Johnson, and A. Valenzuela, eds. 2000. *Prismatic Metropolis: Inequality in Los Angeles.* New York: Russell Sage Foundation.

Boyd, T. 2002. *The New H.N.I.C. (Head Niggas in Charge): The Death of Civil Rights and the Reign of Hip Hop.* New York: New York University Press.

Breitman, G., ed. 1965. *Malcolm X Speaks.* New York: Grove.

Brewster, B., and F. Broughton. 2000 [1999]. *Last Night a DJ Saved My Life: The History of the Disc Jockey.* New York: Grove.

Brown, T. S. 2006. *"Keeping It Real" in a Different Hood: African-Americanization and Hip Hop in Germany.* London: Pluto.

Bucholtz, M., and K. Hall. 2004. "Theorizing Identity in Language and Sexuality Research." *Language in Society* 33: 469–515.

Caldwell, B. 1993. "KAOS at Ground Zero: Video, Teleconferencing and Community Networks." *Art and Social Consciousness* 26, no. 5: 421–22 [special issue].

Cannon, L. 1999. *Official Negligence: How Rodney King and the Riots Changed Los Angeles and the LAPD.* New York: Basic Books.

Carby, H. 1987. *Reconstructing Womanhood: The Emergence of the Afro-American Woman Novelist.* Oxford: Oxford University Press.

Cashmore, E. E. 1984. *The Rastafarians.* London: Minority Rights Group.

Castleman, C. 1982. *Getting Up: Subway Graffiti in New York.* Cambridge: MIT Press.

Chadwick, B. A., and T. B. Heaton. 1996. *Statistical Handbook on Adolescents in America.* Phoenix: Oryx.

Chambers, I. 1985. *Urban Rhythms: Pop Music and Popular Culture*. New York: St. Martin's.

Chang, J. 2005. *Can't Stop Won't Stop: A History of the Hip-Hop Generation*. New York: St. Martin's.

Chideya, F. 1999. "Hip-Hop in the Heartland: MTV as Cultural Common Denominator." In *The Color of Our Future: Race for the Twenty-first Century*, 86–112. New York: William Morrow.

——. 2004. *Trust: Reaching the 100 Million Missing Voters and Other Selected Essays*. Brooklyn, N.Y.: Soft Skull.

Christenson, P., and D. Roberts. 1998. *It's Not Only Rock and Roll: Popular Music in the Lives of Adolescents*. Cresskill, N.J.: Hampton.

Chuck D. and Yusuf Jah. 1997. *Fight the Power: Rap, Race and Reality*. New York: Dell.

Cohen, J., and W. S. Murphy. 1966. *Burn, Baby, Burn! The Los Angeles Race Riot, August 1965*. New York: Dutton.

Collins, Patricia Hill. 1990. *Black Feminist Thought: Knowledge, Consciousness, and the Politics of Empowerment*. New York: Routledge.

Condry, I. 2006. *Hip-Hop Japan: Rap and the Paths of Cultural Globalization*. Durham: Duke University Press.

Coombe, R. J. 1998. *The Cultural Life of Intellectual Properties: Authorship, Appropriation, and the Law*. Durham: Duke University Press.

Crenshaw, K. 1991. "Mapping the Margins: Intersectionality, Identity Politics, and Violence against Women of Color." *Stanford Law Review* 43: 1241–99.

——. 1992. "Whose Story Is It Anyway? Feminist and Antiracist Appropriations of Anita Hill." In *Race-ing Justice, Engendering Power: Essays on Anita Hill, Clarence Thomas, and the Construction of Social Reality*, ed. T. Morrison, 402–40. New York: Pantheon.

Crisafulli, C. 1996. "Project Blowed." *U.H.F*, July–August 1996, 44–48.

Cross, B. 1993. *It's Not about a Salary: Rap, Race and Resistance in Los Angeles*. London: Verso.

Csikszentmihalyi, M. 1975. *Beyond Boredom and Anxiety*. San Francisco: Jossey-Bass.

Csikszentmihalyi, M., and I. S. Csikszentmihalyi, eds. 1992. *Optimal Experience: Psychological Studies of Flow in Consciousness*. Cambridge: Cambridge University Press.

Darby, D., and T. Shelby. 2005. *Hip-Hop and Philosophy: Rhyme 2 Reason*. Peru, Ill.: Open Court.

Das EFX. 1992. "They Want EFX." *Dead Serious*. East/West America.

Davis, A. 1993. "Nappy Happy: A Conversation with Ice Cube and Angela Y. Davis." *Transition* 58: 174–92.

——. 1998. *Blues Legacies and Black Feminism: Gertrude "Ma" Rainey, Bessie Smith and Billie Holiday*. New York: Pantheon.

Davis, M. 1992. *City of Quartz: Excavating the Future in Los Angeles*. New York: Vintage.

———. 2001. "Wild Streets: American Graffiti versus the Cold War." *International Socialism Journal* 91 (summer), http://www.socialistreviewindex.org.uk.

Davis, T. 1988. "Civil Rights and Wrongs." *American Film* 14, no. 3 (December): 32–42.

Dawson, M. C. 2001. *Black Visions: The Roots of Contemporary African-American Political Ideologies.* Chicago: University of Chicago Press.

Decker, J. 1993. "The State of Rap: Time and Place in Hip Hop Nationalism." *Social Text*, no. 34: 53–84.

DiIulio, J. 1995. "The Coming of the Super-Predators." *Weekly Standard*, November 27, 23.

Dimitriadis, G. 2001. *Performing Identity/Performing Culture: Hip Hop Text, Pedagogy, and Lived Practice.* New York: Peter Lang.

Drake, S. C., and H. Clayton. 1970. *Black Metropolis: A Study of Negro Life in a Northern City.* Chicago: University of Chicago Press.

Du Bois, W. E. B. 1975 [1920]. *Dark Water: Voices from within the Veil.* Millwood, N.Y.: Krauss International.

Duranti, A. 1993. "Truth and Intentionality: An Ethnographic Critique." *Cultural Anthropology* 8: 214–45.

Duranti, A., and D. Brenneis. 1986. "The Audience as Co-author: An Introduction." *Text* 6: 239–347.

Easton, N. J. 1992. "Bringing It All Back Home Rebuilding." *Los Angeles Times*, October 26.

Ellison, R. 1947. *The Invisible Man.* New York: Random House.

Epstein, J. S. 1998. *Youth Culture: Identity in a Postmodern World.* Oxford: Basil Blackwell.

Eure, J., and J. Spady. 1991. *Nation Conscious Rap.* New York: PC International.

Fab 5 Freddy. 1992. *Fresh Fly Flavor: Words and Phrases of the Hip-Hop Generation.* Stamford, Conn.: Longmeadow.

Fernando, S. H. 1994. *The New Beats: Exploring the Music, Culture, and Attitudes of Hip-Hop.* New York: Anchor.

Ferrell, J. 1993. *Crimes of Style: Urban Graffiti and the Politics of Criminality.* Boston: Northeastern University Press.

Fine, G. A., and P. A. Turner. 2001. *Whispers on the Color Line: Rumor and Race in America.* Berkeley: University of California Press.

Fine, M., and P. Mcpherson. 1993. "Over Dinner: Feminism and Adolescent Female Bodies." In *Gender and Education*, ed. S. K. Biklen and D. Pollard, 126–54. Chicago: University of Chicago Press.

Fischer, D. E. 2007. *"Kobushi Ageroo! (=Pump Ya Fist!)": Blackness, "Race," and Politics in Japanese Hiphop.* Gainesville: University of Florida Press.

Fisher, L. 1976. "Dropping Remarks and the Barbadian Audience." *American Ethnologist* 3: 227–42.

Floyd-Thomas, J. 2003. "A Jihad of Words: The Evolution of African American Islam and Contemporary Hip-Hop." In *Noise and Spirit: The Religious and Spiritual Sensibilities of Rap Music*, ed. A. B. Pinn, 49–70. New York: New York University Press.

Forman, M. 2002. *The 'Hood Comes First: Race, Space, and Place in Rap and Hip-Hop*. Middletown, Conn.: Wesleyan University Press.

Forman, M., and M. A. Neal, eds. 2004. *That's the Joint! The Hip-Hop Studies Reader*. New York: Routledge.

Foucault, M. 1972. *The Archaeology of Knowledge and the Discourse on Language*. New York: Pantheon.

———. 1980. *Power/Knowledge: Selected Interviews and Other Writings, 1972–1977*. New York: Pantheon.

Frege, G., P. T. Geach, and M. Black. 1977. *Translations from the Philosophical Writings of Gottlob Frege*. Oxford: Basil Blackwell.

Fricke, J., and C. Ahern. 2002. *Yes, Yes Y'all: The Experience Music Project Oral History of Hip-Hop's First Decade*. Cambridge, Mass.: Da Capo.

Gates, H. L., Jr. 1988. *The Signifying Monkey: A Theory of African-American Literary Criticism*. Oxford: Oxford University Press.

———. 1990. "2 Live Crew, Decoded: Rap Music Group's Use of Street Language in Context of Afro-American Cultural Heritage Analyzed." *New York Times*, June 19.

George, N. 1988. *The Death of Rhythm and Blues*. New York: Pantheon.

———. 1992. *Buppies, B-Boys, Baps and Bohos: Notes on Post-Soul Black Culture*. New York: Harper Collins.

———. 1998. *Hip Hop America*. New York: Viking.

Giddens, A. 1984. *The Constitution of Society: Outline of the Theory of Structuration*. Berkeley: University of California Press.

Gilmore, R. 1993. "Public Enemies and Private Intellectuals." *Race and Class* 35: 69–78.

Gilroy, P. 1994. "After the Love Has Gone: Biopolitics and Ethno-Poetics in the Black Public Sphere." *Public Culture* 7: 49–76.

Goffman, E. 1959. *The Presentation of Self in Everyday Life*. New York: Doubleday.

———. 1961. *Asylums: Essays on the Social Situation of Mental Patients and Other Inmates*. New York: Anchor.

———. 1967. *Interaction Ritual: Essays in Face to Face Behavior*. Garden City, N.Y.: Doubleday.

Gold, M., and G. Braxton. 2003. "Considering South-Central by Another Name." *Los Angeles Times*, April 10, section B-3, 1.

Goodwin, M. H. 1990. "He-Said, She-Said: Formal Cultural Procedures for the Construction of a Gossip Dispute Activity." *American Ethnologist* 7: 674–95.

———. 2006. *The Hidden Life of Girls: Games of Stance, Status, and Exclusion*. Oxford: Blackwell.

Gregory, S. 1998. *Black Corona: Race and the Politics of Place in an Urban Community*. Princeton: Princeton University Press.

Grice, H. P. 1957. "Meaning." *Philosophical Review* 66: 377–88.

———. 1975. "Logic and Conversation." In *Syntax and Semantics,* ed. P. Cole and J. Morgan, 41–58. New York: Academic.

Gwaltney, J. 1981. *Drylongso: A Self-Portrait of Black America*. New York: Vintage.

Hall, S. 1996. "The West and the Rest: Discourse and Power." In *Modernity: An Introduction to Modern Societies,* ed. S. Hall, D. Held, D. Hubert, and K. Thompson, 185–227. Oxford: Basil Blackwell.

Halliday, M. A. K. 1978. *Language as Social Semiotic: The Social Interaction of Language and Meaning.* London: Edward Arnold.

Hanks, W. 1996. *Language and Communicative Practices.* Boulder: Westview.

Harris, M. 2000. "Urban Totems: The Communal Spirit of Black Murals." In *Walls of Heritage and Pride: African American Murals,* ed. J. Prigoff and R. J. Dunitz, 24–44. San Francisco: Pomegranate.

Hassey, B. 2005. Medusa Acoustic Live: "Battle of the Bands." www.campuscircle.net/homegrown.

Hebdige, D. 1987. *Cut 'n' Mix: Culture, Identity and Caribbean Music.* London: Routledge.

Hinds, S. S. 2002. *Gunshots in My Cook-Up: Bits and Bites from a Hip-Hop Caribbean Life.* New York: Atria.

Holt, G. S. 1972. " 'Inversion' in Black Communication." In *Rappin' and Stylin' Out: Communication in Urban Black America,* ed. T. Kochman, 152–59. Urbana: University of Illinois Press.

hooks, b. 1994. "Ice Cube Culture: A Shared Passion for Speaking Truth." In *Outlaw Culture: Resisting Representations,* 125–44. New York: Routledge.

Horne, G. 1995. *Fire This Time: The Watts Uprising and the 1960s.* Charlottesville: University of Virginia Press.

Hurston, Z. N., and C. Wall. 1995. *Zora Neale Hurston: Folklore, Memoirs, and Other Writings: Mules and Men, Tell My Horse, Dust Tracks on a Road, Selected Articles.* New York: Library of America.

Ice Cube. 1991. "True to the Game." *Death Certificate.* Priority Records.

Irvine, J. 1993. "Insult and Responsibility: Verbal Abuse in a Wolof Village." In *Responsibility and Evidence in Oral Discourse,* ed. J. H. Hill and J. T. Irvine, 105–34. Cambridge: Cambridge University Press.

Jackson, D. 2003. *Entertainment and Politics: The Influence of Pop Culture on Young Adult Political Socialization.* New York: Peter Lang.

Jenkins, S., E. Wilson, Mao, G. Alvarez, and B. Rollins. 1999. *Ego Trip's Book of Rap Lists.* New York: Ego Trip.

Kelley, R. D. G. 1996. "Kickin' Reality, Kickin' Ballistics: Gangsta Rap and Postindustrial Los Angeles." In *Droppin' Science: Critical Essays on Rap Music and Hip Hop Culture,* ed. W. E. Perkins, 117–58. Philadelphia: Temple University Press.

——. 1997. *Yo' Mama's Dysfunctional! Fighting the Culture Wars in Urban America.* Boston: Beacon.

Keyes, C. L. 2002. *Rap Music and Street Consciousness.* Urbana: University of Illinois Press.

Kitwana, B. 2002. *The Hip Hop Generation: Young Blacks and the Crisis in African-American Culture.* New York: Basic Civitas.

Kool Moe Dee. 1990. *How You Like Me Now.* Jive Records.

Krims, A. 2000. *Rap Music and the Poetics of Identity*. Cambridge: Cambridge University Press.

Labov, W. 1972. *Language in the Inner City: Studies in the Black English Vernacular*. Philadelphia: University of Pennsylvania Press.

Leadbeater, B. J. R., and N. Way, eds. 1996 *Urban Girls: Resisting Stereotypes, Creating Identities*. New York: New York University Press.

Lee, Benjamin. 1997. *Talking Heads: Language, Metalanguage, and the Semiotics of Subjectivity*. Durham: Duke University Press.

Lefebvre, H. 1991. *The Production of Space*. Cambridge: Blackwell.

Levinson, S. 1983. *Pragmatics*. Cambridge: Cambridge University Press.

Lipsitz, G. 1994. "We Know What Time It Is: Race, Class and Youth Culture in the Nineties." In *Microphone Fiends: Youth Music and Youth Culture*, ed. A. Ross and T. Rose, 17–28. London: Routledge.

Lorde, A. 1997. "Uses of the Erotic: The Erotic as Power." In *Writing on the Body: Female Embodiment and Feminist Theory*, ed. K. Conboy, N. Medina, and S. Stanbury, 277–82. New York: Columbia University Press.

Losen, D., and J. Wald. 2005. *Dropouts in California: Confronting the Graduation Rate Crisis*. Civil Rights Project, Harvard University.

Lott, E. 1993. *Love and Theft: Blackface Minstrelsy and the American Working Class*. New York: Oxford University Press.

Madison, K. J. 1999. "Legitimation Crisis and Containment: The 'Anti-Racist-White-Hero' Film." *Critical Studies in Mass Communication* 16, no. 4 (December): 399–417.

Major, C. 1994. *Juba to Jive: A Dictionary of African-American Slang*. New York: Penguin.

Males, M. A. 1996. *The Scapegoat Generation: America's War on Adolescents*. Monroe, Maine: Common Courage.

——. 1999. *Framing Youth: Ten Myths about the Next Generation*. Monroe, Maine: Common Courage.

Marquand, R. 1989. "Feelings Smolder Over 'Burning' Issue." *Christian Science Monitor*, February 24, 11.

McCann, E. J. 1999. "Race, Protest, and Public Space: Contextualizing Lefebvre in the U.S. City." *Antipode* 31: 163–84.

MC Lyte. 1988. *Lyte as a Rock*. First Priority Records.

McWhorter, J. 2003. "How Hip-Hop Holds Blacks Back." *City Journal*, summer, http://www.city-journal.org.

Medusa. 1999. *It's a Gift*. Goodvibe.

——. 2005. "Pimps Down, Flows Up." *Project Blowed: 10th Year Anniversary*. Decon Inc.

Mitchell, T., ed. 2001. *Global Noise: Rap and Hip-Hop outside the USA*. Middletown, Conn.: Wesleyan University Press.

Miyakawa, F. 2005. *Five Percenter Rap: God Hop's Music, Message, and Black Muslim Mission*. Bloomington: Indiana University Press.

Morgan, J. 1992. "Dreaming America: Walking along America's Musical Color Line." *Spin*, October 10, 118.

Morgan, M. 1993. "The Africanness of Counterlanguage among African-Americans." In *Africanisms in Afro-American Language Varieties*, ed. S. Mufwene, 423–35. Athens: University of Georgia Press.

——. 1996. "Conversational Signifying: Grammar and Indirectness among African American Women." In *Interaction and Grammar*, ed. E. Ochs, E. Schegloff, and S. Thompson, 405–33. Cambridge: Cambridge University Press.

——. 1998. "More than a Mood or an Attitude: Discourse and Verbal Genres in African-American Culture." In *African-American English: Structure, History, and Use*, ed. S. S. Mufwene, J. R. Rickford, G. Bailey, and J. Baugh, 251–81. London: Routledge.

——. 2001. " 'Ain't Nothin' but a G Thang': Grammar, Variation and Language Ideology in Hip Hop Identity." In *Sociocultural and Historical Contexts of African American English*, ed. S. Lanehart, 185–207. Amsterdam: John Benjamins.

——. 2002. *Language, Discourse and Power in African American Culture.* Cambridge: Cambridge University Press.

——. 2005. "Hip-Hop Women Shredding the Veil: Race and Class in Popular Feminist Identity." *South Atlantic Quarterly* 104, no. 3: 425–44.

Morgan, M., and D. Bennett. 2006. "Getting Off of Black Women's Backs: Love Her or Leave Her Alone." *Du Bois Review* 3: 485–502.

Mtume. 1983. "Juicy Fruit." *Juicy Fruit*. Epic Records.

Mullen, B. 2000. "Down for the Good Life: A Unified Revolution Called Jurassic 5." *LA Weekly*, June 21, Music Section, 1–4.

N.W.A 1998. "Fuck tha Police." *Straight Outta' Compton*. Priority Records.

Nas. 1996. *Hip Hop Is Dead*. Def Jam Records.

Nettleford, R. 1978. *Caribbean Cultural Identity: The Case of Jamaica*. Kingston: Institute of Jamaica.

Osumare, H. 2007. *The Africanist Aesthetic in Global Hip-Hop: Power Moves*. New York: Palgrave Macmillan.

Payne, J. 2003. "Rhyme of the Century: In the Beginning Was BUSDRIVER, Then Came the Word." *LA Weekly*, June 19, Music Section, 1–2.

Peirce, C. S. 1955. "Logic as Semiotic: The Theory of Signs." In *Philosophical Writings of Peirce*, ed. J. Buchler, 98–119. New York: Dover.

Perry, I. 2004. *Prophets of the Hood: Politics and Poetics in Hip Hop*. Durham: Duke University Press.

Peterson, J. 2003. *Concepts of the Underground in Black Culture*. Philadelphia: University of Pennsylvania Press.

Pollard, V. 1983. "The Social History of Dread Talk." In *Studies in Caribbean Language,* ed. L. Carrington, 46–62. St. Augustine, Trinidad: Society for Caribbean Linguistics.

——. 1994. *Dread Talk: The Language of the Rastafari*. Kingston, Jamaica: Canoe.

Potter, R. 1995. *Spectacular Vernaculars: Hip Hop and the Politics of Postmodernism*. Albany: State University of New York Press.

Pough, G. D. 2004. *Check It While I Wreck It: Black Womanhood, Hip Hop Culture, and the Public Sphere*. Boston: Northeastern University Press.

Prigoff, J., and R. J. Dunitz. 2000. *Walls of Heritage and Pride: African American Murals*. San Francisco: Pomegranate.

Quinn, E. 2004. *Nuthin' but a "G" Thang: The Culture and Commerce of Gangsta Rap*. New York: Columbia University Press.

Raber, E. 2000. "Hip-Hop Her." *Curve*, August, http://www.curvemag.com.

Rap Pages. 2000. "The Beats Heard around the World: Special International Section." *Rap Pages*, May, 43–77.

Reed, A. 1992. "The Allure of Malcolm X." In *Malcolm X: In Our Own Image*, ed. J. Wood, 201–32. New York: St. Martin's.

Richardson, E. 2006. *Hiphop Literacies*. New York: Routledge.

Rickford, J. 1999. *African American Vernacular English: Features, Evolution, Educational Implications*. Oxford: Basil Blackwell.

Rickford, J. R., and R. J. Rickford. 2000. *Spoken Soul: The Story of Black English*. New York: John Wiley and Sons.

Rose, T. 1994. *Black Noise: Rap Music and Black Culture in Contemporary America*. Hanover, N.H.: Wesleyan University Press.

Samad, A. A. 1997. "No Meters in Leimert Park!" LA Watts Times Online, www.lawattstimes.com.

Sansone, L. 2003. *Blackness without Ethnicity: Constructing Race in Brazil*. New York: Palgrave Macmillan.

Sapir, E. 1955 [1921]. *Language*. Orlando, Fla.: Harvest.

Savigliano, M. 1995. *Tango and the Political Economy of Passion*. Boulder: Westview.

Schieffelin, B., and E. Ochs. 1986. *Language Socialization across Cultures*. Cambridge: Cambridge University Press.

Scott, J. C. 1990. *Domination and the Arts of Resistance: Hidden Transcripts*. New Haven: Yale University Press.

Searle, J. R. 1969. *Speech Acts: An Essay in the Philosophy of Language*. New York: Cambridge University Press.

——. 1983. *Intentionality: An Essay in the Philosophy of Mind*. Cambridge: Cambridge University Press.

——. 1995. *The Construction of Social Reality*. New York: Free Press.

Shakur, T. 1995. "Dear Mama." *Me Against the World*. Jive Records.

Shelby, T. 2005. *We Who Are Dark: The Philosophical Foundations of Black Solidarity*. Cambridge: Harvard University Press.

Silverstein, M. 2004. " 'Cultural' Concepts and the Language-Culture Nexus." *Current Anthropology* 45: 621–52.

Simone, N. 1966. "Four Women." *Wild Is the Wind*. Phillips.

Sims, C. 2003. "In Los Angeles It's South-Central No More." *New York Times*, April 10, 1.

Skelton, T., and G. Valentine. 1998. *Cool Places: Geographies of Youth Culture*. London: Routledge.

Smith, F., and B. Bloom. 1981. *Double Dutch Bus*. Unidisc Records.

Smitherman, G. 1977. *Talkin and Testifyin: The Language of Black America*. Boston: Houghton Mifflin.

——. 1999. *Talkin' that Talk: Language, Culture and Education in African America.* London: Routledge.

——. 2000. *Black Talk: Words and Phrases from the Hood to the Amen Corner.* New York: Houghton Mifflin.

"Smithsonian's Black Radio: Telling It Like It Was." 1996. Radio Smithsonian, Washington, D.C., for Public Radio International.

Spady, J. G., C. G. Lee, and H. S. Alim, eds. 1999. *Street Conscious Rap.* Philadelphia: Black History Museum Publishers.

Stanley, Lawrence. 1992. *Rap the Lyrics.* New York: Penguin.

Stavsky, L., I. E. Mozeson, and D. Reyes Mozeson. 1995. *A2Z: The Book of Rap and Hip-Hop Slang.* New York: Boulevard.

Steinberg, L. 1990. "Autonomy, Conflict, and Harmony in the Family Relationship." In *At the Threshold: The Developing Adolescent,* ed. S. S. Feldman and G. R. Elliott, 225–76. Cambridge: Harvard University Press.

Stokes, C. 2004. "Representin' in Cyberspace: Sexual Scripts, Self-Definition, and Hip-Hop Culture in Black American Adolescent Girls' Home Pages." *Culture, Health and Sexuality* 9, no. 2: 169–84.

Stokes, M., ed. 1994. *Ethnicity, Identity and Music: The Musical Construction of Place.* Oxford: Berg.

Sunaina, M. 1999. "Identity Dub: The Paradoxes of an Indian American Youth Subculture (New York Mix)." *Cultural Anthropology* 14: 29–60.

Tolman, D. 2002. *Dilemmas of Desire: Teenage Girls Talk about Sexuality.* Cambridge: Harvard University Press.

Toop, D. 1999. *Rap Attack 3.* New York: Consortium Book Sales.

Totten, M. D. 2000. *Guys, Gangs, and Girlfriend Abuse.* Peterborough, Ont.: Broadview.

Turner, V. 1969. *The Ritual Process: Structure and Anti-Structure.* New York: Aldine De Gruyter.

——. 1974. *Dramas, Fields, and Metaphors: Symbolic Action in Human Society.* Ithaca: Cornell University Press.

——. 1976. "Ritual, Tribal and Catholic." *Worship* 50: 504–26.

——. 1982. *From Ritual to Theater: The Human Seriousness of Play.* New York: PAJ.

——. 1987. *The Anthropology of Performance.* New York: PAJ.

2 Live Crew. 1989. *As Nasty as They Wanna Be.* Skyywalker Records / Luke Records.

U.S. Bureau of the Census. 1979. *The Social and Economic Status of the Black Population in the United States: An Historical View, 1790–1978.* Current Population Reports, Special Studies Series, no. 80. Washington: U.S. Government Printing Office.

Urla, J. 1997. "Outlaw Language: Creating Public Spheres in Basque Free Radio." In *The Politics of Culture in the Shadow of Capital,* ed. L. Lowe and D. Lloyd, 280–300. Durham: Duke University Press.

——. 2001. " 'We Are All Malcolm X!' Negu Gorriak, Hip Hop and the Basque

Political Imaginary." In *Global Noise: Hip Hop Outside the USA,* ed. T. Mitchell, 171–93. Middletown, Conn.: Wesleyan University Press.

Werner, C. 1999. *A Change Is Gonna Come: Music, Race and the Soul of America.* New York: Plume.

West, C. 1993. *Race Matters.* Boston: Beacon.

——. 1999. *The Cornel West Reader.* New York: Basic Civitas Books.

——. 2004. *Democracy Matters: Winning the Fight against Imperialism.* London: Penguin.

Westbrook, A. 2002. *Hip Hoptionary: The Dictionary of Hip Hop Terminology.* New York: Harlem Moon.

Wheeler, E. 1992. " 'Most of My Heroes Don't Appear on No Stamps': The Dialogics of Rap Music." *Black Music Research Journal* 11: 193–216.

Whorf, B. 1956. *Language, Thought and Reality.* Cambridge: MIT Press.

Yasin, J. A. 2001. "Rap in the African-American Music Tradition: Cultural Assertion and Continuity." In *Race and Ideology: Language, Symbolism and Popular Culture,* ed. A. K. Spears, 197–224. Detroit: Wayne State University Press.

MARCYLIENA MORGAN is a professor of African and African American studies at Harvard University and the executive director of the Hiphop Archive. She is the author of *Language, Discourse, and Power in African American Culture* and the editor of *Language and Social Construction of Identity in Creole Situations.*

Library of Congress Cataloging-in-Publication Data

Morgan, Marcyliena H.
The real hiphop : battling for knowledge, power, and
respect in the LA underground / Marcyliena Morgan.
p. cm.
Includes bibliographical references and index.
ISBN 978-0-8223-4362-2 (cloth : alk. paper)
ISBN 978-0-8223-4385-1 (pbk. : alk. paper)
1. Hip-hop—Social aspects—California—Los Angeles.
2. Rap (Music)—Social aspects—California—Los Angeles.
3. Project Blowed.
I. Title.
ML3918.R37M674 2009
782.421649'0979494—dc22
2008053653